Active Voices
II

Active Voices II

James Moffett
with *Phyllis Tashlik*

BOYNTON/COOK PUBLISHERS, INC.
UPPER MONTCLAIR, NEW JERSEY 07043

Library of Congress Cataloging in Publication Data
Main entry under title:
Active voices II.

  1. Readers (Secondary) 2. Readers (Elementary) 3. School prose,
American.
I. Moffett, James. II. Tashlik, Phyllis. III. Title: Active voices 2. IV. Title:
Active voices two.
PE1121.A184   1986   428.6   86-23305
ISBN 0-86709-205-X   ISBN 0-86709-111-8

For information address Boynton/Cook Publishers, Inc.,
52 Upper Montclair Plaza, P.O. Box 860, Upper Montclair, NJ 07043

Printed in the United States of America
87 88 89 90 10 9 8 7 6 5 4 3 2 1

Acknowledgments

Our first thanks to those students who did the writing that makes up nearly all of this book. Their names appear in the Contents and at the beginning of their contributions.

To their teachers and schools we are, of course, greatly indebted for affording these young authors the kind of education that made a collection of such range and quality possible. These selections came almost entirely from inner New York City or from Naperville, Illinois, a suburb of Chicago.

Most of the former came from Manhattan, most of those from Manhattan East Jr. H.S., and most of those in turn from Phyllis Tashlik's own classes. Colleagues of hers who also contributed student papers were Jacqueline Ancess, Gloria Augustine, Adele Gittleman, Mel Jones, Denise Levine, Olivia Lynch, Jack Mollahan, and Gil Rodriguez.

We also thank some other teachers in the New York City area who fed us writing samples from their classes. Thomas Southwick of Grace Church School and Earl Jagust of United Nations International School made especially substantial contributions. Others were Barbara Fenster of Eastern District H.S., Mary Feinberg, Marcella Hirschy, and Cheryl Maye of the Northview Center for Communication Arts, Alan Edelman of Wilson Jr. H.S., Elise Frank of Jr. H.S. 118, Ellen Scheinbach of the Isaac Newton School, Marge Lewis and Patricia Serafin of Scarsdale Jr. H.S., Bill Colavito of the Harbor School, Alice Howard of Community Intermediate School 166, DeeAnne Hunstein of the Spence School, Cliff Williams of Brooklawn Jr. H.S. in Parsippany, New Jersey, and Joyce Duncan and Deanna Keller of East Harlem Career Academy. We are grateful to Helene Steinbuck for arranging some of these channels as language arts specialist at the Alternative Centers for Education in East Harlem.

The writing from Naperville, Illinois was arranged for by Marie Carducci Bolchazy, then director of the language arts curriculum there. Thanks to her and to these teachers in that district: Barbara Boehm, Mary Ann Cyr, Alice Feeney, and Rose Anne Hoekstra of Lincoln Jr. H.S.; Frances Gaydos of Naperville North H.S.; Mary Currier and Ruth Woodcock of Madison Jr. H.S.; Joan Carter of Jefferson Jr. H.S.; Marie Bartolotta, Richard Pierce, and Sharon Weber of Washington Jr. H.S.; and Jeanne Apostle, Marilyn Hollman, Ellen LaGow, Don McElroy, and Alice Shaffer of Naperville Central H.S.

And, finally, thanks to Barbara Friedberg and Gayle Rogers of Martin Luther King, Jr. Laboratory School in Evanston, Illinois and Elizabeth Cornell of Lick-Wilmerding H.S. in San Francisco.

Contents

To the Student

Students in grades 7-9 wrote this book, which is meant to sample for you the wide variety of kinds of writing done in our world. By using for this collection only the work of people your age we wanted to show that what is written out of school can be written in school—and that what your peers can do you can do.

To get these examples we didn't run a contest or save top papers from years of classes or search out aces among schools and students. We drew from certain schools where teachers were willing to widen the range of writing and of learning methods. We felt confident that students writing from real experience and interest, and benefiting from workshop commentary from their classmates, would supply us with plenty of enjoyable material to choose from.

So in selecting from their work we aimed to make this, like any other good book, a pleasure to read. May their writing entertain you while indicating what you might do yourself.

Before each kind of writing you'll find some general directions. These are meant to give the main idea of each kind and to say roughly how to do it. The kinds of writing themselves are gathered into five major groups:

TAKING DOWN (Notation)
LOOKING BACK (Recollection)
LOOKING INTO (Investigation)
THINKING UP (Imagination)
THINKING OVER (Reflection)

The words in parentheses are simply another way of naming the groups so that we have a couple of handles on each.

These groups indicate the different ways a writer turns up material and works it into a composition. So each represents a source and a process for working with that source. The first group, for example, TAKING DOWN, consists of writing down events and ideas more or less when they occur, as in diaries and journals. These are very important because things written down at first for oneself may be written up later for others.

The next group, LOOKING BACK, is based on memory. Shaping our recollections results in autobiography (author-centered) or memoir (other-centered). Memory is a vast, rich storehouse of experience and knowledge important for writing.

LOOKING INTO depends on investigating beyond accidental experience by deliberately observing things, visiting places, interviewing people, and consulting sources of information stored in print and other media. This investigation results in new knowledge written as reportage and research.

For the material of the fourth group, THINKING UP, the writer invents people, action, places, and things by going in imagination beyond the actual firsthand and secondhand experiences acquired through recollecting and investigating. Such transformation results in plays, stories, and some kinds of poetry, which are ways of revising reality so as to illuminate it.

For the last group, THINKING OVER, the writer again goes beyond actual actual experience and factual information, this time by reflecting on them, generalizing from them, and relating them to each other to understand them better. This results in various kinds of articles and essays, organized by ideas, not events.

Within a group, the order of examples is meant to bring out connections and differences among the various kinds of writing so that they can make each other clear. You wouldn't necessarily write them in the same order, and in any case you wouldn't have time to write every type illustrated. Some students can try some kinds, and other students other kinds. The main thing is to experience writing in all five groups and to understand some of the connections among types even though you won't do them all. In this way you can find out what sorts of writing exist, what each does best, which comes easier or harder for you, and how you relate to each. Working in all five areas will cover most kinds of writing and will also help develop all sides of your mind and personality.

The organization of this book brings out how kinds of writing correspond to kinds of thinking. Whether or not you see yourself as doing much writing later in your life, you probably want to develop your thinking ability and extend your knowledge. A kind of writing is going on all the time in your mind as you experience things, recollect them, recombine them in imaginative ways, and reflect on them. By processing experience these ways, you're constantly making your own knowledge; it's part of being human. Writing gets your thinking outside and highlights it so you can become more aware of it, bounce it off other people, and take charge of your own growth.

Any material is fair game when writing is opened up across the whole range. At any moment, look inside, look around; stuff is everywhere. But don't count on remembering it all. Do what nearly every writer does—keep a notebook of possible material. You'll find it much easier to start composing if you have a notebook full of jottings on this and that—observations, random thoughts, dreams, memories, images, overheard conversations, story ideas, or the stray phrase that for some reason intrigues you. Writing begins with the discovery of subject matter you care about. You don't have to stare at a blank page and scratch your head. Store up *too much,* and work from a position of plenty rather than scarcity.

Knowing the kinds of writing and how they relate to each other is, of course, only part of the picture. The rest—the actual processes of composing—concern what goes on *inside* you as you think and write and what goes on *between* you and your teacher and classmates or some other audience. Writing is personal *and* social.

Take the *inside* part first. As a writer, you need to be conscious of what you feel and think when you experience, recall, or reflect on something. (Keeping a notebook helps you capture some of all this.) What's on your mind? What's under your mind? You can find out by taking a little time each day to sit still and relax in a quiet place, close your eyes, and focus attention inward in one or more of the following ways:

- Let your mind roam wherever it wants but witness it like a bystander instead of being swept away obliviously.
- Or try to slow down and perhaps even suspend the inner chatter and buzzing. What comes into your mind then?
- Or review the day's events. How do you respond to them?
- Or choose some subject you want to understand better, perhaps some problem you want to solve, and focus just on that by concentrating on some image or phrase or idea that represents it for you. Such a subject might be one that recurs when you try to still or witness your thoughts, or it might just be some situation, person, object, place, or idea that attracts you. Follow through in this way by giving full attention to whatever is already asking for more attention.

Inner material is not necessarily about *you;* it's what you think and feel about *anything.* It's the main source of what you can write about. If you learn to tune into it and cultivate it, you'll not only find writing easier and more satisfying but you'll probably understand yourself and your world better.

Now the *between* part. Unlike many writers who toil alone, you have ready access to an appropriate trial audience—your classmates. You and they don't have to be experts to help each other. And you don't have to play teacher. All you have to do is to respond as readers and listeners. If you can keep reasonably good track of what you're thinking and feeling as you read or hear a composition, you can help the author a great deal to know how close she or he came to the mark. In return, your partners will give you the same useful feedback before you revise so that you can benefit from a realistic trial before handing compositions in to the teacher or publishing them in some way. Most writers do a draft, try it out on whatever audience they can scare up, and then revise (usually more than once). Of course, your teacher provides very important feedback, but he or she rarely has time to respond between drafts as well as after the final version.

Here are several ways that members of a small workshop group can help each other with a draft:

1. Depending on the kind of writing and on other circumstances, you can all either read aloud your own drafts, read aloud each other's, pass around your papers to read silently and discuss later, or pass out copies to annotate as you read silently.

2. As you read or listen to a paper, think of a title for it and jot this down on a scrap of paper and compare later with others'. (The author should have a title but not place it on the paper.)

3. Let the author say what he or she wants help with or is wondering and worrying about.

4. Describe what you thought or felt at various points in the draft without necessarily advising.

5. Ask the author questions on what you don't understand or are curious about.

6. Play with other possibilities. Tinker. Ask the group creative what-if questions about someone's draft. What if things were changed around or expressed in some other way?

Working with classmates has other advantages too. Help can begin even before the drafting stage, when you're trying to get started. Telling a story to someone or talking over some tentative ideas can be useful ways to sort out your thoughts and decide how to proceed, especially if both you and your listeners ask questions.

While thinking of your workshop group as an immediate audience and your class and teacher as a still wider readership, consider as you write who else you might be addressing. Where might the finished piece *go*? What might it *do*? Scripts, for example, or how-to directions, are meant to be performed or carried out. Many other compositions, like stories and poems, serve well as material for rehearsed readings. Nearly all the types of writing in ACTIVE VOICES II are publishable somewhere because they illustrate what can be found in various publications. Consider local newspapers and newsletters and regional or specialized journals. Look and ask around. Exchange suggestions with classmates.

Now read and enjoy. See how some other students your age have done the kinds of writing practiced in the world at large. Try your hand and practice too. Be a writer among writers.

James Moffett
Mariposa, Callifornia

Taking Down
(Notation)

Journal and Diary

Writer's Journal

Keep a lightweight notebook handy and write down in it any time all sorts of ideas and events that interest you enough to want to save. Put in the date when you write in it. Carry your notebook between home and school as much as you can so you can write down things as they come to you—your reactions to events, your feelings and moods, observations of what is going on around you, stories you imagine, dreams, memories, lists and plans, and so on.

In this general writing journal you can store a treasury of ideas and experiences to rerun and make use of later. Some of this material you may want to read as is to certain persons, or let others read it on their own. You can choose what you let others, including the teacher, read.

Like professional writers, you can pick things out and re-write them—fill them out, change them around, and polish them up for others to enjoy in various ways. Putting a lot in your notebook will keep you rich in ideas and material to use for all of the other kinds of writing to follow in this book.

Journal Entry—Beth Katz
February 8

Dear Journal,

Hi! I'm writing to you somewhere about 2:30-3:00 a.m. I'm sorry that I am writing so late and so sloppy, but I'm in pain now and I can't sleep. Not only is there a pain in my leg since about 11:30, but there is this burning feeling. I know that I promised not to talk about my leg any more, but this pain is killing me and I have to take it out by doing something. I'm writing on the floor of the kitchen because there is a fluorescent light on now and I can't put on the light in my room 'cause I would wake my sister up. Ouch! A sharp pain just went through my leg again and I'm trying not to scream. I'm really dying! I know that I am going to look like hell in school tomorrow because I'm going to be up all night. I'm trying to ignore the pain, so please excuse me. I am writing like I am delirious. I'm sitting here holding back my tears because if I start crying I'll start sniffling, and somebody will wake up.

Journal Sequence—Whitney Savage
9/14

I am really excited about going to high school in New York City. You see, I came to New York two years ago in 6th grade and was thinking that 6th grade would be the highest grade in the school. But it wasn't. It was the lowest grade in the school. I was upset, because in Virginia, 6th is the highest grade in elementary school. Then I came to Manhattan East and found myself in the same boat. Now I'm in 8th grade, and I'm finally at the top!

Well, anyway I'm so glad to be going to high school here in N.Y.C., probably because you can try out for special schools such as Music and Art. Down in Virginia you don't have a choice of schools, you have to go to one, and that's it!

9/24

My weekend was fairly nice. It started on Saturday morning. My day was to be very spread out and free. I woke up at about seven, had breakfast, and then went out to walk around. I was planning on going to the high school fair at around 12:30, but I didn't go until 2:30. I found all the information on all the high schools that I wanted, except for Music and Art. After that I went across the street to Lincoln Center, to watch a friend of mine's college teacher perform in the Library Theatre.

That night, my mom, David, and I went down to Little Italy, to see the San Gennaro Festival. It was pretty much fun but very tiring.

On Sunday, I woke up at about nine, I had breakfast, and then I got dressed. At 1 o'clock I went to my tutoring session, and stayed there for about three hours. I pretty much enjoyed it. Then I walked around on Columbus Avenue, looking at all the things on the street.

9/25

I'm so mixed up at the moment. I have so many thoughts running through my mind. I guess the main thing that's bothering me is the tutoring for high school. I have 268 words to study a week, and I have homework. I'm very worried about what might happen on the tests. I'm trying out for Stuyvesant, but I feel that I won't get in. The h.s.'s that I really want to go to are Music and Art, and Humanities. I'm not a really good test taker, so I'm very frightened about the tests. I feel like talking about this to someone, but I can't. I really don't want to go to Stuyvesant, I just want to see really how smart I am. I want to go to Humanities for English and Social Studies, and I want to go to Music and Art for the humanities and the arts.

9/28

Yesterday was probably the worst day of my life. It all started when I realized that I had to do my social studies homework, my English h.w., study for a science test, read my book, study vocabulary words, and study for h.s. exams. Well, I got through my English h.w., and I managed to slip by my science, but the thing that took me so long to do, was my s.s. It drove me up the wall. I was on my last question when my mother said something to me about my social studies, and that threw me off. I was planning on being done with my homework by around 8:00, but it took me until 8:30. As I was just about to go to bed, it dawned on me that I had lost my math. I was going to give it to Mr. Solomon yesterday, but he was too busy playing with his computer. So I folded it up and put it in my pocket. The next thing I knew, it was gone. Well, I did my math this morning while eating breakfast, and also finished my s.s.! Thank Goodness.

Journal Entries—Marcos Mercado
10/4

Then we went to Pointe du Hoc, a strategic line of bunkers occupied by the Germans originally. Their strategic value lies in the fact that they are on a sheer rock cliff overlooking Omaha Beach. A division of U.S. Rangers scaled the cliff and after grueling fighting reached the top. Their objective was to knock out the big guns that could bombard the beach. After heavy casualties they captured all the bunkers, only to find that the guns had never been placed and were in a field a half mile away. They captured those guns and held their positions against successive German counterattacks until they were relieved on the following morning.

The remains of the bunkers still stand today, most torn apart by mortars and grenades. It was fun to walk through the dark dank underground bunkers, and wonder what was there 41 years ago. One large bunker was lit up and had been repaired; it was neat to walk through it and see the walls. There were huge bombardment craters everywhere. They had been created from naval shelling on D-Day, and mortar bombardment. They are now overgrown with grass and weeds, but they are still very deep and formidable craters. The rusting steel bars that hold the bunkers up will soon be gone, but I think the bunkers will be there for another 50 years.

10/29

Poetry, Feelings Toward It

I can not sit down and write poems or anything poetic. To write poems within our walls is dreadful. The pen and the paper I feel also inhibit one greatly; they just give me a poetic block. What I like is being outside alone, and suddenly I'm inspired and the words gush out as I recite. I listen to myself and become intrigued with what I've said. I'm usually inspired by the atmosphere, the weather, the mood of the day and myself. I do this mostly in the fall and spring, but I also do it at other times of the year. I seldom remember what I said.

Journal Entries—Luke Ratray

9/26

Death

I walk along the shore
Where the walls exist no more
And the bodies lay
All night and day
Calling those not there
        Before.

10/2

When I draw, I color.
When I color, I finish.
When I finish, I accomplish.
When I accomplish, I feel.
When I feel, I think.
When I think, I live.
When I live —
        I draw.

10/2

Question

If there were four persons
And the 1st person
Told the 3rd person
A personal thing about the 2nd person
And the 2nd person

Was mad at the 1st person *and*
The 3rd person because the
3rd person told a 4th person the
Same personal thing that
The 1st person told the 3rd person
And the 4th person told
The 2nd person that the
1st person told the 3rd person
      who told him,
Should the 1st person and the 3rd person
Be mad at the 4th person
Because he told the 2nd person
OR should the 2nd person be
Mad at the 1st person because
He told the 3rd person?

10/15

A tear,
      Falling to the cold ground,
            so soft.
Moisture and feeling,
            mixed together,
      To tempt the soul.

11/4

Goodbye, wasted time
            wasted strength
            wasted effort.
Leaves have been turning
                  over.

"Speaking indifferently to him,
Who had driven out the cold
And polished my good shoes as well.
What did I know, what did I know
Of love's austere and lonely offices?"

—From *Those Winter Sundays*
By Robert Hayden

   That's my favorite line out of the whole poem, so much feeling in so few
words. What goes through my mind when I hear that is a young boy that lives
alone with his father getting up in the morning. His father is a very cold person

and his son doesn't get much love from him, but sometimes his father does small things like polishes his shoes or making the house warm again. . . .

Journal Sequence—Tarik Campbell
9/14

I am looking forward to this weekend when the Riverside Church Hawks hold their winter basketball team tryouts. I hope to make the team, not just for the name but because of the great trips they go on. They go to Phoenix, San Diego, Boston, and many more cities. They also give out jackets, bags, shirts, and the coach will buy you sneakers. Most of all they try to get you into a good school, mostly Catholic. Some Catholic schools they help you get into are Hayes, Tolentine, All Hallows, and Rice.

9/17

On Saturday I went to tryouts for the Riverside Church Hawks basketball team. When I got there with my brother and my friend Pate, we were all a little hesitant about entering the gym, not knowing what to expect and all. Then we got up our courage and entered the gym. We knew a lot of people that were there and had a good time. First, we ran a drill where the guards would run up and down the court, passing to the people on our sides. We played well and made the team. The coach told us that we were going to go to places such as Phoenix, Florida, Virginia and Boston.

9/18

I have a very hard decision to make. I have to find a way to tell my old coach that I quit and play for Riverside Church. I don't know how to break it to him or how he will react when I tell him, whether he will be mad and start screaming at me or will understand and still be friends. My brother and my friend Pate and I are in this situation together. We all quit at the same time and went to tryouts together. Pate said he would call Tommie, my coach, yesterday, and then call us back to tell us what happened, but he didn't. I guess we'll have to find out whether he did or did not today after school when I call him.

9/24

Last week I finally told my coach that I quit and that I played with Riverside Church. Actually, the word got around that I quit and he called me.

He called to ask why I'd quit. I told him because of the benefits, such as free trips, schooling, bags, jackets, and shirts. He kept trying to make excuses, saying that I was in a private school, which I'm not, and that they're going on trips but their trips aren't free. He almost made me tell him I'd still play, but I got up enough courage not to. I don't know if he'll be mad at me and hold a grudge, but that's life. I had to try new things and I did, and will continue to try new things.

Journal Sequence—Vince Adam
3/8

A Tragedy

It was a warm May day, and the sun was shining through the windows of the red little fort. Chris was still sleeping, but I woke him up. His brown, thin hair was sticking up. We had already started the day with a laugh. Just then we decided to go to town. We both approved of this idea, so we prepared to leave.

3/10

We went outside. The wind was blowing fiercely. It was going to be a tough bike ride to town. On the way we passed Ted's house and decided to get him to come with us. Ted came and then we were all on our way. We got to town, and lots of people were there hurrying around all the shops.

3/10

After about two hours of this hectic mess we decided to start on our way home. The only thing we bought was a dozen sweet smelling flowers for Ted's mom. The ride home was very easy, the fierce wind was now to the back of us, and we glided half the way home. When we got to Ted's house to drop off the flowers we decided to stay at Ted's place and play there.

3/10

Ted gave the flowers to his mom and she loved them. Ted told his mom that he wasn't going to the Flea Market with them but instead play on this nice day at home with Chris and me. With a little bit of persuasion Ted's mom agreed that we would be ok.

3/11

We got ready to play one of our favorite games, War. We got dressed up in all our camouflage clothes, got an old bullet belt on, and gathered three guns. Chris got a double-barreled pistol, which he held with a tight grip. Ted got an old wooden rifle which as soon as he got it, he dropped on the damp, muddy, ground, and I got the green and plastic rifle I usually used, which I swung around. Just before we started to play, the Scolf family, all but Ted, left for the Flea Market. We set up the green two-man tent in Ted's backyard. The game had just started. Ted and I jumped the fence and sprinted for the front yard while Chris climbed the tall sappy pine tree to be a lookout.

3/12

Ted and I went diving over bushes while Chris towered the prickly, sticky, green pine tree in the backyard. Just then this fun-filled game seemed to become boring to us. What we needed was another person. We decided to call Dan and see if he could play. Ted went inside to call up Dan, and I ran out in back to ask Chris if he needed help, but before I could ask this, Chris yelled, "Vince, come up here, it's great." Without any objection I started for the black iron fence where the old sappy pine tree was and started up the tree. When I got to about the fifth skinny branch I felt a painful tingling feeling run through the sappy branch and into my dirty hand. After that a loud buzzing sound followed.

3/17

The painful feeling was getting much stronger. I looked up the tree and only saw thick, grayish smoke hovering slowly around the pine tree. I asked myself what was going on, but nothing came to my mind. I knew that something was wrong and I couldn't take any more of this painful feeling going through me. I jumped down the sticky tree at once and noticed a couple of flames flickering at the top violently. I ran to the back door that led to Ted's kitchen just as Ted opened the door. "Ted," I said, "Call the police. There is a fire in the tree, and Chris is still there. Hurry!"

Ted nervously picked up the phone and dialed nine one one. The operator got on and quickly Ted explained the situation to the operator while I looked at the fire and my friend.

Suddenly there was a loud bang that shook the house and something on fire fell from the tree. I ran outside and grabbed the hose. I turned it on, and out came cool, clean water. I ran to the flames, and as I got closer I recognized that the thing on fire was my best friend Chris. As I poured the cool water on Chris' brown blistered back I heard the sirens of the fire trucks and the police. I slowly realized what had happened on this day at the Scolf's house to my best friend Chris Tobin.

Journal Entry—Claudine Fields

11/24

unconnected
self-divided
future predecided
mystic soul
confused poet
restless dreamer
pressure points
sleepless nights
sea air breather
city lover
suicide thoughts
paranoid ideas
advice giver
Hated by mirrors
animal lover
clock watcher
who cares

11/25

Journal Entry—Pamela Spiegel
December 3

Dedicated to Jackie,
With Love, Pamela

We met at the shopping center, I on roller skates, you on roller skates. You called out to me, "Hey you're good!" I stopped and turned around. There you stood, in old metal skates, with your short hair, and your long, spindly legs (filled out since then). I said, "Me?? Thanks!" and our friendship began.

That happened the summer before sixth grade. At that time we were not close. We met in the street every now and then. I, always with skates, bike, or glove and ball. You, still practicing on those metal things you found in the janitor's closet. We played together and talked together.

Over the course of the sixth grade year, I came to know you and understand you. I came to know your family. Your mother, father, brother. I admired you. You had many friends, where I had hardly any. You introduced me to Lisa Lovello. The three of us became the musketeers. You taught me things I never thought I could do. Like gymnastics on the grass behind our building.

And then, just before the end of sixth grade, you tried to do a front handspring on wet grass. You slipped, fell, and broke your ankle. Your pain became my pain.

The summer came. The friends you had visited you and gave you their best wishes. Then they left. Our Lisa did the same. For most of the summer, you had a cast all the way up your thigh. All of that summer I spent with you. Day and night. You couldn't do anything really, but it didn't matter. We made up our games, we sat in the sun together, we talked together, and we came to trust each other. I painted your cast, we cut doll's hair, we made cheese raviolis, we drank chocolate shakes.

I think it was there that we became *best* friends in the true sense of the word. We had our fights but always resolved them.

Even though we said it was our worst summer, I think now that it was our best. (You must admit, Jackie, the sleep-overs were fun and the photographs I took of you and that cast were great!)

Since then, we have grown together, I with your family, you with mine. Your mother considers me her third daughter, your little sister someday will consider me her (Aunt) Pamela, and you, you consider me your most special and best friend. I thank you for saying this to me on our last sleep-over. It holds a place in my heart that I will keep forever. You too are my most special and best friend. I hope our friendship can withstand many, many more years of growing. I think it will.

You and I are alike in more ways than we know.

You are the most important thing in my life. And since I am not one for expressing my feelings for you openly in our talks I dedicate this to you, Jackie, my best friend, with

Love,
Pamela

Journal Ending—Pamela Spiegel
March 25

The journal, in the beginning, was something I did not want to do. I struggled over it every night. I then realized that if I didn't think about it, things would just come to me and I would actually want to write in it. Usually these times were at night.

Looking back on the pages that I wrote, I find that I have changed drastically, even though it's only been a matter of months. The journal in time became the legacy that I have searched for. In the journal I think I have captured many things I would have lost had I not written then down. I also find this whole thing sad in a way. Journal Ending—that makes me feel like I'm losing a friend. I think I'll probably keep writing in the thing anyway, even if you don't collect it.

I don't really know what you might have learned about me from the journal, but I know that I have learned a lot about myself.

Rewritten Journal Material

Use something from your journal as a basis for writing a story, poem, essay, or any other kind of writing. Select some memory, image, idea, event, or some sequence of such things and work this material up into a finished piece you can read to others, print up, perform, or otherwise share.

You might just pick something you like that you think would interest others too. Or if you're working in one of the later sections of this book—Looking Back, Looking Into, Thinking Up, or Thinking Over—and are looking for something to write about that fits one of those kinds of writing, glance over your journal and see if you can find material you can use.

Feel free to change the original material as much as you need to create what you want—add, subtract, rearrange, and reword.

[The first example below includes the original journal material from which the final version was written.]

Journal Notes—Kristen Berger
Sept. 13

I was sailing in Long Island Sound from the Thimble Islands to Essex, both on the Conn. side. With me on the boat were my father, my mother, my 2 brothers Ian (9), Colin (3) & my aunt & uncle & their 2 children Amiee (11) & Reena (9). As we got out to deeper water me, my cousins, & Ian were sitting on the bow telling jokes. I could see the next buoy & a large fish what I thought was a tuna was in front of it.

Oct. 1

Baby
whale

about 13 ft.
Fast
likes to roll under water
beluga
female
sailing
Essex
Thimble Is.
Long Island Sound
cute
soft
rubbery
sprays water out blow hole
saw boat again 2
wet
lost
famous
on tape
LOVED

BABY
Kristen Berger

Two summers ago I sailed on my boat with my family for a month in Maine. During this time we looked for whales because Maine is famous for its marine wildlife. We never got to see any whales on that trip. But over the past summer while I was sailing with my cousin and my family we were very surprised by some unexpected visitors.

We were sailing on Long Island Sound on the Connecticut side from the Thimble Islands to Essex. On this four-hour sail we were blessed with the presence of a female beluga whale that we named Baby. She wasn't really a baby whale; she was actually almost full-grown. She stayed with our boat for 2½ hours. All of that time we were busy petting her.

Beluga whales are also known as white whales because of their color. Females tend to be more gray than males. Beluga whales are native to northern waters but are attracted to inlets. Baby somehow got lost and ended up in Long Island. Baby was about 13 feet long. She had absolutely no problem with staying at the speed of a sail boat under power.

It was really special to see her. We even noticed little things she liked to do. At first she liked going under the boat from side to side, but when we started to pet her, she settled down. When she went back under water she would roll over and swim on her back and roll over and come up for more petting. She liked it when we revved up the engine; she would start surfacing some more. The second time she came to our boat (three weeks later), she didn't receive as much attention, so when nobody leaned over to pet her, she would knock her body against the boat.

When we petted Baby, she felt soft and slippery, almost like rubber. Since she had her protective layer of blubber, when we pushed down on her skin it felt as if it would sink right in.

She has been in the newspaper (a short article in *The New York Times*). There is also a special place to call to report whale sightings. When we called we found out that there have been attempts to lead her out to sea by some marine organizations. She just won't go! Now one of the groups wants to take her out of the water and put her in the aquarium.

For now, though, she's Long Island Sound's very own whale. I think that this was a once in a lifetime experience, one I will never forget.

Characterization of a Class Member
Kris Hanson

As she chewed on her sandwich, her blue eyes laughed at the joke someone made across the table. She put down her sandwich, reached for the imaginary necklace around her neck, and started swinging it back and forth. For no reason at all, she started to laugh hysterically, her strawberry blond hair shaking as her head went up and down. Her small hands went up and covered her mouth as if she didn't want anyone to hear her laughing so loud. It couldn't be done, everyone heard her. I started laughing and we couldn't stop for about five minutes, like we always do. When we got up to go outside, she picked up her green coat and put it on in a manner that suggested that she didn't have a care in the world.

Penguins, Penguins
Jessamyn Backe

When I started collecting penguins, I was, oh about 7 or 8. Our third grade teacher had read us *Mr. Popper's Penguins.* Since then, I've loved penguins. I don't know why I was so attracted to them. I guess they are just likeable. They have a certain quality about them which no one can resist. Maybe some people are against them, but I personally can't think of anyone, or why they wouldn't like penguins.

In my collection are candles, pins, buttons, earrings, rings, necklaces, pens, pencils, glasses, mugs, erasers, salt & pepper shakers, photos, an album of stickers, an album of pictures & cards, posters, statues, an electric one, a stained glass one from Mexico, boxes, magnet, stapler, tape dispenser, stuffed animals, wallet, books, shirts, and a scarf.

Penguins aren't ornate or intricate such as a peacock, but they are bold, simple, and adorable. I've grown to love them, and everyone knows I love them, too. See, once someone knows you like something, they tell others, and it gets around. Then for Christmas, or your birthday, they try to get you a present with that particular item. For instance, I have six of one particular penguin statue. People know I have this one kind and keep getting me more of this kind, because it makes a cute chorus line.

Anyone in my family knows how to shop for me and my sister and our two cousins—penguins for me, clowns for Christel, unicorns for Nancy, and hockey stuff for Lauren. It's really a pretty easy system to follow. One Christmas, 95% of all I got was penguins. (Everything else was clothes from my grandmother.)

Someday I hope to get married to someone who also likes penguins, and our whole house can be PENGUINS! PENGUINS! PENGUINS! Our kids can be penguins, our house will be otherwise lavender. The only thing we won't do with penguins is eat them. I refuse! Even if they taste like barbecued chicken, I will NOT eat penguins! That's really gross! Oh Boy! Well I don't want to excite you any further (nor myself) so I won't go on about how we'll have penguins in our freezer, bathtub, etc. etc.

Whenever I see someone on the street with a penguin pin, bag or shirt, I think to myself (Obviously! I don't think to anyone else, do I?), "If I ask them where they got that pin, bag or shirt, would they give it to me? You see, lady, I um, collect penguins, may I have that?" Would they? I keep hoping and maybe someday. . . .

Pastries in a Shop Window
Gillian Shaw

Sugared shortcake and strawberry preserves,
Pastries and layered cakes with an ice-cream surprise,
Blueberry croissants and chocolate chip cookies,
Fresh jelly doughnuts and banana cream pies.

All in a shop window, staring at me,
The cakes, cookies, doughnuts and pies
Look at me saying,
    "Can't help yourself, huh?
    Come in and try us . . ."
With mysterious eyes.

So, I look back at them and try to help myself
From going inside,
But will power—I had none,
And walked in with disguise.

Bought a little of this, and a lot of that,
Cookies, cakes, and a "spit and a spat!"
>One pound of mint biscuits, and half a cheese cake,
>(With strawberries and cream,—oh, what a make!)
>Five vanilla puddings, eight banana cream pies,
>(Who gives a "fudge" about my size!)

Next thing I knew, I had bought out the store,
Bought one little thing, and then . . . more and more!
Now no cakes from inside, to stare back at me,
They're gone and I'll eat them with glory and glee!

Soon as I got home, I opened my mouth,
Popped in a cupcake, and smiled north to south!

Soon I'd devoured all cookies and cakes,
(And thought, "What a funny sound my stomach makes!")

Suddenly, my face turned green,
My stomach flipped over twice,
My eyes changed to a bright, bright white.
(Sorry to say—I wasn't feeling too nice!)

My head felt all dizzy,
My earlobes were quivering,
My hair stood on end,
My kneecaps were shivering.

Everything became light.
Chocolate chip morsels flew in front of my face,
My throat grew all tight;
To breathe—I felt I had no space.

I tried to stand up,
But the apple pie à la mode
Sank down in my stomach,
And sat like a load.

Get me to the sink,
Before I . . . think . . . .
Get me to the door.
Woops! All over the floor.

Diary

Keep a diary for a number of weeks, making at least four or five entries a week. Allow ten to fifteen minutes to write down whatever seems important for the day or the previous. This is meant to record events and how you feel about them. It can be general or you can use it to focus on some special pursuit or aspect of your life. Write with enough explanation so that you—and possibly someone else, if you want—will be able to understand it later. Although you may want to offer all or portions to others as is, one purpose is to provide details of the moment that you can summarize from a later vantage point.

You can invite others to read it as you go and give responses and suggestions. Select parts that stand well alone and present them in some way to others, rewriting if necessary. Often the complete diary, or edited version, is readable and interesting enough to deserve an audience for its own sake, whether or not you also summarize it.

Diary—Kaori Kono
11/24

Dear Diary,

Today I was supposed to go with Judy, Judy's mom and Claire ice skating. Well, on Thurs. Judy called and said that she had a bad cold and couldn't go. I thought, "Fine, Claire's still coming," so I didn't mind. This morning Claire called and said that she also had a bad cough and couldn't come. I thought, "Oh great, just what I've always wanted." This happens a lot to me. For instance, on my birthday no one could come. Well anyway, my father and I went to walk around on 5th Ave, and then since we were early for a movie we went to Central Park and went to the Children's Zoo and I met a friend there and that was a surprise (for me). We went back to the movie. The movie was French, and you had to read sub-titles, and this guy's head was in the middle of my vision of the screen. Well, I really didn't mind because it was *boring*. Do not see a movie called *Sunday in the Country*. Well, after that we went to a small store which was stuffed with people.

My father's friend and family came in from Maine and came over for a while and we had Chinese food. After that at about 8:30-8:45 we left to go to the Village and walked and walked and walked and walked and walked (I guess you're getting the picture). We got back at about 11:30, and there was soda in the fridge, and so I drank it and now I'm regretting it because I can't go to sleep.

11/25

Dear Diary,

Remember yesterday I told you that I was supposed to go ice skating with Judy & Claire and instead I was to go today? Well, we did (my mom and I). The session was from 3-5 p.m. and I met a girl who was in my old school. She was there with her mother, sister, and friend. They were celebrating her sister's 15th birthday. Well for once I didn't fall down at all. My right ankle always goes in when I skate, so now it aches. I have a terrible headache! *and* I feel *sick*. I have no idea why.

Well, there's nothing else to say, so I'll write another time.

11/26

Dear Diary,

Hi! Since this is the day after ice skating my right ankle hurts whenever I turn my foot. Well, it seems that nothing unusual happened today except that I got everything right in Spanish. So there is nothing else to say.

12/4

Dear Diary,

I just had a Soc. St. test and I think I did horribly. I mean *bad*.

There were 7 parts to the test and we only had to do 5 and I only could finish 4. Ms. Lynch (Soc. St. teacher) said she might let us finish the next day or grade it on how much each person did.

Wish me luck! (In getting a miracle.)

12/5

Dear Diary,

Ms. Lynch did let us finish as much as we could today in 15 min. Well, I noticed that I really finished six parts. (Boy I cannot count.) I also found out that we have a Spanish test tomorrow (Oh no).

Well, wish me luck again!

12/6

Dear Diary,

Well, I don't think I failed, but I know I didn't get a hundred. I'm talking about the Spanish test. We didn't get our Soc. St. tests back. Boy, during recess me and like 3 or 4 of my friends were being bothered by about 10 boys, so we taught them a lesson. One guy in my group calls me "Shorty." Can you believe that! I am not short, so I called him "Tally."

Well, I guess that's all.

Bye!

12/24

Well, this is great I'm alone on CHRISTMAS EVE. My parents went to a party and my sister is always out (with her boyfriend). All I have to do is watch TV or call a friend. I'm so alone. Well, I think I'll ruin my mind and watch TV.

12/25

Well, I opened my presents today. Oh, that's not all that happened. We spent all morning preparing for our unknown guests. Well, we knew they were coming, but we didn't know who they were. You see, a Japanese dance group came to America and they wanted to get families that would give them an American Christmas dinner, so we did. Three people came for our dinner. They were really "in." It was great. During all this I had the chills and a cough, but I was having a lot of fun. At 7:30 they left, and I felt real sick. So I went to sleep then. At 8:00, as planned, 2 more people came but I was asleep and really dead to the world. Oh, and that whole day Miyo was asleep and sick.

12/31

Well, it's the last day in *1984*. Did you know that they might move the apple—you know, the apple that drops every new year. They might move it because that building that it falls from is gonna be torn down. You want to know what I think of that. I think that it is X?*X!

This eve I was with my family.

I have to go.

1/1

I went to see *Breakin and Electric Bugaloo.* It was really good. That was the first time I went out after Christmas. You see, I was sick for the longest time.

Nothing to write. Bye.

1/1

I've just gone over my diary entries, and one things stands out, I complain a lot. Oh also, I list the things that happened that day and if nothing happened then I wrote that. I guess I just needed something to tell what has happened to me that day because no one asks me, "What happened today in school?" NO ONE.

I also notice that I don't like to be alone, and if I was I just complained more. In fact, in one of my entries it's all practically complaining about being alone.

Diary Summary

Write an account of the material covered by your general or special diary. Eliminate the dates; summarize and retell so that you blend things into one continuous whole. Feature what seems most important to you and that you think will most interest some audience you have in mind. You are free to cut and add material and to reorganize according to your purpose as you look back. Fit length to whatever the main subject seems to require. Choose the audience according to the direction this takes. Your summary might take the form of a sketch or essay as well as a story

A Second View
Cara Wall

Looking back on my diary entries, I wonder "How could I have thought that about someone?" or, "How could I have done that?" I never realized how much my feelings change from day to day, or how differently I look at the same things on different days.

I kept saying that I didn't do anything, and it seemed true at the time, but as I re-read my entries it dawned on me that I did do things. The funniest thing that happened in the five weeks fortunately didn't happen to me. It was one of my friends' birthday, and I had given her little heart sachets. I was going to warn her not mistake them for candy, but she seemed to know what they were for, so I let it pass. Well, the next day she called up and asked me what they were for. I told her and when I asked why she answered, "Because I just ate one!"

The most exciting and embarrassing thing that happened to me was when we went to see *The Human Comedy*. When we were walking down the stairs Carolyn said, "That's Tony from *All My Children*." He was walking down the stairs in front of us. We doubted it was him, but when we saw him again later we were quite sure. We decided to get his autograph, but is was easier said than done. It seemed like twenty minutes of giggling and uncertainty until Carolyn finally asked if he really was Tony. When he answered yes, she was so startled that she just said, "Oh my God!" We finally did get his autograph, but we were all thoroughly embarrassed before the ordeal was over.

Throughout January and February a lot of people I know have birthdays, and sometimes their parties get a little wild. At one party someone received a box of Ju-Ju Beeds. BIG mistake. You see, at a party a long time ago given by a person they didn't like, the guests at this party had thrown Ju-Ju Beeds into the light fixture. So, the remainder of the evening was spent seeing how many Ju-Ju Beeds landed in the light fixture.

Also in January and February a lot of people get sick. The eighth grade especially. One day there were only thirteen people there. It all seemed to move in shifts. One week half the class was there, and the next week they were there but the other half of the class wasn't.

One thing that we started these five weeks was the play. A lot of eighth graders were disappointed because seventh graders got lead parts, but we've gotten over it. The play is pretty fun, but Mr. Levy is just into his guilt trips.

There is a lot in my diary about my pets. My kitten is really cute, but she has grown a lot in the past five weeks. She is more of a cat now. My other cats have had fleas and ear and eye infections. My dog saved the hamster when it got out by chasing the cats away.

I have spent my time at school and home. I have watched T.V. and played with my pets. I have led a normal life that I can always remember because I have written about it in my diary.

Herself
Jennifer Collet

This is the story of Jennifer, a girl who did not like much. She has a brother Christopher who comes and goes a lot and a mother, of course, whom she loves a lot. At this point in her life, her family seems not to be having a very large impact overall on her. At least it's not too apparent to her.

Her weeks are very repetitious. Monday she goes to school, always complaining how much she dislikes it. On Tuesdays she can't deal with the fact that she is going to have to be in school for three more days. She thinks Tuesdays are boring and she always wants to rid the world of someone or something. Wednesday she dislikes too, because she has to go to chapel. She's been going every Wednesday for nine years in school. Thursdays aren't that bad, mostly because the next day is Friday, and she doesn't have to go to school the day after. She lives for Fridays. It sounds very cliché, but it makes sense. She lives for Fridays because the next day is Saturday and she can see *Rocky Horror* on Friday & Saturday nights. Saturdays are pretty boring until the nighttime. Sundays, she finishes her homework and mopes around because she doesn't want to go to school the next day. Also on Sundays she seems only to be doing some sort of Latin homework.

On Saturday night, while at *Rocky Horror,* she and two friends decide to sit in front of these two rows of seats with newspaper over them. All of a sudden in walked Harvey Fierstein and the cast of *Torch Song Trilogy.* They sat in the rows right behind them. She was really annoyed. She kept on saying, "Oh my God!" and, "I can't believe it." Her friends thought there was something really wrong with her. She kept on saying, "Do you know who is sitting right behind you?" The reason this was so weird for her was because her brother had just left the Broadway production of *Torch Song*. She and her friends might call that evening an accomplishment, because they made her laugh. It was a deep scratchy laugh. It's something they'll never forget.

The thing she likes about *Rocky Horror* is that she sees no one she knows. It's an escape from her normal everyday world. She can be anyone she wishes, or act any way she wishes and no one cares. It's something that she knows better than a lot of people. It is a place she knows that many others don't. One thing annoys her though—when people she knows and doesn't care for, personality-wise, are there. It annoys her because it's an escape, yet someone found it.

Her brother, Christopher, is like all older brothers, a stereotype. He's always teasing and bothering her. He can be nice if he wishes, although, she's noticed, he's much meaner to her when he's around her friends. He, being an actor, isn't always around. He's been out to California twice in the past eight months and is supposed to go out there again soon.

She tries to see people as they really are, not as they appear to be. There are many people who appear odd or have an unhinged personality, but usually they are just unsure of themselves or shy. A lot of people act or dress as they do just because they want to fit in. It's all right to do something if you really believe in what you're doing and aren't trying to be like everyone else. This is her justification for her oddness. She believes in the way she acts and she doesn't care what people think.

The way she sees it, in one way or another everyone follows some type of trend. A trend could be a stereotype that one tries to follow. She believes in one way or another we all follow a cult. Some may think "cult" is too strong a word, but it all depends on how you look at it. With some it's the way you dress, with others it's a common person, and still with others a frame of mind. Most people though are interested in all three.

As mentioned before, she doesn't like much. There is no half way with her; it's either she likes or hates something or someone. Most of all she dislikes people. People mostly in general she dislikes, because they can be very insensitive and uncaring. She'd rather have a few close friends than a lot of people whom she doesn't care for. It's not as if she's not nice at all to everyone; she realizes it is important to keep in contact with all types of personalities. She also dislikes people who she thinks are going to invade her privacy or harm her. She also dislikes things that are supposedly good for her, school especially. She's not apt for change that she feels won't benefit her or anyone else, and she believes more often than not that through most change things usually come out worse than before. Another things she hates is people, adults or otherwise, who believe they're superior. Or at least act that way. She has a lot of teachers who act like that, present company not included. She doesn't like people who spend all of their time putting themselves down.

She doesn't like the beach, mostly because of the sand. She hates sand.

There is too much of it, and all of it is different, just like snowflakes. She doesn't like bad sitcoms and toy dogs. She has more dislikes than likes, but what she likes, she likes quite a bit.

Of the few people she likes there are David Bowie, Tim Curry, and Boy George. All three fascinate her.

David Bowie is amazing because he has been so many people at different times. She's recently discovered Tim Curry, as Frank-N-Furter. He's beautiful, as is David Bowie and Boy George. This is a quality you don't find much in males. Tim Curry has a certain air of oddness. She has seen him dressed up in a corset and fishnet stockings, but he is said to be quite a man. Boy George she likes because he does his own thing and doesn't seem to care what other people say about him.

It's not like she hates everything. She likes her cats, music, musicians, her family, good movies, big sweatshirts, and the Wheaties commercial with the football players.

Looking Back
(Recollection)

Memories

Look around at your surroundings until something you see reminds you of an event or person or place from your past. Write that down. What does that memory in turn remind you of? Keep the chain of memories going. Write pell-mell as a sort of notation for later without worrying about completeness or correctness. Get down a lot of material to choose from later.

With the help perhaps of partners with whom you talk over these notes, you can go a couple of ways at this point. One is to pluck out a single memory that seems to have promise and to expand it by jotting down more details about it. A second is to look for threads or themes across a number of apparently jumbled or unrelated memories and to make notes on the connections you now see among them.

Now compose a memory piece understandable and interesting to some audience you choose. Use your notes, but feel free to go as far beyond them as you need to do justice to the memory or memory thread that has emerged. Starting to compose may trigger more details or more ideas about a theme. Try out a draft on partners and revise it for a final version to print up with other memories by you or others, or deliver as a reading to some audience.

This activity may result in a kind of writing illustrated further on in this section of the book or in a poem or essay. [The first examples here include the notes from which they were written.]

Memory Chain
Zoe Garcia

Njameh → Patricia and I met her, the third day of school last year → the school was smaller → now we have the complete fifth floor → walking up these stairs → very tiring → legs hurt → I get thirsty → drink water → *in Vilma's house the kitchen floor was flooded with water* → we had buckets and mops trying to get rid of the water → janitor came to help → poured liquid in sink to stop the water from coming up → dirt, food came out of the sink → the sink was greasy → my hands → when I wash greasy pots & pans → used for cooking, boiling → my brother burned the pan and his hotdogs when cooking → I don't know how to → only a few things → as pancakes, eggs, → my brother threw away the egg because it splatted all over the pan when trying to do fried eggs → I like them juicy → juicy fruit gum is really good → I saw a real good movie Sunday → Animal House → that reminds me of my house when my brothers and I argue → or my mother and my brothers argue → they're screaming from the top of their lungs → get a sore throat.

Vilma's Kitchen Floor
Zoe Garcia

A few weeks ago, something terrible occurred to my friend Vilma. The kitchen floor of her house was flooded with water. The water was coming out of the sink, but she had no idea why the sink had backed up. The water was greasy and the floor was slippery.

I went over to her house to see if I could help her and the water had spread to the living room. I almost slipped when I stepped into the kitchen. They had buckets and mops and were drying the floor. I started to help them and my hands got greasy. I felt horrible.

We scooped water out of the sink with pots and poured it into the buckets to keep it from overflowing. But water was still coming out of the sink with food, dirt, and grease. We were all furious.

Finally, we went to look for the janitor, to see if he could help us. He poured acid into the sink. It helped to clear the clogged sink, and the water stopped overflowing. Then everything was controlled. We spent around two hours or more trying to control it.

Immediately, I went home and took a shower to get the grease off of me. I felt so good after that shower. And hoped never to be in a situation like that one, again.

Memory Notes
Joel Rivera

flowers→(funeral of my brother)→my father and mother fighting→my father leaving home→(my grandfather's funeral)→(spend Christmas and my birthday alone without my mother)→my grandmother→(being with my grandparents for one year)→falling in love→getting in trouble with some people of my church

Turning Point of My Life
Joel Rivera

May 3, 1980 my brother died of pneumonia. Everything went crazy. From that day on everything changed for me and my family. My father is the one that changed. When we went to Puerto Rico to bury my brother, we stayed there for one year. My father stayed here. My father changed. He started drinking and smoking again. I think another thing that messed him up was that he found his other wife and three kids. We found out a few months later when he brought us from Puerto Rico. My mother found a marriage certificate. That's what started all the fighting.

It was hard to get over it. It was not easy; you just can't get over it one-two-three. It took a long time, especially for my mother and father. I think my father and mother are still not over it. That's what makes me different from my parents. I really loved him, but I know he is in heaven and that is a better place than here.

My brother was loved and still he gave love right back. Sometimes we fought but we used to love to get into trouble. My brother used to get hit when I got in trouble, and I did the same thing for him. I don't know what kind of love the teachers had for him. But after he died, on a Saturday morning, my father went to school on Monday to discharge us from school. When he told the teachers that my brother died, even the teachers cried. To me everything went too fast.

A lot of things happened from 1980 to 1983, like one incident in Puerto Rico. When we were watching my brother in the funeral my parents were going to stay all night. So they sent me home so I could sleep. That night I was scared. I was crying and just fell to sleep.

It is hard. Well, to finish, my family is never going to be the same as before. It is like a jigsaw puzzle all broken up. Nobody knows how to fix it, and half the pieces are missing, and I don't know where they are.

Memory Notes
Smokey Fontaine

Globe → London → Elvaston place → young life → brother → punk → Toby
→ party → Jenny → ugly → Deidre → Thanksgiving → tennis → tests → pail
→ motorcycle → wreck → money wasted → fights → father → late →
Grandma → Angelo → court case → war → no money →

Court Case
Smokey Fontaine

Three years ago at the time of my elementary school graduation my
grandmother won a court case against Macy's Department Store.

She was in Macy's trying to buy a new dress to wear to my graduation.
She had bought one the day before and she had found out that there was a
defect in the dress, so she had gone back to the store to get her money back.
The sales clerk whom she had bought it from said that they would gladly
refund her money if she would go down to the basement with this slip and tell
the lady.

She went downstairs and waited for about half an hour before she finally
got to the head of the line to speak to somebody. By this time it was 6:00, and
the store was getting ready to close for the weekend. She gave the lady behind
the counter the slip, and then the lady proceeded to tell her that she had
gotten the wrong slip and to go back upstairs and get the right slip if she had
actually bought something.

At that my grandmother became quite mad, because she had been accused
of finding a slip on the floor and of trying to get some money for it. Since she
had really bought something, she had to go back upstairs again and come back
down to find another line to wait on. She told the lady that the sales clerk
must have given her the wrong slip and that if she could call him on the 3rd
floor she would find out what happened. The lady abruptly said no. A kind of
argument then broke out, and after a couple of minutes of arguing the lady
called Security. They came to pick my grandmother up!

The plainclothes guards arrived (two of them) and took my grandmother
downstairs to the security headquarters. She got there and was with all the real
shoplifters and others. They took her to see the Chief, and he heard her
argument and called the head of the third floor and said he was really sorry
that this happened and that he would clear it up. The head of the department
came down, and he went to the sales clerk and they sorted it out, and my
grandmother got her money back. The lady then apologized on behalf of
Macy's for the trouble.

Everything turned out okay, but my grandmother proceeded to sue
Macy's for false arrest and harassment. The case came up, but before it

started, Macy's settled out of court with my grandmother for $4,000.00! Macy's did this because they did not want the publicity of being in court. My grandmother settled because she did not think that she could win if it actually went to court.

Ellis Island
Darcy Magalaner

On the ferry to Ellis Island I could smell the unmistakeable stench of the river. The ride was short but fairly pleasant. On approaching the island I first saw the outside of the very large main building. This was where the immigrants would first come after getting off of the boats. I felt almost as though I was an immigrant getting off the boat.

We entered the gigantic baggage room. This is where they would leave their bundles. I could imagine the huge number of courageous people who left their country and came to America with practically nothing and without knowledge of the language. They would get off the boat then hurriedly ascend the stairs, unaware that they were being evaluated by doctors who were watching them.

The tour climbed the stairs as well, and I could almost understand how the immigrants might sense a feeling of doom. For although they were unaware that they were being watched at that moment, all knew the chance of being deported. We were shown a room where people were checked for disease, a room equipped with certain things that were used at the time. For example, an actual, original old-fashioned wheelchair and original medicine. The room was not offensive in any way, but I felt considerably uncomfortable in it. Perhaps I have an aversion to doctors and pain, or perhaps it is because of the rushed and formal treatment I thought the immigrants were given.

We also surveyed the dining room. I heard the guide say that often people were seated at tables where nobody else spoke their language and they were totally isolated from one another. We visited other places with importance on the island, and each left a permanent mark in my mind.

Ellis Island is sometimes called the Island of Tears because so much emotion was displayed there. Sometimes it was a joyous feeling because maybe every member of the family was allowed to stay in the U.S., but sometimes it was very sad when families were split up. I couldn't stand the thought of never seeing my family again, especially at such an early age. Suddenly, Ellis Island seemed to hold more meaning and importance for me than it ever had before.

A Haunting Reality
Nina Keinberger

Above my bed, I notice a gruesome object hanging in the dimness of my room, glowing a bright green. I focus my attention on it, and in amazement, I recognize what it is. I bought it last June at the Haunted Mansion in Disney World. I stare at it for a while; it amazes me.

A fake skull glowing bright green with long, shiny black hair is the only thing possible to notice in such darkness. I stare at it again and dream about the day I bought it. . . .

It was last June in Disney World when the heat was on. I was determined to have a great time. And I did. My favorite rides were—Thunder Mountain, Pirates of the Caribbean, and my absolute favorite, the Haunted Mansion. I went on the Haunted Mansion over and over, again and again, fascinated by what I saw. I wanted to reach deep inside and touch the terror, feel the fright, and talk with the dead—but of course, that's just my fantasy. It was all fake . . . every bit of it. Of all people *I* should know.

On my second to last day there, I was on the ride, situated in a buggy, in a hall of darkness, moving along, observing the sights such as big, fluorescent spider webs covered with spiders. When my buggy neared the end of the hall, it suddenly stopped, and a voice came out of the speakers behind me. "The spirits are having troubles contacting you. Please stay seated in your 'doom' buggies. Haaaghghghaaa!" The haunting voice and the frightening laugh started again, saying the same thing. There I sat, alone, at around 10:15 a.m. when the park had just opened. There were seven other people on the ride, but their buggies were farther back from mine. In complete darkness, there I sat. After five minutes of hearing the voice again and again, I got bored and realized that I knew this ride inside and out and it wouldn't hurt to observe it a bit closer. I squeezed out of the safety bar on the buggy and got off it. "I can't believe I'm doing this," I thought.

I began walking alongside buggies out of the Wall of Darkness and into a candelabra to see a coffin lid move up and down with green, hairy hands attached to it from the inside. I lifted the lid with great force and saw a machine attached to two hands moving up and down. I walked on, wondering if I would get caught by anyone and get into trouble. Nah. I walked on alongside the buggies and still heard the voice say, "Please stay seated in your 'doom' buggies." The buggies still weren't moving, so I walked on to the section where ghosts were flying about the darkness in a graveyard. The part where ghosts passed right in front of the buggies is where I observed that the ghosts were images on film, because when I reached out my hand to touch one, I saw the shadow of my hand in the light. I searched for where the light was coming from and found a projecter hidden high up in a corner, camouflaged in the dark above a shrine.

Suddenly, I heard a loud screech, and the voice stopped. The buggy I was standing on began to move. I squeezed back in through the safety bar, and went on with the ride, knowing how everything was done. All mechanics, all technical, all fake. Every bit of it. Where's reality?

After the ride, I stepped outside to meet my uncle. He gave me ten dollars to spend. I then went to the giftshop and came across a glowing green skull with long, black hair that amazed me. There was one next to it with white hair, but I picked the one with black hair to remind me of the complete blackness in the hall of darkness where I first explored the so-called "Haunted" Mansion.

Sensory Memory

Suspend some moment in time by recalling every detail you can remember about it. Note down exactly what you saw, heard, smelled, tasted, touched, thought, and felt then. Select and compose later from these details to recapture most vividly the outer look and inner feel of the experience.

Try it out on a few people. Revise. Print it up in a book with other memories of your own or others.

Reactions to Death
Chad Luning

Two times in my life I have had to cope with a feeling of death. This feeling has come at different times, and in different situations. Certainly my grandaddy is more important to me than an adopted baby bird. The feeling still is one of the most powerful feelings I have ever encountered. I reacted fiercely when my grandaddy died, resisting death's painful attack in a psychological war. With the bird's death, I let pain roll over me, wave after wave.

The bird was dead. Death was expected, but a cold, dark lump still formed in my throat. My weary eyes, still adjusting to morning light, gazed down at the twisted shape of the dead sparrow.

Cream brown feathers covered the bird's body. Thin jagged stripes spilled down his wings. Each black stripe was specked with small particles of grey dust that had found a new home on the lifeless bird. At the end of every other stripe there was a white square rippled with individual tiny feathers. His short rectangular tail stuck straight up in musty air, and was made of inch-long feathers.

The stiff bird's head was buried in a pile of brown, dry leaves, which lined a broken-down, large cardboard box sitting awkwardly on an old, scratched chest. Sunlight flying from the bubble skylight unmasked dust fleeing about in the small room. All sounds were muffled by the eerie silence of death.

Ruffled breast feathers reminded me of white caps on a rough ocean. Tail feathers overlapped like wind-blown sand on a lonely beach. Leaves covering the bird's head were shells delicately covering the dead. The faded brown box was a mighty Viking ship with no rowers. An ignored fly became a mourning seagull flying over this isolated beach.

Soon the omnipresent waves will sweep the bird away, and memories of this bird will be cast into the ocean to join lost dreams at the dark bottom.

As I let the horrible feeling of death envelop me, and painfully pull away, I reflected back to the first time this feeling had ambushed me. I reacted differently then, viciously resisting the attack.

The battle had begun. Unknown to onlookers, a fierce battle raged in my throat. The sadness of death thrived, and grew inside me. As I sat in a hard grey chair, shrill whistling wind whipped my hair to and fro. My gaze stretched past the short, plump preacher, past the array of colorful red flowers, past the silver majesty of my grandaddy's coffin, and out, into the past.

The evergreens hugged my face as I knelt, looking onto the red-tiled porch. My grandaddy sat on a white-washed metal chair, facing down into the dark woods. He was unaware of my game, so I sat there looking, and smiling. His body slouched comfortably in the chair, and his legs stretched to their limits in front of him. His brown eyes wandered randomly over his hill. Wrinkles in grandaddy's face sagged with his body. Black-rimmed glasses covered bushy eyebrows as well as soft eyes. His light green shirt had a little hill for each bend of his body. Grandaddy rested his hands on curly-cue armrests beside him. His whole body seemed to be saying, "Oh, how peaceful it is...."

Snapped back to awareness by a loud accent from the preacher, I found myself still under attack. I could not tell when this battle would be over, but that is true in every war.

Every human has to deal with death in one way or another. Pain is necessary but not in mass quantity. Resisting death inflames the wounds, as I found when my grandaddy died.

Autobiography

Autobiography: Incident

Tell an incident that happened to you some time in the past, an incident being a specific occurrence that took place only once, on a certain day or mostly on one day. You might do Memories *first to recall some material. Or you might think of some "first," the first time you did or experienced something.*

Think of who might want to hear or read this, where and how.

Head over Heels in Love
Debbie Steltser

   One day in early spring my family and I were going home from my grandparents' house. The car stopped in front of our home in Parsippany, New Jersey. And who do you think was standing by the front door of the house but the paperboy. Not just any old paperboy, but the one I liked. So I ran out of the car and towards the house. Then all of a sudden I fell right flat on my face! Boy, was I embarrassed! I could not look at the paperboy's face for at least six months after that incident. Even now I still feel embarrassed when I see him, because I remember the time I not only fell head over heels in love but flat on my face as well.

The Fair
Jonathan Winslow

   I can't remember exactly when it was, two maybe three years ago, I guess. We were just going for a walk, kind of a family get-together. We didn't know anything about a fair, yet there it was, stretching up the avenue, lines of people and shops—a giant constricting snake.
   We walked out into that sea of faces. I bought a soda as we were walking. I remember I couldn't drink because of all the people pressed against me. I could feel them brushing against my body, smell their sweat and their rancid breath.

My head began to throb, I broke out in a cold sweat. I pushed my way through the press, colors flashing by my eyes. Help me! I felt like screaming. Finally I broke through the crowd, my 7-Up still clutched in my white-knuckled hand.

Since then I've not been able to go into any large crowds. Call it psychological, call it physical, but no fairs, no carnivals, nothing.

The Audition
Alison Tucker

The very second my foot landed on the hard pavement, I realized what I was doing. I watched the bus pull away and then turned to face the big black CBS building, in which I would audition for a television movie. I'm pretty sure I was trembling from head to toe.

I slowly walked through the revolving doors, then, looking down at my watch, ran for the elevator. I was quickly stopped by the security guard, who showed me to the front desk. I signed my name on a sheet that said "Visitors of the day," and they loaned me a little plastic CBS card, which I showed the guard.

When I reached the 22nd floor, I was sweating like anything. I went to a small desk in the middle of the room, with a long-nailed, high-heeled secretary seated (nail file in hand) in a small chair behind the desk. She told me to sign in again and take these two portions of the script that I would be reading for them.

When I first read it, I wasn't thinking about whether it was good or not, but in the 20 minutes I was waiting, I learned to really dislike the black print that was before me. It was an over-dramatic story about a girl (my part) who sees her mother for the first time in something like nine years. She gets pretty hysterical or something like that. I really hated it, but on the other hand, soppy, over-dramatic scripts are easy to act.

The lady who auditioned me was really nice. I think she was English. She led me through about seven long, dark halls, then we came to a small, dark room. The only thing I could see were some flowers on a table that were really well spot-lighted. That's why it surprised me when these two ladies asked me to have a seat.

I had to read with the casting agent. I kept trying to get involved with the scene, but the lady was staring straight down at the page. I didn't have any time to be scared. I couldn't think about anything but those stupid words on the yellow sheet I was holding.

In my own opinion, I read well, but it's about a month later, and they haven't called me. That's one thing I really hate about acting; they never tell you when you don't get it.

Just Once Again
Ivelisse Rodriguez

One sunny spring night when I was about 11, I was at home, doing my housely chores that I was too lazy to do during the day. Suddenly there was a knock on the door. I went to investigate who it was. I looked through the peek hole but didn't recognize the man, so I called my mother and went back to my room. After a few minutes my mother called me, so I responded, "Yes, wait just a minute." Then I soon went and saw this man standing near the kitchen.

I was puzzled because here was a stranger in the house, an unexpected stranger. My mother had told me to get closer. So I did. My mother told me his name, Eliezer Rodriguez. She said to me, "Ivelisse, hug your father." I was startled to hear this. A man I hardly knew, and only from letters. And my mother expected me to hug him. I did so no one will think wrong of me. My hug was unemotional. In a way I was happy. After all these years he's finally here. That night we all sat down. We talked a little. I did most of the listening, about how good a girl I am, how big and pretty.

It was getting late, so my mother decided he should stay overnight. The next day I woke up and found him home. I had no idea he had stayed over, but I was glad. He was making us breakfast when we got up. In the afternoon he left but soon to return to take me to see my grandmother. Then he took me to Connecticut.

It was fun while it lasted, for he was bound to leave me again. I said goodbye and wished him well. He was soon off to Puerto Rico. I only hoped to see him once again. And I did.

A Bright Spot on a Gloomy Day
April Sexton

One of the scariest days of my life was my first day of school. I felt like I was being taken away and would never come back. My mother reassured me that everything would be all right.

That morning was hot and humid. My clothes clung to my body as I stood by the door, waiting for the bus to come. I had looked forward to this day with such eagerness that I drove everyone else in the family up the wall. My favorite thing to say was, "When I get four I can go to school, like Audrey!"

Audrey is my sister. I always was jealous of her because she could do so many things that I couldn't. I always cried when she left for school.

Now, as I stood by the door, I was shaking. I was so afraid of what I was going to have to do in school.

The bus pulled into the driveway, and I called to my mom. She said for me to have fun, and I told her I probably wouldn't. I ran outside and went into the bright yellow school bus.

From the moment I stepped on the bus, I knew I wasn't going to like it. Most of the boys were climbing all over the seats and getting mud everywhere. Just then, I remembered that I forgot my umbrella. The bus was already out of the driveway, so I just did without it.

I sat next to my friend, Adam. Adam was a really nice kid. He had straight black hair that was always combed neatly and millions of freckles. The only thing that I didn't like about Adam was that sometimes he was too neat. Adam said hello to me, and I said hello to him. Somehow he knew that something was wrong. "What's the matter?" he asked me.

"Nothing, I'm just a little scared, that's all," I answered. We sat there a little longer, and then we started talking about our pet turtles. We each had one turtle. I named mine Adam, and he named his April.

By the time we got to school, I was laughing and so was Adam. I think Adam was just as tense as I was when he got on the bus. I asked him about it, and he said that he wasn't scared at all. I looked closely at him. "You're lying," I said.

"You're right!"

I started to laugh again, and so did Adam. We were still sitting in the sticky seat of the bus because Adam didn't want to push his way into the crowd and get his pants dirty.

I told him, "If I were in that aisle seat, I would have been out of the bus already!"

"Well, go ahead," he said, making room for me to go.

"No, I'll sit here and wait for you."

"All right, but no more yelling. These are brand-new pants."

As we walked up the green wooden steps, we ran our hands along the wet, green railing. The paint for some reason was still wet. I stared at the globby, green paint on my hand. Adam got it all over his pure, sparkling pants.

I started to laugh so hard that I couldn't stop. Adam looked at me like I was crazy. Then he looked at his pants again. His freckled face turned from a look of horror to a smiling face, glowing with friendship.

He started to laugh with me, and we walked up the stairs and into the school house.

Fire
David Bock

It felt hot at first
Then hotter.
Then finally it started to burn.
White hot pain surged through my finger.

I dropped the lit match on the rug
And ran into the bathroom.
When I returned
The side of the room opposite the door
Was an inferno.

Red, yellow, blue, and green flames
licked along the walls and ceiling.
The acrid smell of smoke was everywhere.

I tried to put it out with my hands
but the pain was too great.
I ran into the living room yelling
"Fire! Fire!"

Ten minutes later
My mother's room was totally incinerated.

My First Experience with Death
Cathy Cronin

My first experience with death was when my nine-year-old cousin Mary died. It seemed impossible because just the week before it happened we were at her house visiting, and she wanted me to come out and play a game with everyone. The others went out to play, and while they were outside playing I fell down the stairs in her house. We had to leave early because my leg swelled up so bad. She was so caring, even though she was three years younger than I.

The next week, the morning before my swimming lesson, my mom and sister came in to wake me up. My pink room was unusually grey, but as mom lifted up the shade, a beam of light rushed in. When the room was bright again, I noticed that my mom's beautiful brown eyes were now red and watery. "What's the matter?" I asked.

My mom was slow in giving me a reply, so finally my sister answered, "Mary was hit by a car and died!" I looked at my mom with a questioning tear in my eye, and all she did was nod her head. I burst into tears and immediately wanted to know everything that had happened. My mom said that Mary had been standing on a corner talking to two friends when a drunk driver drove up onto the curb and hit her from behind. The car had hit her so hard that she was knocked half a block, and her shoes flew off. She broke her neck instantly and died. One of the other children standing with her had died in the hospital the next morning.

When the time came to go to the funeral, I promised myself that I would not cry. We entered the funeral home with its green carpets and white walls. My legs started to shake. The rooms smelled from ladies' perfume and coffee from the lounge. We slowly entered the room, and I grabbed my mom's hand. Mary was in a coffin at the far end of the room. Now that I saw her I burst into tears, and worst of all I couldn't stop! My aunt held me and told me it was okay, and we walked up to see Mary. When we got up to the front, she looked so peaceful. It made me so angry that the man wasn't put in jail. Before we went back to our seats, I gave her a kiss on her forehead. I was shocked to feel how cold and hard her skin was. We went down to the lounge for a while and to the smell of cigarettes.

Before we left I went to see her one more time, and this time I walked over to see an arrangement of flowers that caught my eye. There was a small card attached, and I opened it to see who they were from. But, all it said was, "I am sorry!" A chill went up my spine, and we headed for the car to go home.

Standing on Water
Chris Brown

The first time I tried waterskiing, I was terrified. But, there I was, all sixty pounds of me, standing in the icy cold water of the St. Lawrence River. My father had instructed me to lean back in the water with the tips of my skis perpendicular to the surface. As he revved up the boat, I kept myself calm by staring at the island on the horizon. I was going to tune everything out to keep my courage up.

Just as I went into my trance, the boat took off and began to drag me through the water. I was totally unprepared for the pull, and it pulled me right over on my face. Since no one had told me what to do if I fell, I didn't let go of the rope. The boat dragged me about ten feet under before I thought to turn loose. My life preserver, though, brought me back to the surface, where I coughed out half the river.

Once again I tried it. Shivering violently, I leaned back and placed the mammoth skiis into position. This time I was alert, ready, and terrified. When the engine's pitch went up, I stiffened my legs and rose right onto the top of the water. There my fear turned into exhilaration.

The cool wind soon dried me off, and I felt as warm as ever, inside and out. I felt even better when I knew I had shown up my cousin Robbie, who was standing on the dock. Those things are very important to ten-year-olds.

Now that I had overcome my fear, I began to notice all the finer points of the river I hadn't noticed before: the way the water sounds without the roar of a boat engine, how it feels under your feet, and how it smells when not smothered by the smells of shore. I soon lost my concentration, though, and I fell on my face for the second time. But this time I didn't mind, for I had skied for quite a long time by now. Besides, I could smell the water even better when it went up my nose. I was never afraid to try something new again.

First Terror
Hannah Aitchison

The day began green and golden. Sunlight sifted through the dew-tipped morning trees as we three strolled through the bright front yard. My grandmother, silver-haired in a green paisley shift, walked slowly, and I, feeling at the moment in a particularly companionable mood, trod along beside, short and fat-legged in my pink sunsuit. Ahead of us my baby brother Willie scampered along, bare feet flying as he toddled along, gurgling, clad only in his diaper and tee shirt, blond hair glinting in the friendly glow of the nine o'clock sunshine. Occasionally he would fall to his knees in the dew-dampened grass but leap up immediately to continue on his way, more energetic than before.

We were approaching the brilliant, many-colored flower bed that was located conveniently along the property line, to serve as a boundary keeping us out of the neighbor's yard and, according to my mother, trouble. But the warming golden glow and morning freedom had made my brother giddy and unobservant of rules; heedlessly he plowed directly through, his bare feet crushing jewel-toned snapdragons, pansies and jonquils until at last they landed and swiftly began to carry him across the neighbor's lawn. His destination was obviously their patio, which lay in the dim, gray shadow of the house, but still visible on it were a bag of charcoal, a grease-blackened barbecue and, in plain sight, a full paper cup.

Willie, who was known at the time to drink anything available, immediately trotted forth with greater speed than before. From above my head grandmother caught her breath, and I looked up to see her face creased with worry. She bent quickly.

"Honey," she said, her kind voice anxious, "run and catch Willie. I'm not fast enough." Then, as I still hung back, her voice became stronger. "Hurry!" she cried urgently as my brother at last reached the cup. "He mustn't drink that! It's propane fuel!" She gave a little shove and I began to run, short fat little legs gaining speed as I reached the flower bed and clambered through. A slight breeze came up to tousle the trees as my brother picked up the cup in his fat fingers and drank it in one gulp.

Immediately he fell to the ground, coughing and retching, his tiny face contorted in pain. The paper cup tumbled empty from his fingers to the ground, where it rolled along the cement, rattling mockingly. My grandmother had come up behind me, and when she saw my brother doubled over, his stomach in screaming agony, she let out a little shriek of despair and scooped him up in her arms. She then began a slow, staggering process of carrying him across the lawn to our house. For some reason the air had taken on the consistency of gelatin; none of us could move quickly enough. All the while poor Willie's breathing became more labored and urgent with the pleading desperation of one who is being deprived slowly and inexorably of life. Grandmother herself was breathing in short, rasping gasps as she staggered slowly to the front porch with him in her arms. I had run ahead, confused and frightened, to open the door, and now, a hundred confused emotions jumbling through my head, I watched them enter.

Grandmother placed Willie gently on the battered blue sofa; and I ran to get a pillow, which she then placed under the tousled blond head. Willie's eyes were closed now and his breathing was harsh and labored—short, rasping, shallow breaths, a horrible, agonizing sound. Blood flowed in tiny rivulets from his nose and over his upper lip. I remember the first huge drop trickling down his face and falling to the floor; I choked and turned away. Grandmother went into the kitchen and got ice wrapped in a terry towel to lay on his flushed forehead, and as she turned away again, I felt a choking panic rising in my now-dry throat.

"Grandma, where are you going?" I cried, leaping up and running to her, blocking her way.

"To call the *ambulance,* stupid!" she hissed, pushing me out of her path with impatient hands, reaching for the glossy black telephone. Hurt and nearly frozen with confusion and fear, I approached the couch and kneeled beside it, staring with unseeing eyes at my baby brother. He lay unmoving and stiff, his hair matted with sweat that glistened on his flushed forehead, and only when I leaned close could I hear his choked breathing. A grayish splotch suddenly appeared on his shirt, and then another. Startled, I reached my hands up to my face and felt my own wet tears sliding down my face. A knot developed somewhere in my stomach, tight, numbing cold.

I didn't look up when my grandmother came in or go to her for comfort when I heard her sit down on the folding chair by the window.

"I'm sorry I called you stupid, honey," she said softly, and I ran to her then, crying, to fall to my knees in front of her and plunge my wet head into her lap.

"There," she said gently. "There, there now," she stroked my hair softly.

Sirens wailed outside, a metallic scream, as two men in white suits came in and took Willie away. When Grandmother said the word "poison" to the men, my heart lurched suddenly and I felt suddenly dizzy and sick.

Grandmother lifted me onto her lap and held me very close, and I clung to her with all my might as one would to a final reprieve. She rocked me gently and crooned for what seemed an eternity until the telephone rang. When she went to answer, I followed uncertainly, my short, curly hair wet with tears and sticking to my face. She spoke with trepidation at first and then with increasing relief and happiness. After she hung up she turned to me and smiled.

"He's all right," she said gently. "They were sure he was going to die. It's a miracle."

I cried again, with joy this time, and I clutched at my grandmother gratefully.

"He's gonna come back then, isn't he," I said, and grinned through the tears.

Break-In
Dave Elish

Just this last spring break I went to Houston, Texas. I was visiting my sister and brother-in-law. The event I am writing about took place the first night I was there.

I was almost asleep in the living room, next to a large sliding glass door, when I heard a kind of pounding sound. I got up and walked to the curtain to see what it was. I couldn't believe my eyes. There was a man standing maybe 50 feet away, trying to break into a Stop-N-Go store. Their apartment is on the second floor. The back faces the store. I could see everything clearly. I just stood there and watched, too scared to move. My mouth was dry, palms were sweaty, heart pounding rapidly, and I felt hot and sick. Something snapped, I guess, and I jumped. There was my brother-in-law, Mike, standing there.

"What are you doin' makin' so much noise?" he asked.

"Sssh!!" I whispered, "look outside."

He moved to the window to look. Now, to understand Mike, you have to know what he's like. Mike's kind of big, about 5'11", oh, I'd say 200 pounds, and a tough character. Mike always boasted that if anyone ever broke into his house, he'd shoot him. Mike is a hunter, so he has all kinds of guns and other weapons. He also has a good knowledge of weapons and a cunning mind. Unfortunately, he wasn't thinking too clearly. If he had been, he would have thought of a plan to catch the burglar. Anyway, Mike's standing there and, all of a sudden, it hit him like lightning. He realized what was happening. Mike dove for the floor, like a frog jumping for a lily pad, and crawled to where I was standing.

"What are you doing?" I asked, looking at him strangely.

"Get down!" he whispered. "Don't wake Cin up or she'll have a baby."

Little did he know that in October of that year he'd be a father. But that's a different story.

I did as he told me and got down.

"Okay, okay," he talked quickly, "I'll get my gun and try to surprise him."

"Go ahead," I said calm-like. Really, I was so scared that I was numb.

"Okay, I'm goin'."

Mike crawled back into his room and got his .357 Magnum. He silently slid the glass door open and crawled out onto the balcony. I got next to him. We looked through a place where he had broken the glass. Mike whispered, "Okay, here goes. . . ."

"Wait," I tried to say, but nothing came out.

"Hey, you!!!" Mike yelled in a coarse voice.

The robber turned around, and I saw his face. I'll never forget that face. He was ugly. It was dark, but I could see every last detail. He was a Mexican or Puerto Rican with dark curly hair, a black moustache, and, to top it off, a scar on his left cheek. He wore a red bandana, and, I think, he was carrying a knife. He also had a gun.

Two shots rang out in the night sky. I covered my head and curled up in a ball. Mike just stood there, probably too scared to move. He still insisted that he didn't want to hurt the guy.

I was soaking wet from sweat and totally dry in the mouth. The robber jumped through the door and ran away.

A Lesson
Anson Chan

It's hunting season in the northern forests of Canada. The wild geese can be seen exhibiting their much coveted plummage in their transcontinental migration. As usual, hordes of hunters make themselves known. The country up here is a hunter's haven. Whether you are a hunter of bears, antelope, or birds, it does not matter. Coming up from the States to my uncle's country house perhaps was a mixed blessing. I knew he loved to shoot birds for sport; it was his "hobby." I had finished packing and sat down on the lawn idly when my uncle started to shout at me. "Anson, get up and put the dogs in the car." I never had a very close relationship with any animal save my own. As I approached the shed, the customary dog noises (and the smell) overcame me. I began to retreat when my uncle shouted, "Hurry up, you (unprintable)!"

"Go, I must," I sighed. As soon as I came into the view of the two German shepherds, they began to growl. "Nice doggies," I gasped. I inched closer. Growl! Snap! Snap! I was on the verge of running for my life when I decided that it was my duty. So, in my most authoritative manner, I said, "Looks like you're gonna be all alone." But they still didn't budge. I took a bone that was lying on the grass and baited them. Sure enough, they began following me. I hated dogs and, at the same time, I feared them. My uncle stood by the car, his arms folded against his chest.

We got into the car and my uncle consulted his road map. Life is sure pleasant when you're eight. It began to rain as the engine whirled and chugged. It revved and purred like a kitten. Pitter-patter! Pitter-patter! Pitter-patter! Pitter-patter! The rain beat relentlessly upon the window. I stuck my head outside and tasted the rain. A drop fell on my tongue and sent a tingling sensation through me. A lady-bug struggled to remain attached to the slippery windshield. Akwardly, it crawled, but suddenly a blast of windshield wiper knocked it away. Pokey the Pig lay next to me, apparently bored, but I wasn't. The dogs were in the back watching me with their small eyes. I turned around nervously and eyed them. Yes, I was afraid of dogs and simultaneously I thought they were stupid. Pitter-patter! Pitter-patter! The rain continued. Pokey the Pig lurched forward and fell on his face when the car hit a pothole.

Now the yecch was all over his face. Oh well, I didn't call him Pokey the Pig for nothing....

A nudge on my shoulder brought the reply, "Mom, don't tell me it's time for school!"

"I'm not your mom, dodo!"

The car screeched to a halt. Something in the air was entirely different. I got this impression when we were unpacking. The gnats were driving me crazy and I felt uncomfortable. It was the first time in my life that I ever went to the country. I stood on the lawn, looking up at the mountains towering above me like majestic kings, showing their advantage over me. The gnats were still pestering me, until I got so angry that I smacked a couple of them. I ran across the lawn and began to climb a tree. I perched atop a limb and surveyed the area. Here was the American spy on a reconnaissance mission. The gate over there was the Berlin Wall. Those little ants: tiny soldiers guarding the entrance. The two pebbles in my pocket were hand grenades. I climbed down and hid behind a bush. The great spy stole up to a jeep, hopped in and drove off, heading toward the wall. Machinegun fire, and I ducked. I blasted them with my hand grenades, rammed through the defense and leaped over the wall, unscathed.

My uncle was watching me all the time and applauded. "Bravo! Bravo!" he yelled. Even I was quite pleased with my performance.

It turned out that we didn't go hunting, much to my disappointment. My uncle was fixing up the house the next day, for it needed much repair. Insects had eaten through some of the wooden beams that helped hold the house up. After all, I didn't want the house to fall on top of me. I was filled with ennui, so I decided to go outside. I threw on my jacket and sneakers, then flew out the screen door. I climbed up a tree and tried to repeat yesterday's performance. I surveyed the terrain and began climbing down, but the worst thing happened. I lost my grip and I ended up falling several feet. Thud! My right arm was in pain ... searing pain. My god! It hurt! I started to scream, and loudly at that, but silence save the chirping of birds hurt my ears and heart. There I was, a good distance out of earshot, wounded in a fall....

Uncle was sitting beside me, watching the heavens. My arm was heavily bandaged and resting beside me. I felt lousy, why even Pokey the Pig can't match my degree of lousiness, no matter how many times he fell into the mud. "Better rest 'til tomorra," my uncle said with a smile. Feeling lousy all over, I dozed.

It turned out that somebody heard my cries for assistance. But that somebody was not my uncle. It was one of the dogs. Yes, the dogs, which I condemned, had saved me. Those dogs which I feared perhaps saved me from the hands of death. After all, my arm was in terrible shape. "Those dogs," my uncle said, "made me follow them." You know, it's weird and it doesn't make sense. I had misjudged them, and I can now say that the dog is really man's best friend.

Autobiography: Phase

Tell what you did or what happened to you during a certain period of your life covering months or a year or so—some "phase." Allow plenty of wordage to do justice to both what happened and what made it a phase, that is, a period having its own beginning, development, and end. This could become an installment in a full-dress autobiography comprising all the phases up to now, or it could be offered separately.

The Operation
Anthony C. Gibson

I dedicate this to Bobby—wherever you are.

I can't at this moment remember the exact date, but I do remember the shock and terror I felt after being told I may not be able to hear ever again . . . I would be deaf the rest of my life!

The thought of being deaf the rest of my life scared me and in a strange way also made me ashamed. It scared me because the loss of any of my senses at the mercy of a cold even scared me half out of my wits. I felt ashamed in a sense because I would grow up in an environment where when someone said something to me out in the street, and they did not realize I could not hear, I would not actually have a way to communicate to them that I was hard of hearing. Never being able to hear my friends, the honking of horns, or the noises that bothered me. I didn't like a lot of noises but when you are told you are going to "die," almost everything you disliked becomes precious.

I refer to my loss of hearing as "dying" because that is how I felt about it. Most of my communication was done verbally and by listening carefully. You may think, "It was only your hearing" (not that you would), but I felt a strange nakedness.

My hearing failing in leaps and bounds, I was told I would be totally deaf in a matter of months. The decibels at which I heard in a whispering manner were those of a discotheque in full swing. If you've ever been to a disco, you know how much noise there is. With that in mind, you now know how bad my hearing was.

The summer of 1979 I was hospitalized for a tympanostomy tube placement. In plain English, they put tubes in my ears to drain the fluid build-up in my middle ear. The idea of having my own television and room (my mother was pregnant and I already had two younger brothers) was a luxury. It was the only nice thing about being in the hospital. The only friends I had in the hospital were my mother and Doctor Linn, but I could not consider them close friends. They were not my peers. The only peer friend I had was Bobby.

I don't remember Bobby's last name but we had a special friendship at that time. Bobby had something wrong with his legs and had spent most of his ten years in hospitals. He had a wheelchair which he drove better than some people drive their cars. We would pretend his wheelchair was a limousine and I was the chauffeur. Bobby and I would zoom through the traffic in the halls, and sometimes we would race each other. Even though Bobby would give me a head start he would always beat me in his wheelchair.

I remember cruising through the hall with Bobby one day. I suddenly decided to pop a wheelie with his chair. When I did the wheelie I pushed the wheelchair very hard and caused Bobby to get hurt. Bobby wheeled away from me and didn't talk to me again until after my operation. Bobby came into my room and apologized to me, but it was my fault he got hurt.

The day of the operation, a nurse came and gave me an injection about 6 o'clock in the morning. After that injection things got very hazy in my mind. After being rolled into the operating room, I remember seeing a man whom I had seen earlier that summer while I was getting x-rays for a head injury. The man was about average height and looked very young even though he was bald. He had some strange device attached to his head. It was a little like the device Lobot, from *The Empire Strikes Back–Star Wars Saga,* had attached to his head. Thinking back to the emergency room visit, I remember the man shaking violently. Seeing him in the OR preparation room, he seemed to be shaking even more violently. The last things I remember before the operation were the OR people bringing down some strange object towards me and flipping me over my stomach while I cried "STOP!" Then the anesthesia finally blocked out all conscious thought.

In the recovery room I remember my private pediatrician's nurse, Terri, saying, "Look over there. It's your mother." I recall lifting my hand to wave but I was too feeble and sleepy.

When I awoke for the second or third time, I immediately reached over for a cup. I must have known it was there because I did it without spilling it all over myself. I bit the ice because it soothed my aching throat. I was still eating the ice when my mother returned with my aunt. My aunt wasn't in the room a minute before she said, "Don't eat the ice. It takes away something or other from your teeth. It will also scratch your throat!" Then she said, "Hello Anthony. Feeling better?" You may get the impression that she is a person who is hard to get along with, a pain in the neck (keep the thought and remember when you meet her), but she is actually almost as nice as I am.

I thought I still had my hearing disability the next day because everything still sounded the same. This however was not true. Dr. Linn came in and said, "Hello. How are you feeling?" I grabbed for my ears. He apologized and said he thought he had spoken in a rather soft voice. The operation was a success.

It had already started taking effect. All those hours I was sleeping must have helped. I was getting better with each passing second. It seemed as though I was already cured.

Later in the day I was informed that I should be excluded from all water activities or taken out of summer camp. My mother chose the second of the above. You may have already started thinking, "How's he going to take a bath or a shower?" Very simple, cotton in the ears and extreme care. With that taken care of the only problem was rain. My only defense against the element was heavy protection for my head. I almost forgot waterguns. My favorite recreational item. I was a fine marksman. No more.

The estimated time for when the tubes were to come out was six to nine months. They'd be out before summmer came again. I'd be able to swim next year. Wrong! Big dreams die hard. It took a year and a half. Many times I thought I had felt the tubes come out. Every time No, Nyet, Nien, Non, Negative, NO! NO! NO!

When the tubes finally emerged I was startled to see their size. They were about the size of the nail on my pinky. For eighteen months I had had to wait for two things no bigger than the size of my nail. Still, the anguish they caused me just wouldn't stack up to the joy I felt upon their removal.

There was only one strange thing that had happened. The last place I had gone swimming before the operation was the exact same place as my first swim after the tubes came out—Bear Mountain State Park. Two different camps, different group leaders, and counselors. However, the same pool, and the same wonderful love and friendship I received from the counselors and family members.

Breaking Away
Reka Koerner

I dedicate this to my grandparents, who made this experience possible.

I think it is an important stage in one's life when one separates from one's parents for over three months. With some people this happens when they are young: others grow old before they have this experience. With me this happened when I was quite young. As a matter of fact, I was eight. At first I went to Germany just like every other summer when I go to visit my grandparents in Munich. That summer and the year following were to change my life! I feel that I became more independent and courageous. You would too if you had to cramp all of your feelings inside of you, depending only on yourself for consolation. Try to imagine how I felt going to a new school in a new country, not knowing the language or children. Well, I felt very scared, and I am sure you would feel the same way.

In New York at that time my family was renovating a brownstone. There was no water because the pipes were lead and you can get lead poisoning from drinking or bathing in that water. It was extremely uncomfortable because there was no heating or air-conditioning. There was no privacy because workers were in every room of the house.

It was almost impossible to live in my house, so my family agreed that my sister and I would stay in Germany and go to school there. So I settled down in my grandparents' two-story house and got ready for school.

On the first day of school I knew no German. I had to learn it during the school year, so I got no report card. Even though I was not graded on my work I did everything that everyone else did. I learned as much or more than if I had stayed in America.

I noticed on the first day of school that there were no boys as far as I could see. This is how I found out that the Sophie Scholl Gymnasium was a girls' school.

Let me explain the German school system. From 1st to 4th grade you go to Grund Schule (Elementary School). Then one goes to the Gymnasium, which is where I went. It is from fifth to twelfth grade. Then one goes to the Universität or university. One starts walking from class to class in fifth grade.

I was in fifth grade, even though I was supposed to be in fourth, because I wanted to be in the same school as my sister for moral support, and also because she knew a little German.

In school I had trouble because we got out at 1:15 but had four hours of homework. It took me eight hours a day in the beginning because I knew no German. I was not too popular with most children because they were jealous that I was a favorite of most teachers, but I had five good friends.

Some nights I would not get to sleep and just cry all night, for my parents. Nobody who hasn't been separated from their parents for such a long time knows how it feels. Even though I had my grandparents and sister, whom I loved dearly, it was not the same as having a parent to yell at you and nag you. I was a tiny bit lonely because it is hard to tell anybody about feelings like that. (I was afraid they would not understand.)

My favorite part of Munich was, and is, the Englishe Garten (the English Gardens). It is like stepping into forest and meadows. There is no dog mess, and it is three times as big as Central Park. It is amazing that there are about fifty deer, 500 rabbits and a few thousand ducks. In the river, the Isar, there are many fish. When I lived in Germany I went every day on walks or bicycle rides with my grandparents and sister. Those walks were the highlights of my day.

Another landmark is the zoo. There are no cages. Instead there are big enclosed meadows with heated houses or shacks. The zoo was so big that it would take a week to go through it and see all the animals. Once my grandparents were to have some of my grandfather's students over. So my grandmother had made some deviled eggs. I wanted to go to the zoo before the guests came, so we went. We came home after three hours. The whole house was in smoke. My grandmother had not turned off the stove. The whole house smelled like rotten eggs. The eggs had exploded and were plastered on the ceiling. I had the wonderful job of scraping them off .

It was funny. I knew no boys except for my grandfather's students, who were 30 to 35 years old. My school was a girls' school. Gymnastics was all girls and so was swimming. Somehow I didn't miss boys.

At night, before I went to bed, my grandparents would tell me of their childhood adventures and pranks. I'll give you two sample stories. My grandfather's class had to stand up when the teacher came in until he said you may sit. Well, the chairs had springs, so the class put walnuts under the chairs, and when they sat down, all the walnuts cracked. You should have seen the teacher's face.

My grandmother took to school some very valuable Persian rugs for a play. When my grandmother's mother came home the door was open and the rugs gone. Of course she thought the rugs were stolen, so she called the police. After the police had gone, my grandmother came traipsing back from school with the rugs. My grandmother's mother tried to slap my grandmother as soon as she saw my grandmother had the rugs, but my grandmother ducked, and my great grandmother broke her hand on the doorknob—and she never hit my grandmother again.

I went almost every weekend and vacation to a small town called Zankenhausen. I love it there. It is so tiny! There are only 250 inhabitants and almost all of them are farmers. It is very near a lake called Amersee. When there is good weather, one can see the Alps.

This village has its problems, too. All the toothbrush and sewage water goes into a small stream which is now very polluted. The village cannot ship the dirty water and sewage to the next sewage plant because the pipes would have to go through forest and field, and another slight problem: the sewage plant is fifty miles away. I saw hundreds of fish lying dead in the stream. That makes me extremely sad, but what else can the village do?

The people I know best in Zankenhausen are farmers. Their names are the Selbernagels and the Hopflos. They are extermely nice. I have stayed with them a number of times. I do the things I love there—chase cows, call cats for food, milk cows, play in the woodpile and many other marvelous things. The Hopflos have three children, the Selbernagels, four. I like all the children except for a girl who belongs to the Hopflos. She is a big brat.

One week one of the Hopflo boys was not there, so I took his place. It was fun but hard work. There were 14 cows under my care and all the cats. Each cow got three wheelbarrows of grass. That was a good muscle builder. I also had to get the pigeon feathers out of the hay because the cows cannot digest the feathers and they can poke a hole in one of their organs. It is a lot of work because the hay loft is as big as Manhattan East! The work and sweat I shed were worth it because of the fun I had.

One day we found that there were pigeons living in the hay loft, so the Hopflo children and I took long sticks and hit the pigeons until they fell to the ground. It was a gruesome job, but to us the cows were worth more than the pigeons. After the pigeons had fallen we brought them to a man who trained them to be carrier pigeons.

One day after *stall zeit* (stall time) we went to a funeral of an old preacher. After *stall zeit* we always have a snack called *brotzeit*. Well, that day we did not have time before the funeral for *brotzeit*. In the middle of the funeral I fainted. I think you would have too if you did sweat work four hours straight. I can assure you that I did not feel well.

It was fun getting up at 4:30 in the morning to feed the cows. The children and I went back to sleep after the cows were fed, but the Hopflo grownups stayed up.

On that farm I learned how to drive a tractor. I sowed a few fields with it and drove some vegetables to the next town to be sold. I was extremely scared, but I did not want to have coward as a nickname. In Germany farmer children are allowed to drive as soon as they learn how. Surprisingly enough there have been no recent accidents in the area.

In school vacation I went to the mountains for fourteen days. The snow was higher than my head. Several times I was thrown head first into the snow. I got thoroughly wet. I went on many walks in the deep snow; it takes you an hour per mile! The hotel had a German shepherd guard dog. She could catch snowballs in the air without breaking them. She was very fierce until you got to know her. She saved many people from avalanches. She was trained to dig out people, and she already has a medal.

As you can see, my visit had its ups and downs. Fortunately most of the time I had upsies. From Germany I learned not only of culture and the language, I learned a lot about myself. I still go every year to Germany and Zankenhausen to visit my friends.

Memoir

Memoir of Another Person

Tell someone else's story as you witnessed it. This may be an incident that occurred on one occasion or what someone you knew or observed did over a longer period of time amounting to a "phase" in that person's life. Mention yourself only to tell how you came by the knowledge and how you reacted to it. (The other "person" might be an animal if you want to show its personality.)

You might place this in a collection of your other memoirs. Or, if it makes a certain general point, consider how you might get it to an audience that would appreciate that point.

The Burden
Toan Huynh

This morning, when my teacher came into the class, I recognized she carried a new bag with her. Looking at her bag suddenly reminded me of the school bag of a friend of mine, not only its style and color, but also the stretch of the bag and the heaviness of it expressed by the carrier.

Peter Smith, whom I admire, is an unfortunate person. His mother died when he was eight or nine. The father then brought home a strange woman who would be his stepmother from that day. Since then, everything was changed. How delightful the past, how gloomy the present time! He has a little sister. But both of them were maltreated by the irresponsible father and the cruel stepmother.

His father is a college professor. When his wife was still alive, he had been a nice husband and a good father. They often took their children for shopping or a picnic, teaching them how to be polite to people. Somehow, since their mother's death, he changed a lot. He got out of the house every day from early morning to midnight, even on Saturdays and Sundays. He was rarely with his children side by side. If so, it was just for a yell or a command.

Furthermore, Peter's stepmother forced him to get the produce from a company which is near their house to sell. And each day, he had to return to her the money he earned. She, on the contrary, never worked but painted herself all day and dressed like a peacock.

Therefore every morning, besides the books for studying, he also brought to school in his bag a box which contained candies or cookies. He came to school early and stayed there to sell them after school. In the middle of the day we had a short break in the playground. Diligently and pitifully, he sat down at a corner with the box that was a part of his life then.

Peter studied hard. He is good in math. Because of his miserable situation, he became boorish and taciturn. Many students in the class hated him for his character. He's been jeered by some of the bad guys. Between them, there were fights, but every time he never wanted to be beaten.

He walked to school tired with a face in the blues. On his back, the school-bag stretched heavily like a storm that is going to cover his little lonely boat on the open sea.

The Fluteplayer's Son
Brandon Buth

He was a quiet guy and shy as hell. I only knew him for a year, but it was the best year I ever had with *anybody*. It was a Saturday morning in April. I was bored at home, so I decided to go down to the Citicorp Centre to eat and listen to some of the bands. I didn't have too many friends at the time. I guess that's the reason I did a lot of stuff by myself.

At the time I lived at 94th and Madison, so I could take the Lexington bus down to the Citicorp. I had a lot of fun on the bus. My favorite pastime was staring and smiling at people. It was fun to watch the people's reactions. Mostly, they'd pretend they didn't see me and look out of the window. A few seconds later they'd look up again (very quickly) to check if I was still staring.

When I arrived at fifty-fourth I got off and walked to the Citicorp building. The streets were pretty crowded. That's one thing I really hate in New York is the unfriendliness. Always when I bumped into a person I'd say "Sorry" or "Pardon me." When I said that people looked at me with the strangest faces.

In the building I got some ice cream and a brownie. I decided to sit down to eat. I found a place right next to the flowers. It was great fun since this really great flute player was playing on the stage. But even though it was good I couldn't help hearing this kid crying. I finished my food and looked around to see where the sound was coming from. There was a guy my age right behind me crying. Even though this was New York I asked him what was wrong. He wouldn't answer. He just said "Thanks a lot for your concern but I'm all right." Realizing that people actually heard him he jumped off the edge of the flower pot and left.

I wouldn't have thought much of it if I hadn't met him again at Donnel Library in the record section. It's there I really got to know him. I looked at the record he took out and said, "That's a neat record, I've got it at home."

"Oh, that's good, I usually like their music." That's how we blabbed on for hours. After a few weeks I really became good friends with him.

We even went to England together in the summer. I found out a lot about him and his life. His parents got divorced recently and he went to live with his father in New York. He missed his mother a lot. The reason he cried at the Citicorp was the fluteplayer reminded him of his mother. She also played the flute. I don't know how he coped with the tremendous guilt complex he had. He always felt that he was the reason for his parents' divorce.

After the summer he went back to live with his mom. I really hope he's happy. We write sometimes, but I'm losing contact with him.

Only Memories
Bosi Cohen

Death

Their death broke our hearts.
It left us with only their
          memories,
And they were not many for
          me.
My mother had her whole life-
          time filled with them,
And my father, a few more
          years more than me.
I only had four years,
Four very precious years,
But they were not long
          enough.
They were way too short but
          some of the sweetest years
          of my life.

Being Four

The sand runs between my toes while the little waves rush over me. Riva, my sister, is a little deeper than me, about a foot. She runs around falling and laughing when the waves reach her. I remember when I was her age. That was a great and sad age. When you're four, you see the world through fantasy eyes. The world opens and closes opportunities. When you were three, you just started realizing the opportunities. But by the time you are four, you start reaching for the opportunities. Grabbing them, not stopping till you reach it. That is the great part of being four.

The sad part for me was my grandparents on my mother's side. . . . They were in a rush to get home from Florida, where they were visiting my other grandparents. My grandmother wanted to get back to her school. At 66, she was going back to school!!!! They got stuck in a storm on the way back; they were very near to the airport in New Jersey. The airplane crashed against a fence. My grandmother was killed instantly, and my grandfather was rushed to the hospital. They were sitting in the front of the plane, and their seats were loose. My grandfather died in the hospital a month later. They said he did not suffer, for he died in the night. I always thought if he had not died, then he would've died later of a broken heart.

Darkness

Darkness,
Nothingness,
My life is filled with this.
There is no end,
No way out.
But until I was four
I never felt it,
Didn't know it existed.
It had no use for me nor I for
    it.
But, yet, it made its way to my heart.
It played with my emotions,
It rearranged my life.
I wish it hadn't.
'Cause I loved my grandparents
    too much

More Memories

My grandfather's pipe was always sitting in an ash tray next to the white leather spinning chairs. The pipe smoke would make the air smell nice, and the smoke would travel upwards and disappear halfway between the ceiling and the ashtray.

My grandfather's smile could calm a thunderstorm. It could make all your worries go away. I have never seen my grandfather frown. I doubt that he ever knew how. When I sat on his lap, I would suddenly smile. His hands were big, compared to my little hands, and smooth. They were perfect to play paddie-cake with.

My grandfather didn't deserve to die. He had too much to live for. He hadn't seen my sister who was born about three and a half years after his death. Why did he have to die?!? Why couldn't someone else have died? But not him. Not my grandfather. Why did God take him? I hated God for some time but what could I do? What could a little girl of four do?!? Nothing, just sit and wait. Well, I've waited too long for something to happen. The waiting just left me with memories, but the Africans say, "No one has died unless no one remembers them."

Heaven

His pipe's smoke went
    up to the ceiling in
    circles.
Although it never made
    it up to heaven, it
    tried.
My grandfather didn't
    try,
But he went.
God took him up to his
    domain,
Up, up in the clouds,
Where I can't see
    him.

Walking and Sitting

I love Wildwood. The beach and the boardwalk. My grandmother and I would take walks along the beach and I felt as if I was in a dream where everything was perfect. I still walk the beach with the same dream but it is missing something. Someone . . . my grandmother. I feel her but I don't see her. Her memories go through me in her old house, on the beach, on the boardwalk. My grandfather's memories do the same thing. His pipe's smell fills the air as I think of him. He would sit on the white leather chairs with his pipe in his mouth. I'm sitting on his lap and nothing seems to matter.

Now the chairs are black. They changed the color. But when I sit on the chairs, I smell the pipe, see his face. I wish they were with me now. Then they could see how happy I am. Maybe they can . . . . I wish they could. I wish they were alive again. I know this is a wish which can't come true but it would stop me from wishing.

"Baulder the Beautiful"

My grandmother's red hair would move with the warm summer breeze. The setting sun's rays made her hair glow and twinkle. This is one memory which comes to my mind when her name is mentioned. Her face was so perfect. To me, she looked like a movie star—glamourous. She bore four girls, the oldest, my mother. None of her daughters resemble her. Some say so, but my grandmother had no twin. She was one of a kind, maybe an angel sent from heaven. Her personalities were like Baulder's, a Norse god who brought purity to the world. So bright and gay were they both. She could cheer up anyone, no matter what the situation. . . . When I heard she'd died, the light faded into darkness, nothingness. I wondered how my mother felt if I felt this bad. It felt as if I was losing everything and there was nothing for me to grasp—just the air, which felt heavy and dry. It seemed like evil had attacked the good and won. Evil was taking everything I loved. But I told myself that if evil ever got my parents, too, I would fight it, and if I didn't win, I would leave this earth and live by myself instead of living in total darkness.

Kevin
Amy Billone

A dark figure quietly occupied the desk next to mine. Tense and withdrawn, Kevin huddled in his chair, concentrating on a crack in the corner of the wall. I had rarely heard him speak, except in one of his uncontrollable fits of rage. These outbursts, triggered by unpleasant remarks from classmates, were characterized by screaming fits and blind swings at nearby offenders. Kevin was large for his ten years. This, in addition to the fact that he was black, had given him the reputation of a person to stay away from.

Suddenly I noticed that Kevin had turned timidly towards me, his face solemn. As I looked into his soft brown eyes, I noticed that they seemed gentle, that there was a certain sadness in them, almost pleading.

"I. . . ." he began, then stopped, as though the prospect of speaking frightened him.

"What is it, Kevin?" I asked. My surprise that he had finally spoken made me respond almost too quickly.

"I don't . . . I don't understand," he said softly. I glanced at the blank math worksheet on his desk. Taking the pencil into my hand, I began to explain the concept of long division to him, slowly, waiting for some sign of comprehension. Still, his eyes remained blank as he looked down helplessly at the unyielding paper. Soon the teacher caught sight of me and made me return to my own seat. Kevin's paper remained untouched throughout the day.

That afternoon, as I traced my usual route home from school, I became aware of footsteps a few paces behind me. Turning slightly, I saw Kevin. He was lost in the depths of a bedraggled blue overcoat, several sizes too large. I had never seen him walk this route before, and I was sure he didn't live in my neighborhood. Southeast Evanston, with its restored Victorian mansions and lakeside, courtyard condominiums, was not Kevin's domain. Was he following me? Rounding the final corner before reaching our two-flat on Michigan Avenue, I could still hear the shuffling sound of his feet on the pavement behind me. When I reached the walkway leading to my front door, I turned to face him. He looked down shyly. At last he raised his head.

"Can I come in?" he asked in a voice barely above a whisper. I hesitated.

"Sure you can," I said finally. We reached the front door, where I turned the key in the lock. As we walked inside, Kevin's eyes quickly scanned the front hall, finally resting on the ten-gallon fish tank I had inherited from my grandfather. He stood transfixed, his eyes wide. At last he pulled himself away from the aquarium and followed me into the kitchen. Taking out some milk and chocolate chip cookies, I sat down across from him at the kitchen table. He ate ravenously, without raising his head until he was finished. We sat together, then, in silence. He seemed content just to be there, quietly, and I soon began to go about my business, washing the dishes, and finishing up my homework. Still he sat. He must have stayed for two hours, never once speaking or moving from his chair. At 5:00 my mother arrived, announcing that it was time for supper. Kevin rose heavily and followed me to the front door. Lost once more inside his enormous coat, he slipped out into the cold November night.

The next day at school everything was quite the same as it had always been. Kevin spent the afternoon staring at another blank worksheet, occasionally glancing at me, but for the most part, withdrawn as usual. Walking home from school that day, I could once again hear the shuffling sound of feet behind me, but this time I did not turn around. When we reached my house, Kevin waited patiently for me to unlock the door. Once inside, he paused momentarily to look at the fish, and then followed me into the kitchen. He sat in the same chair as before while I got out some string cheese from the refrigerator. Once again he devoured his food hungrily, without lifting his eyes. When he was finished, I cleared the table and began washing the dishes. For the next few hours Kevin watched me silently as I puttered about the house. Finally it was time for him to go home. Taking one last look at the fish, he turned and trudged out the door. I followed him with my eyes until he disappeared into the darkness.

For the next few days the ritual was exactly the same: Kevin would accompany me home from school, and I would let him in. Then he would stop and look at the fish before following me to the kitchen, where he would sit for the next few hours, without speaking or rising from the chair, until it was time for him to go home. One day, however, I was asked to stop at the grocery store after school to pick up some bread and milk before heading home. That afternoon I explained the situation to Kevin.

"Kevin, today I'm going to the store instead of straight home. Do you want to come?" He nodded, and we set off in the opposite direction from home. The air was cold against my face, and I was glad to have a change in the monotony. I noticed suddenly that Kevin was by my side rather than a few paces behind, as usual. We walked in silence for a while, each wrapped up in our own thoughts. Suddenly Kevin turned to face me.

"Do you think I'm dumb?" he asked. I was startled. It took me a few seconds to react.

"No, of course I don't," I reassured him.

"Well I am," he said flatly.

"What makes you think so?"

"The teacher told my mama I got a learnin' disabled or something, and I axed her what it was and she said it meant I was real dumb, 'cause I don't do math or read good."

"That doesn't mean you're dumb." I struggled to find the words to comfort him. "It just means that certain things, like reading and math, are harder for you than other people. It doesn't have anything to do with how smart you are."

"Oh." He seemed skeptical but at the same time slightly relieved.

From then on Kevin and I spent our after-school time outdoors, wandering the streets or riding the buses to the end of the line—somewhere in the depths of the city—caught up in the thrill that came with wondering whether we'd ever get home. Day by day we roamed the streets together. Kevin's fascination with fish resulted in many trips to the "Fish Bowl" (the local aquatics shop), as well as the public library, where he would sift the shelves for books even remotely pertaining to the subject of fish. On days too cold and windy to wander the streets I would read to him from books on fish. The idea of a mystical underwater world in which every creature was a major part in the life cycle kept Kevin captivated for hours.

To adjust to the harsh reality of life, Kevin's mind, it seemed, had become very literal. Perhaps because he himself was such an open human being, the thought of anyone else as less than this did not enter his mind. He took everything seriously. One day we stopped at the Fish Bowl after school. My family was going out of town for a few days, and to save the trouble of having someone come in and feed the fish, I had decided to pick up a weekend fish feeder that would feed the fish slowly over a period of two days. While I paid at the counter, Kevin stared uncomfortably at the fish feeder.

"Weekend fish feeder?" he repeated hesitantly. "Why'd you get that?"

"I'm going out of town for a few days next week," I explained.

"When?" he demanded.

"Next Tuesday," I said, rather impatiently.

"You can't do that!" he exploded.

"Why not?" I asked simply, nothing else coming to mind.

"Because your fish is gonna die!!" His voice shook, and his body began to tremble. I put my hand on his shoulder to comfort him.

"The fish will be fine, Kevin," I said gently.

"No! No they won't! They won't be fine! They gonna die!'' he stammered.

"Kevin, why would the fish possibly die?'' I asked rationally, trying to calm him down and discover the cause of his agony.

"They'll starve!'' He was near tears now.

"Kevin,'' I said calmly, "that's what I got the fish feeder for.'' He shook his head violently.

"No! It ain't gonna work! You said you was leaving on a Tuesday!''

"Yes, and I'll be home Wednesday night. That's two days. This is a special kind of fish feeder. It lasts for two days.''

"No! It says on the box, weekend fish feeder, and you're leaving on a Tuesday!'' he wailed. It suddenly dawned on me why he was so upset. I couldn't help but laugh at the situation. I explained to him the loose meaning of "weekend,'' and he seemed somewhat pacified.

The next day after school I asked Kevin where he wanted to go. It was beginning to snow, but it still seemed like a fine day for walking. Kevin hesitated for a moment.

"Could we . . . you think we could stop at my house? There's something I got to show you.'' I had never seen Kevin's house before, and my curiosity had been gnawing at me for some time. All I knew was that he spent little time there—wherever it was—and that whoever took care of him did not seem to mind. I agreed readily, and we set off into the falling snow. Kevin led me through a complex network of darkened alleys and narrow breezeways, each branching off into a seemingly darker path. My lashes were wet with melted snow. Having lost all sense of direction, I followed him blindly. Kevin came to an abrupt stop in the middle of a deserted alley. Directly in front of us was a steep set of cement stairs descended into the ground. I followed Kevin down the stairs and into what seemed to be a typical basement. There was virtually no light. Cobwebs clung to the walls. Pipes jutted out rudely from the low ceiling. In the center of the room stood a small rickety table. Behind it a refrigerator leaned weakly against the edge of a rusty counter. Kevin led me out of the kitchen and into a room barely larger than a closet, which I took to be his. The room was empty except for a broken-down cot in the corner. Suddenly a faint iridescent glow illuminated the far corner of the room. Kevin guided me to the source of light.

"See?'' he said proudly. In front of me towered a magnificent twenty-gallon fish aquarium alive with a multitude of bright orange swordfish, angelfish, and tetras. I did not ask where he had possibly gotten the money to put this incredible treasure together. Nor did I ask where he had found the time to nurture a thriving world of healthy, exotic fish. I merely gazed in silent awe.

"I clean it every day,'' Kevin beamed with pride.

"I can see that. It's beautiful,'' I murmured. For a while I just stood there, entranced by the slow movement of the fish. Finally I announced that I had to be getting home for supper. Kevin led me out of the darkness of his home, and out into the cool, snowy world above. For many days and nights afterwards the image of Kevin's fish tank, radiating in the corner of his cold, bare house, remained with me.

In the days that followed, Kevin amazed me time and time again with his acting ability. He had a wide range of characters he loved to play, some of them comic, and others painfully serious. I carried with me a red, flowered bandana, and when I held it in front of his face he would change personalities. I had no control over what character he would choose to portray at any given time; that was solely up to him. I could merely persuade him to change from one character to another with the bandana. Soon Kevin's range of characters had expanded to such an extent that I began to find it hard to keep track of them. I would carry the bandana with me wherever I went—including school. Kevin, however, would never let anyone else watch during the transformation, and I suppose they wouldn't have understood if he had. It frustrated me that he had such incredible talent but wouldn't allow it to be discovered. He was constantly on guard, afraid to open himself up to the world for fear of rejection. The anger inside of him would still erupt occasionally into fits of rage, where he lost his tight control and struck out at his cold surroundings. Once, David Whitney, the class trouble-maker, had referred to Kevin's father as "a no-good bum." Kevin had attacked him—it took three teachers to pry Kevin away from David. David had been rushed to the hospital, where he was treated for head injuries and a broken arm. Kevin, meanwhile, had been suspended from school for three days.

One day, as usual, we were walking aimlessly through the streets of town towards no particular destination. A biting wind was coming in from the lake. The sky was ominously dark, despite the fact that it was only mid-afternoon. My ears pounded with the rumbling of machines, the clank of metal, and the shouts of construction workers, as a building was being torn down. Kevin's eyes were glazed as he stopped to watch the workers.

"My daddy was a construction worker," he said suddenly. The reference to his father startled me, for I had rarely heard him speak freely about either of his parents.

"I don't got a daddy no more," he said softly, his eyes on the ground. I suddenly felt an overwhelming pity for Kevin, standing weak and vulnerable by my side. I, too, stared at the ground, no words coming to my throat.

"He died and now he's gone and I don't got a daddy no more." I drew a breath of cold air into my lungs, his words echoing in my ears.

"I was five years old and my mama wasn't home. I was playing outside and when I came in I saw my daddy lying on the floor. I thought he was asleep and I tried to wake him up but he wouldn't. I didn't know what to do, so I sat in the corner and cried 'til my mama came home." Kevin's voice was so soft that I could barely hear him above the sound of construction.

"They took him away to the hospital and I never saw him again. I could have . . . I should have done something but I didn't know . . . I didn't understand. . . ." His voice trailed off. I felt a desperate urge to do something for Kevin, to comfort him in some way, but I just stood there helplessly by his side. We stood together until the sound of construction faded and the sky grew dark—more sinister than before—the last hints of daylight melting into the deepening shadows of night.

From then on, Kevin rarely left my side; throughout the school day and outside at recess, Kevin was my constant companion. His familiar presence molded into my life; without it I felt an emptiness, as though something wasn't quite right. Kevin's loyalty was immeasurable, provoking him to direct the buried rage inside of him towards my protection. Anytime anyone so much as looked at me, Kevin would jump to my immediate rescue. This did create some serious problems. I spent many lunch periods with him at the principal's office, promising to try to control Kevin's seemingly abusive nature. But for the most part, Kevin was gentle and subdued.

One Saturday night as I was walking into the house with my family, the shrill sound of the telephone penetrated my ears. We had been gone all day, visiting friends on the other side of town. Throwing my coat down onto the nearest chair, I hurried into the next room and picked up the phone. Kevin's soft voice greeted me.

"Amy? Can you meet me in the alley behind the school in a few minutes?" His voice sounded strained.

"Sure, I'll see you in a little bit," I said, a feeling of urgency descending upon me. Grabbing my coat, I rushed out the back door and into the icy night. I ran breathlessly through the streets of town, around the school, and finally down the dark alley where Kevin was already waiting. When I reached him, I noticed that he was more tense than usual.

"What is it?" I panted.

"Amy, there's something I got to tell you. Today I was looking for you but you wasn't home."

"No, we were visiting some people," I explained.

"Well, I couldn't find you nowhere, so I was looking for you. I went across the street to Robby's house, but he weren't home neither, so I went all down the street, ringing people's doorbells, and if they was home I axed them if they knew where you was." He talked hurriedly, and I had difficulty catching what he was saying. "Then I saw this police car in the center of the road and this policeman was staring at me. He said to get over there so I did and he axed me lots of stuff like what did I think I was doing, and how old I was, and stuff. I said I didn't do nothin' and I answered all his questions but he didn't look like he believed me. Then he axed me if I knew about all the robberies in the neighborhood and I said no, 'cause I didn't. He told me to get in the car. I tells him I wasn't supposed to get in cars with strangers but he just smiled real mean and grabbed my arm. Then he drove me to the police station and called my mama. She came and he told her if he ever saw me in your neighborhood again, I'd get in big trouble. My mama brought me home and whipped me real hard." Kevin paused for a moment. "It's because I'm black, isn't it?" he asked me directly. I looked at the ground.

"You don't know that." My voice sounded flat, and there was no real feeling behind my words.

"I'm scared," he said softly.

"I know."

"My mama says I got to come right home after school and wait for her. I can't let anyone in the house ever, and I can't come over to your house no more." He looked away, down the street into the darkness beyond. "I gotta go now or I'm gonna get in trouble." Kevin turned and I watched his dark figure get smaller and smaller in the distance, until he became one with the night.

During the next week Kevin was transferred to another school, and I heard rumors that he had joined a street gang. Later I heard that Kevin's aunt had fallen sick and his mother had sent him to South Carolina to care for her. So I suppose I'll never see Kevin again. Now, when I think of Kevin I remember his gentle eyes, his fierce loyalty, and his quiet sensitivity. But most of all when I think of Kevin I am haunted by the injustice that stalked him throughout his childhood and finally overtook him.

Memoir of a Group or Place

A different version of memoir writing would be to tell what some group did once or used to do habitually. You were there but not central to the action. Give your reactions as observer or participant.

Another slant is to tell what some place you remember was like or what used to go on there. Whatever feeling or idea makes this memory stand out now may provide a mood or angle to give it in telling others about it.

Could this be a feature piece for some newspaper or magazine? Or include it with your other memoirs of people and places.

How Was the Wedding?
Rania Calas

"How was the wedding?" asked my little niece Elleni.

How do you explain a Greek wedding to a three-year-old? How do you explain a Greek wedding to anyone? Greeks, after all, are not like other people. They are a species by themselves.

Imagine, for instance, the hot kitchen in the house in Athens the day before the wedding. Five husky women are standing around, gossiping, chainsmoking and arguing over what to serve eighty guests the next day.

Meanwhile, visitors arrive at the house to bring wedding presents to the bride. But the bride is not here. She went to pick up her dress at the dressmaker. It still needs some adjustment and a big bow of lace to be sewn on in the back. And where is the bride's mother? She has gone to the flower shop to order huge baskets of pink roses for the church. Someone better give some cool drinks to those visitors!

And where is Aunt Emmanuella? She just remembered that she forgot to pick up her wedding dress at the dry cleaners and it is Saturday and the cleaners are closed! Isn't anybody going to clean up the house? It's a frightful mess, and tomorrow is the wedding.

Does anybody know if the groom's parents from Chicago have arrived? They'll probably drop in anytime now. Oh, god! If they saw this mess, would they really want their son marrying into this strange Greek family, and the wedding taking place in Athens instead of in Chicago?

The pandemonium lasts way into the night. Furniture is moved about. I am delegated to clean up the bathrooms. That sounds easy. It isn't. Standards of cleanliness are not the same all over the world.

On the big day, everything somehow seems to fall into place. The house is spotless; the food is cooked; and the best tablecloth, silver, crystal, and chinaware grace the table. The bar is properly set up, because the bride wants to serve cocktails to her guests in the American manner. She has all the proper supplies. The groom asks, "Where is the ice?"

"Ice? What ice?" There is no ice. The refrigerator has broken down hours ago under the load of foods it is stuffed with.

I am one of the helpless bystanders who is delegated to procure ice. We are going to five different restaurants and ten different hotels to gather two bags of ice cubes. They melt in the Greek heat. So let's hurry! We have to be in church in an hour!

The bride looks stunning. The groom perspires. He is nervous. Maybe he thinks, "What am I doing here?"

I guess all this wouldn't interest Elleni. She would want to know who the flower girl was, and what she wore, and why do people throw flower petals at the bride and groom. She would want to know whether everybody got sugar-coated almonds and what did they do with the baskets of pink roses. I'd have to make it sound like a fairytale. I too wish it would have been a fairytale.

It Was All Over
Zoe Gilman

All was quiet at the dinner table. I could guess what was going on in their heads. Why!? What was I to say? How was I to act? How do you act when you're sitting at a table with a wife and two kids after they have just found out that their father/husband has cancer of the liver? The expressions on their faces were nothing that I had ever seen before. He was going to die, and there wasn't anything that anyone could do but pray that the cancer would go away. **They were all torn up inside, and nothing could help them.**

While I was eating (pushing my food around) I was thinking about how I would cope if it were my father who was dying, and my conclusion was that I had no idea. One by one they solemnly left to put their dishes in the sink. I just sat there. I heard outbursts of crying, and as I sat there tears built up in my eyes until I couldn't see. Then they made their way down my face. I heard sounds of terror from the kitchen, and this was only the beginning. I wanted so badly to give Gemma (my friend, the younger daughter) a hug, but I thought that she might just want to be comforted by family.

That night I couldn't fall asleep. All I could think of was how lucky I was to have two healthy parents. What was I to say when Tom came home? What is there to say when they're going to die? Nothing would ever be the same.

After the cancer began to affect Tom's life, money was needed. My dad helped out a lot with trying to sell Tom's paintings and prints. Tom slowly got thinner and tired-looking. His brother Paul from Texas came to visit. This was very touching because they hadn't seen each other for about five years. At this point, when Paul visited, Tom was using a wheelchair to get around. He now began to forget names—sometimes of his daughters—which was really up-setting. Very disturbingly, he would sometimes get out of his wheelchair and rush into his bedroom. He became very moody and was upset easily.

During all of this, I never really spoke to Gemma about exactly what she **was feeling. I always felt uncomfortable talking to her about this traumatic** experience. I never really knew what to say.

Every time I looked at Tom I thought about death. When I saw him it **was like looking at death itself, his eyes limpid and sad, his face thin and** bony, and his speech confused.

Now money was getting very tight, so my father and Phyllis (Tom's wife) had to try harder than ever to sell the office and its supplies. Rooms around their house began to get messy and crowded with papers, prints, paintings, books, and boxes because Tom was a professional artist who illustrated many books and did advertising and packaging for cosmetic companies. He was a very talented man, and I always admired his work. I especially loved his **paintings of flowers, which were all done from imagination and were beautiful. He would sometimes paint even after the cancer had a great effect on him.** These paintings became cluttered and confusing as the disease became worse.

Tom was my dad's best friend, so he tried his hardest to help Phyllis in any way possible and did a good job. Besides helping to sell Tom's business he also took care of legal papers and documents that had to be filled out. At times (quite often, in fact) I became jealous because it seemed like all of my dad's **attention was centered around Tom and Phyllis. This was true, and it was right** for my dad to center his attention around them, but this did not stop the jealousy that I felt.

Sara, Gemma's older sister, was 17; we're also friends. Once or twice when we were both home alone she asked me if I wanted to go shopping with her. She said that she had to get out of the house because it was depressing. We would go to Woolworth's on 110th street and Broadway to buy cheap make-up. It was nice spending time with her. She's a great person, and I always have fun with her. It's nice that we are close because I have always thought of her as the older sister that I never had but always wanted. Sara and Gemma both had been so strong throughout this whole thing. Gemma kept going to school and stayed up late doing homework.

Family and friends came to visit. Many would say, "Gemma, how are you doing?" She would sometimes say, "All right" or just be honest and say, "Not too good." I used to think to myself, what a question to ask, How are you doing? I guess they were just trying to acknowledge that they cared and were concerned. I cared more than I could ever express, but it was hard for me to show it. I always felt like I would say the wrong thing. It was probably a mistake not to say what I felt because she probably would have liked to hear about my concern for her and her family.

Tom began to eat less and get thinner. He only ate mushy foods like bananas, and he drank nutritious milk shakes. He became weak and had to be helped to the bathroom. For showering he would sit in a chair under the water. He stayed in bed almost all the time now. A nurse would come from Sloan-Kettering to massage his body in order to keep his blood circulating. He was going through a large amount of pain, so he would occasionally take morphine. Phyllis now got Tom a hospital bed so he could be more comfortable. Now he could go to the bathroom in the bed and the urine would be transferred into a sac. It was very hard for Tom to communicate with anyone, so we had to guess what he was asking for, which was difficult. He remained in his house until he died because he made my dad and Phyllis promise that they wouldn't take him to the hospital.

Now he stopped eating, and this meant that the end was near, a week at the most. A few more days went by and now he hardly had enough energy to drink out of a straw. Phyllis and my dad would have to wet his lips every fifteen minutes or so because he had stopped drinking and his mouth had to be kept moist.

One Friday night I made plans to sleep at my friend Jenny's house. My dad called me at around 6:00 or 7:00 that Friday evening. He told me that he thought I should come home because this would probably be Tom's last night. I didn't want to come home, I was afraid to face Tom's death even though I knew it had been coming for months. I told my dad that I'd be home at about 9:30, and he said okay in a deep, solemn voice.

I rode home in a cab with great anticipation about the news I would receive when I entered my lobby. I began to get butterflies in my stomach as the cab rode through the noisy streets. I began to get hot and a bit dizzy. The ride seemed like forever until I arrived in front of my building. I couldn't believe that I was already there. As I stepped out into the cold night air I could see my dad waiting for me inside the lobby door. I didn't want to face it. I knew that everything was over. My dad opened the lobby door and looked at me with sad red eyes. I said, "Dad, please don't tell me until we get into the elevator."

I knew it was all over, but I ignored the truth and had to wait and see what my dad would say. As we rode up in the elevator I asked the question, "Did Tom die?" The answer was yes. I felt like I had been stabbed with a knife, right through my heart. It was all over, everything. I was scared to enter that house—then I would truly have to deal with his death.

My dad and I went inside, where many people sat in the dining room. Nicole was there with her family; she was Gemma's best friend and my very close friend, too. We went into the living room and began to talk. She was happy that I had arrived so that we could be together and talk. Gemma was in her room the whole time talking with her tutor, teacher, and close friend. She remained in her locked room for a couple of hours. I was wondering what she was saying and how she was feeling. I had an idea of the suffering that she was going through, but I was still wondering how she was dealing with her enormous loss.

Nicole and I sat in the living room waiting to see if we could go in the bedroom and see Tom. We were scared to go in because we didn't know what to expect. We were told that we could go in so we slowly made our way into the bedroom, me first (shaking) and then Nicole. As I entered the room Phyllis looked up at me. I was surprised; she had a look of relief on her face, and she looked relaxed. She said to me, "Don't be scared. It's okay. Come over here." I walked over, looking at the lifeless body that lay on the hospital bed before me. The expression on Tom's face was peaceful. I saw a slight smile on his face, and his eyes were slightly open. Phyllis explained to me that Tom now had no more pain, and that was a relief to her. At that moment I felt so close to Phyllis, closer than I had ever felt before.

Then Sara (the older daughter) came in, climbed onto the bed, rested her head and arms on her father's lifeless body, and cried. I was sitting and watching this whole thing. I couldn't believe it.

It got later and the doorbell rang. It was men coming to take Tom away. They brought a cot into the bedroom as I sat in the livingroom. Suddenly I heard screams of terror worse than ever before, and they were coming from Phyllis as the men began to carry away Tom's body. She began to walk with the men hoping to stop them from taking her husband away. He had to go, and nothing could keep him—he had already gone.

While I watched Tom being carried through the house, tears poured down my face. I couldn't control them. They just kept pouring out, but I didn't say a word, I just kept crying. There was nothing to say. Just the expressions on everyone's face was enough to say more than a million words. I looked up and saw Gemma's face. She was looking at me as I sat there crying. I wasn't really sure what was going through her head as she looked at me. She had a look of agony on her face; I'll never forget the expression. I can still see it clearly in my mind. I couldn't believe that this was happening: a man's body was being carried through a dining room and this man was like part of my family. I just sat there and cried. That was all I could do.

Epilogue

I decided to write about this particular trauma in my life because I wanted to share this experience with others and it seemed easiest to do this by writing about it. As I wrote, the words seemed to be coming out of the tip of my pen. Writing the story came easy to me and I felt good while I read over the pages of thoughts that I had written days before. I hope that the reader of this story can picture the scenes and can experience some of the feelings expressed in my story.

Two Rooms at the Children's Free School
Kerry Adelson

The room we used to work in at the Children's Free School was the room for the middles (ages 6-9) and the littles (ages 4, 5 and sometimes 6). The tables that the middles worked at were parallel to the big storefront window that looked out on 119th and Morningside Dr. The window was lined with bean plants. The table seemed huge to me at the time. It was painted bright orange and I remember clearly sitting at the end of the table scribbling on it, then smudging the scribble and trying to erase the smudge. Since the smudge didn't usually come off, the table was covered with pencil smudges.

The table that the littles worked at was blue, I think. It has been painted so many times that the paint bulged out in certain places. In other places there were holes where children had scraped away at the paint, and you could see layers of red and yellow under the blue.

The library was off the room where we worked. I remember doing my reading work in the Dick and Jane type books in the library. I was the furthest advanced in my group because I was a year older than most of the other kids. I was so proud to be the furthest ahead. At the time that seemed like a big thing.

When you walk into the library, to the left and right of the door are many orange crates filled with books. On the wall in the back of the room are many cushions. The two I remember best are two large corduroy cushions. They were as big as I was. In the center of the room I remember the tables the littles worked at. It was in both age areas but I guess at different times.

I was young then, and the differences between ages 7 and 8 seemed like forever. Those huge cushions were probably tiny. Those were my carefree days, and I wish I could have them back. I can't though. Now the old storefront building is a huge Columbia dormitory.

Martha's Vineyard
Andrew Liebhafsky

The plane had just landed on the little Martha's Vineyard airport, from polluted N.Y.C. When I stepped off the plane I was hit by a sharp gust of cold sea air. I was freezing. It was about fifty degrees, and I was just wearing my soccer uniform. (We had just beat Berkeley 4-0.) We crammed into our little Volkswagen beetle. When we arrived at the farm (Brookside Farm on Middle Road, my Dad's), it was still dark. I could just barely see the horses grazing in the upper pasture and the moon reflecting on the pond. I took a warm bath and had some delicious clam chowder and went to bed at eight.

When I woke up the next morning it was still dark. I slipped on some clothes and crept downstairs quietly. I turned up the thermostat and ran down to the barn. Bill, the man who takes care of the animals, was there. I filled the horse stalls with feed and brought the oxen up from the lower pasture. When I came back, Bill had already gone. He had left me a bucket of feed for the ducks, who were quacking like crazy down at the pond. After I had fed the ducks I gathered some firewood. When I looked up I could see an orange line streaking across the sky. The sun had almost come all the way up. I walked back to the house, and everybody was still asleep, even my dog, who is an early riser. I lit all of the fires and read until my parents were up.

My Dad was the first one up. He immediately went out and got the bikes ready, filling the sacks with food, drink, etc. After we had some delicious pancakes we started on our thirty-mile bike ride. We went up our driveway and on to Middle Road, which is probably the hilliest road on the Vineyard. We rode all the way down the island to the tip of Menemsha. I had a tall hot chocolate. My dad and I then sat on the docks and watched the boats unload the morning catch. There were nets and nets of big fish, all squirming. It was really neat to watch the men get them on the dock. From Menemsha we took a road going up island all the way to Oak Bluffs, where we sat for a little while in the community square. There were people playing soccer and singing songs. It was enchanting. In Oak Bluffs you can see right by the community square the gingerbread houses, which are very small, very old houses which people still live in. From Oak Bluffs we took a road called Edgartown Road past the airport and through the state forest on a bike path. The forest was really beautiful; all the leaves were turning, and at a certain point if you looked around you could see the ocean with all its white sails. When we got out of the state forest, we got on a road called Old County, which eventually led us home.

The bike ride was a little over thirty miles. This particular one was really nice. It was chilly, and there was almost always a sharp breeze. All the leaves had turned, and we passed many farms with cattle and sheep grazing. Bike riding, I think, is also one of the most exhilarating sports, attacking hills on the way up and flying down again in twelfth gear. Then on the flat stretches you just pace yourself all the way.

A New Experience
John Bermudez

My cousin one day invited me to visit friends he knew who lived up on a farm. I thought this would be a new experience and my chance to get away from the city. During my stay I had a lot of fun and did things I'd never done before like milk and feed cows. It was fun but the bad thing about it was that I had to wake up at six in the morning to do it. We also drove tractors, went hunting, water-skied, and took walks through beautiful fields and woods in which there were tall colorful trees, streams and ponds.

One of the most interesting and exciting things I did there was help to remove a calf being born from the mother. It was a wonderful thing, and actually helping and witnessing the birth of an animal being brought into the world was an experience in itself. Even when it was all over it gave me a wonderful feeling. This was something I had never seen and something I never thought I would see.

One day while I was there I had another experience. While walking through the field my cousin and I saw what we both thought was the back of a dog. But as it came over the hill we saw it was a full-grown black bear. I've seen many pictures and movies about them on T.V., and I've seen bears in the zoo. But seeing it in the wild, free seemed like a whole different thing. We both did have rifles because at the time we were hunting for woodchucks. If it were to attack we would probably have had to shoot it, but I'm glad it didn't. The bear didn't even care about us; it just looked at us once and kept going like we weren't even there. I'm glad it didn't attack for two reasons: one, because I really wouldn't want to see it go; and two, because I wouldn't want such a wonderful experience to turn into a tragedy.

I think everyone should get a chance to get out of the city at one time or another to go experience a new type of life with new and different challenges. For instance, instead of facing cars and people and all the crime you hear about, you could try to face challenges like moving, feeding, and milking cows. You could also try fun things like riding cows and hunting, and hard things like lifting bales of hay onto wagons in the hot sun. I'm planning to go back soon, and when I do I know I'll enjoy it and experience more things.

The Lighthouse
Damian Eckstein

The memory now is faded ... but is still there. The place is somewhere on 170th street near the Hudson River.

The time is 1974 sometime in late Spring. My father would play tennis over near what I would call "The Big Rock." I would get overly bored and beg my mother to take me home—the nice *cool* home. But no, I had to wait. Damn! Then my mother, noticing my fatigue, would take me by the hand and lead me into what seemed to me a whole new world. I could spot it a hundred yards away.

My little red lighthouse ... the lighthouse that was written about in the childhood classic. Although I have never seen it without the George Washington Bridge over it, I still loved it.

The dappled sun winked against its rusted paint, and red chips were falling to the ground. Two stories up, the black-topped lighthouse had lost some of its luster, but it was still in stable condition.

I would jump up and down trying hard to reach the porthole. My mother would heave me up by the armpits. I would squint, and squint again, my eyes not yet adjusted to the darkness.

Inside, the floor was higher, so somehow I would tumble in. Standing up and dusting myself off, I would look around. Turning my head to one side then the other, I would see more portholes winding up, and in the faint light was a winding and twisting stairwell.

"Mom," I would say, "come in." But she would answer, "I can't, Damian. I'm too big. Go yourself."

So I would turn to the stairwell winding up and take a first reluctant step. Fear swelled up inside me; with a gulp to protect me from vampires and demons of the sort, I would take a few more steps, winding ever upwards. Reaching the first porthole, I would look outside to see if my mother was still there. She would wave at me; sticking my arm out of the porthole I would wave back. So I continued to trek onwards.

Almost halfway to the second level, my eyes adjusted to the dark, I would see the dim wooden stairs, and the glowing door ... the glowing door.

Repositioning my neck back from a twisting crane upward, I hastened my steps. Finally the dim white stairs. Visions started to dance in my head: me suddenly losing my balance, falling in some kind of eternal deepness, finally landing, my neck askew in an awkward state. The visions disappeared as I ascended the steps. There it was, my one true point, but with the old vision gone, a new one came to take its place: I was opening the sun-outlined door, and out comes a mangled dead body, falling to the floor with a sickening thud.

Although something told me that that wasn't going to happen, I hoped against hope that the glowing door wasn't locked. My trembling hand took the cold dirty metal, the knob twisted, I opened the door, and the sunlight greeted my face. At last I was out! I had conquered new heights! The water sparkled, the bridge was alive and roaring, my mother seemed like a waving speck. I waved back, on top of the world.

It's a shame people can't do that any more. People need to find new horizons, even if it's a closed-down lighthouse.

Memoir of an Eyewitness Incident

Tell anything you saw happen once that was a brief incident you merely witnessed as a spectator, something of some significance to you but not necessarily very unusual or dramatic. Would this go well with some of your other writing? Or would it fit into the theme or subject characterizing some publication or audience you know of?

Undaunted
Sallima Khan

I was looking through my window on a cold, dark and lonely morning. I didn't want to go to school because it was snowing. As I looked out onto the streets covered with snow, I saw a girl waiting for the bus. She was dressed for the weather. Her bright-colored outer clothing caught my eye as I was looking through the window.

The bus came coasting down the street. It appeared dirty and battered. Instead of stopping, the bus went right past the girl, splashing her with slush. The dirty water and ice dulled her bright colors. Instead of throwing her books on the ground and crying, she walked back home.

After seeing this I ate my breakfast, then went back to look out the window. I saw her again, but this time she was cleaned up and ready for a bus ride to school.

Replay
Jennifer Rockford

It happened about eight months ago, and I still dream about it. I still shiver about that horrible night.

From my apartment living room window you can see across the street into this couple's living room. Now, I usually don't go around peeking into other people's lives, but this night I could hear some awful yelling going on, so I decided to investigate. This couple never pulled down their shades; I had a perfect view of what was going on.

The two of them couldn't be over the age of 27. They had just moved in, so I took it they were newlyweds. Anyway, the girl was in her nightgown (a flannel one), and the man still had his overcoat on. She was crying. Even though her eyes were clouded with tears, I could see the passion piercing through. It was not the normal love-passion though, and that's what worried me. Suddenly with no warning the man whirled around and shoved the woman against the wall. He then started slapping her, not once, but twice, three times. Over and over again he slapped her until she was a blur of tears and blood.

I finally just couldn't stand it any more. I stole away from the window as though if I were caught, I would be punished like a child or like that woman. I slowly made my way across the apartment until I finally reached my bedroom. I shook my clothes off as though they were infected and slipped into my bed.

How many times before had I seen that same scene, but the actors changed. This time my own parents. How many times had I sat in the darkness of my room while I heard my mother scream out of pain and agony. I'd tried over and over to forget it, but it finally caught up to me. As I felt myself drift off, I knew it wouldn't be a peaceful night. I'd be haunted with memories, memories of two words that went hand in hand together in my world. Childhood and terror.

A Moment of Anger
Zeph Landau

I was sitting on a stoop on Mormeck St. It's one of those quaint city streets with three- or four-story brownstones. The cars were parked one behind the other. Trees stood in front of every house, each with its car on guard. The pieces of sidewalks, cemented at different times, looked like a patchwork quilt. A pedestrian walked by from time to time.

A taxicab whipped down the street and came to a screeching halt a couple of houses past me. A man dressed in a business suit and a hat took his briefcase out of the cab. He was mad about something. He shouted at the taxi driver, "What the hell is your problem, you drive like a maniac. I've got valuable things in here." He pointed to his briefcase. I started to listen more carefully. I was curious about what was in the briefcase.

"I'm sorry, sir," said the cabby, "but you did say 'The end of the block'?"

"I don't care what I said," bellowed the businessman. He was turning red with rage. He was no more than a couple of feet away from the driver. "I've never heard of such a monstrosity in my life." He looked as though he might punch the driver.

The cabby just sat there. He wasn't obnoxious or vulgar. Somehow, without saying or doing a thing, he managed to stay polite.

The man, expecting an answer, was taken aback. He huffed loudly and stalked off.

"Sir, you haven't paid." It sent a chill down my spine. Evidently it did the same to the man, for he stopped and turned around. The man came back, thrust his money at the driver and then kicked the door with his shiny shoes. The cabby didn't twitch a muscle, and before I knew it, his cab had turned the corner and was gone.

The street was quiet again, one of those quaint city streets.

Memoir of Nature

Give an account of some action you witnessed in which people played little or no part, such as some animal behavior or weather that particularly impressed you. Give your own thoughts and feelings, however.

You may include this in a collection of your memoirs, to diversify them, or make it part of a booklet of nature memoirs by others.

For the Shortest Time
Craig McCord

I woke up out of my deep sleep to find myself being shaken by my older stepbrother, Scott. "Wake up, Ginger's had a baby!" he yelled.

I looked out the window at the rays of the early morning sun. It was very early in the morning, about six o'clock. I had had only four hours of sleep. My usual morning argument started up within me. "Scott's lying through his teeth," said Voice A. "Go back to sleep!"

"Maybe he's right! Ginger [my horse] has been looking fat lately," returned Voice B.

"No, everybody but you and your old blind grandmother say she's just getting overweight. Scott just wants you to make him breakfast."

"You're right. You win," said Voice B.

"You're crazy," I said to Scott.

"I'm serious," he said.

"Really?" I jumped out of bed.

"Let's see about this," said Voice B.

"Oooohh—[disappointed]. Do we have to?" asked Voice A. "Well, all right, let's go."

I walked out of my room to find myself being pushed downstairs among a flurry of nightgowns belonging to other members of the family running to see if Scott was being truthful or if he was just hungry. As soon as we got downstairs, we peered out the windows in the direction of the pasture. Sure enough, hobbling behind Ginger was something that looked like a large dog. But looking closer you could see that it was a small foal with a bit of the umbilical cord attached to its stomach.

"I told you," said Scott behind us, but we were not paying attention to him. He may have said, "Hey guys, I'm hungry! Make me something to eat," and we wouldn't have noticed.

So we went out to see what sex it was. It was a male. He was really cute. He was very thin though, and his tiny ribs were visible. He was a medium red-brown except for his white rear-end and white legs. His coat was still moist from his mother's womb. His tail looked kind of deformed, for it was short and bushy. It looked a little like a deer's tail except that it didn't stick up. He also had a white spot about two inches in diameter between his eyes on his forehead. His little rear-end stuck up in the air almost higher than his head was. He looked like a sprinter at the "Get set" position before a race. He kept filling his little body with the rich milk from his mother.

Ginger was relying only on instinct, for this was her first foal. She looked a little nervous and confused, though, and got a little crazy every time we got near her. But she seemed to be taking good care of her foal.

Later on my dad and our neighbor Gary came over. Gary is an expert on horses, having many of his own. We went out to the pasture to check on the foal and his mother. After we got their trust, we were able to get near them and pet them. Gary gave the foal some shots, and then we went around looking for the afterbirth. Soon we found it.

"Oh wow!" said Voice B.

"Oh sick!" followed Voice A. "Throw up, now!"

"What do you mean? It's pretty! It's got a little red, a little white, a little purple."

"Stop it! It's sick. I don't think I've been more revolted in my life," interrupted Voice A.

"It's a little bit of nature," said voice B. "Since you keep winning those arguments about TV, we've been inside all day watching soap operas. There's a whole new world outside! The green grass, the blue sky, the animals...."

"Yeah, and the manure, the flies, the heat," added Voice A. "Does this mean we're going to be outside all of the time, instead of watching soap operas?"

"Probably," said Voice B.

The next day, before we had even thought of a name for the foal, he died. We went out to see how he was, when we saw Ginger trying in vain to make him get up. We went closer and found out that he was dead. Ginger looked pleadingly at us. My dad got a huge shovel, picked the foal up, and took him away.

Suddenly Ginger went mad. First she went after my dad, but he made it out of the pasture before she reached him. Then she went after the rest of us, who were just standing around gloomily. She started charging at me. I quickly woke up out of my daze and ran for my life toward the fence. I had just barely climbed over the fence when she reached me. She looked at me desperately and then turned around to see who else was around to run after. All the others had escaped except for Scott. So Ginger went after him. Scott reached Sonny, another one of our horses. Scott and Ginger went around and around Sonny, who just stood there as if nothing were going on, like two boys playing tag around a tree. Ginger eventually gave up, and Scott made it to safety. For days after, Ginger searched the pasture in vain for her lost foal.

Later on we put the foal in a hole and filled it up again. I watched the whole process quietly, and when it was over, I walked off alone. I looked at everything around me. Summer was in full blast, and the air was filled with the sound of birds. The grass was rich and thick, and the trees, once bare in the winter months, were full with leaves. The rushing creek was rumbling in the distance. I decided to walk down to it and skip stones off its surface. The dogs joined me and, realizing the mood, walked quietly and slowly next to me.

On the high banks of the creek, we saw a dead oppossum. Flies covered it, and the dogs bent over to sniff it. "Well, everything dies," said Voice A. "Not only the stiff they just buried but other things also."

"True," answered Voice B. "That's the first smart thing you've ever said."

"Great. So are you going to stop this sulking garbage? *Days of Our Lives* is on in five minutes."

"Shut up," said Voice B.

As I skipped stones on the creek I realized for the first time that everything is born and then dies, whether there's a long time period between the two or a short one like the foal's.

The Bridge of Flowers (in Vermont)
Jillian Atkin

Brown water slipping all around. Nothing could stand out over that water. I was wrong because when I looked up I saw flowers parading over a small grey bridge embedded with stones.

I ran around to the entrance. I could no longer see the dull water but pansies, daffodils, lilacs, and every other flower you could name.

I saw bees buzzing along the branches of the flower trees. I had to shrink away because I still had not conquered my fear of bees, but besides that, it was a beautiful day.

When I was with people on the road by the side of the water, it appeared to be a gray day, but once I had entered the bridge, everything was sunny and wonderful.

The smell drove me closer and closer to the bridge.

I have to go back ... someday.

The Butterfly
Lucia Rambusch

Out of my window I could see the mist rising from the wet ground. Finally after a while the sun was shining bright, and the mist was gone. I had to mow the lawn. After I had finished I went to lie down out on the soft green grass with an ice-cold lemonade. After a while I took a sip, and on the sweating glass was a black and white caterpillar. I screamed and dropped my glass and shook my hand as if I had just touched a poisonous snake that had almost bitten me! I was about ready to get up when I saw it; it seemed as if it was hurt. So I thought for a minute and looked at it. I finally picked it up and then noticed that the glass had barely missed him by a hair! After looking at it for a while I thought it became sweeter and sweeter.

When I went into the house I put it on the counter, thinking it wouldn't go away while I went to the other room to get a coffee can to put it in. When I returned, it was hanging upside down under the counter spitting on itself. I put the can back, realizing that the caterpillar was making its chrysalis from which it would emerge a butterfly.

I watched it all day. After a couple of hours the green threads started to look like a chrysalis. It was fascinating! I got a headache watching it go up and down, up and down, never getting tired. Soon it was dinner time, and so I set the table next to the now half finished chrysalis. Throughout dinner I watched it, always moving, never getting tired. After dinner I watched again but it was time to go to bed.

The next morning I woke up and went down to the kitchen. I had forgotten all about the chrysalis and ran my hand under the counter. I hit it softly and then remembered. I quickly knelt down to check on the damage I had done. I hadn't done much, but that didn't matter now that I was watching it! It was a brilliant electric spring green. I watched it day after day, and day after day it got darker and darker and also seemed to get a little smaller as if it were clinging to the caterpillar. Soon the chrysalis turned a brownish black and I could see the veins of the almost formed wings. Soon the chrysalis was shriveling up.

One morning I went downstairs and checked up on my chrysalis, and there was the butterfly halfway out of its chrysalis, all slimy from its protective coating of spit. I wasn't quite sure what to do because if I touched it after it came out of its chrysalis I might hurt it, and if I touched it now I might hurt it too! I decided to take it out now! I slowly and very carefully took it off of the shelf where it was hanging and laid it outside on the bench. Slowly it emerged from the chrysalis. Though it was still wet its colors were brilliant, orange, yellow and black. It was a monarch. The butterfly was lucky I had put it in the sun; because of this it dried a lot faster. Soon it went for its first flight. It flapped its wings but couldn't get off because it was still wet. Then finally it got off the ground for a couple of seconds. Then it tried again and it was off, so light that the wind carried it away.

I thought about it everyday, and when I did think of my butterfly, I thought about how much it had contributed to my life, watching one body turn into another.

Memoir Profile

Show what someone was like or is like by telling typical things about their behavior that you know from knowing him or her. Use their actions and habits and words to sketch the main lines of their character or their relationship to you.

A Real Smile
Lana Lin

We were leafing through a photograph album in her dimly lit room. Her room itself was an illustration of her whole self. It was in a shambles because she never bothered to clean it up, but it was cozy in its own way. Books on Zen and Hinduism lay scattered on the floor along with Shakespeare and Hans Christian Anderson. She had a strange poster on the wall called "The Birth" or something close to that, and she had created a strange little sculpture out of a lightbulb, a syringe, and a deodorant can. Polly was unique, different, all out for nonconformism. Her room and everything she owned and did showed it. The grown-ups called it a "phase," but it would never leave her, it was her being.

I noticed she never smiled in her earlier pictures, and in the later years it was only a strange contortion of the mouth. She couldn't be fake like that, couldn't light up a brilliant smile for the lense of an inanimate camera. There she was costumed in an ugly straw hat with a ragged dress, her feet pointing out sideways. When I tell her I think some of her clothes are strange she only replies that she knows, but they are different. Purple was her favorite color at the time. All her clothes were purple, not blue or red or something "normal" like that. Then she switched to what she called "barf green" and bought an army cap to accompany the change of taste.

Her taste in food was also out of the ordinary. With her around we had to settle for spicy Indian foods with names no one knew how to pronounce or salads with fresh alfalfa sprouts, spinach, and avocados. Now she is into teas of every nationality in the world.

In the picture of her friends, my eyes met no sparkling smiles of pretty pom-pom girls and cheerleaders. Pom-pom girls made her puke. They giggled too much, and the whole group of them were the same person, no individuals, no differences. They dressed the same, they acted the same, and they always smiled those fake smiles. Looking at those ancient pictures of a little girl with a solemn face, I knew she could never be one of the crowd. Polly would always be Polly. Her name was even different, and she would always be a little different. "Nonconformist" was her favorite word. I looked up at her, and she looked back, throwing off one of her hilarious smiles, a "real" smile.

The Manager
Karl Thompson

My brother Kevin is six years old. I see him daily in a wide variety of situations. Sometimes, when he is with his friends and having fun, he is full of confidence, even bratty and mischievous. Other times, however, when he becomes frustrated, he is inattentive, quick to cry, and very temperamental— not unlike the manager of a baseball team. When his team is winning, he will be happy, jovial, confident, and entirely different from the same manager of a losing team.

One Friday, after a hard day at school, Kevin's team was losing. He sat at the kitchen table struggling with math problems, trying to right a jumbled batting order. His body was slumped and relaxed. His legs hung limply over the edge of the chair. His feet were angled slightly downward, and pointed in odd, contrasting directions. His thighs pushed his knees to the edge of the chair and seemed to flow from his waist. The lower half of his back was curved like the arch of a baseball glove, slipping into slumped harmony with his drooping thighs. His upper back seemed disorganized, with one shoulder slouching below the other. His face bore the weight of his drooping head to a barely upright arm. The manager's free arm hung limply from his lowered shoulder. He made no noise and seemed a melancholy cloud, wasting away the final innings of an impossible game.

The next day, Kevin had a good game, and his team won. I saw him running across our backyard, out of the dugout to congratulate a homerun hitter. His brilliant red T-shirt and faded blue jeans were blurs of contrasting color in the moving streak he made as he ran. His arms were bent at right angles, with fists tightly clenched. They swung busily at his sides, extending far forward and up, and swinging down in a dipping arc to extend behind his body. The manager's head was cocked to one side, and his face tight with clenched teeth. As he ran, his legs moved in mechanically contrary motion with his arms.

After the game was finished, he sat down to rest. I noticed his face, arms, and voice as he enthusiastically contemplated his victory. He often lifted his forearm in small half-circles and drummed his small, dirty fingers on his pants. His skinny, frail arms were very smooth and white. Kevin's face was framed by an entangled mop of wild hair. It was long and nest-like and hung about his head like a lion's mane. His face was the same sort of white as his arms save two pale pink semi-circles that covered his cheeks. His nose was small and triangular, as were his eyebrows, which formed small, blunt arches over his dark, withholding eyes. His voice was a high-pitched sing-song, a bird-like sound that floats out of his mouth and through the air like wisps of steam. All through his body, a confident, proud air is present, telling all that his team has won.

The trait that I notice most about my brother is the way he changes with the situation, environment, circumstances. This response to environment is strikingly similar to the way a baseball manager feels during and after each game. Both Kevin and the manager find themselves different people in the space of an hour. This sort of response to environment may be a common characteristic in people, but I noticed it clearly in my brother Kevin, the Manager.

Lessons of Life
Laurie Paul

He understood my fears, my sorrows, tears and happiness before I did. He explained what he could of life to me. He showed me that people are individuals, with different needs and feelings. This person was my grandfather.

One incident I recall occurred when I went to church with him one Sunday. My grandfather gave me the choice of either sitting in the congregation or going downstairs with the other children to Sunday school. I chose to sit with the congregation. While sitting there, a lady in her mid-forties nudged me. "Go downstairs with the other children for Sunday school," she said sternly. "Why are you up here?"

Frightened, I obeyed. Walking away I looked behind me and saw the lady sitting down in my seat, for there were no others left. I realized that she only wanted a seat, and I had done nothing wrong.

After church my grandfather said to me, "You must realize, Mrs. W. did the wrong thing, but do not condemn her for it. She knows no other way to assert herself." From this, I learned that people have different qualities, good and bad, but one must try to cope with both patiently.

I was a little chubby, and one day, having gotten sick of slim fashion models, I decided to lose six pounds. My grandfather came to me and said, "If you want to diet, it will be up to you to stay away from candies and sugar. Nobody but yourself can be blamed if you don't stick to it." I stuck to it and lost the six pounds. The experience taught me responsibility for my actions and helped me to learn to repress actions that were not correct.

My grandfather treated me as a person, not a child, and showed me I was worth something. He taught me how to treat other people, and myself. Without my grandfather, I feel I would not have become a whole person.

Tiffany
Jody Mecklenburger

My cat's name is Tiffany. We named her that when she was a kitten because of the way she pranced around as if she knew she was something important. At the same time there was her mischievous side. This was the Tiffany that chased our toes and nipped our fingers. Her mischievous self and her sophisticated self were competing for her name. Tiffany to me was a playful name. When I thought of "Tiffany," I could see a young girl swinging in a playground swing, or playing hopscotch in the park. But I could also see a fancy old lady sitting down to "tea," at noon. So Tiffany was the name I chose. And she fits it perfectly.

Tiffany sometimes lies sprawled out loosely on her smooth gray back. Her front paws are curled up against her chest. Her back paws are in the air, and her tail lies limply between her stockinged legs. Her ears flicker with every sound, and her whiskers twitch to every movement. Her wet pink nose catches aromas as they drift in the air. Her eyes open wide and stare vacantly out into her own transparent world.

When Tiffany relaxes this way she's as easy going as can be. But sometimes she tries to appear mellow when she really is not mellow at all. She may appear to be loose, and at ease. But never take that for granted. Because under that disguise she's really as preposterous and feisty as a kitten. Tiffany's mischief carries her into spirited and sometimes foolish behavior. But she will never let herself be deceived or victimized. She is far from stupid. She just likes to have a good time.

Sometimes I can see a twinkle of mischief gleaming in her suspicious green eyes. Her long flowing tail quivers awkwardly. She sits, ready to pounce. Her long legs are tucked under her body, ready to heave herself from the chair in the wink of an eye. Her long alert whiskers twitch with excitement, and her listening ears wait for a sound to shatter the silence. She springs from the chair and is gone, leaving only the sound of her pattering feet against the wooden floor.

Tiffany's personality seems so full of opposites. That is why we had such a hard time naming her. But her many contradicting moods make her all the more interesting. When I feel tired, Tiffany will lie by my side and put me to sleep with her soft purring. But when I feel restless and bored, Tiffany will always perk me up with one of her clowning acts. She adds spice to my life and joy to my days.

Looking Into
(Investigation)

Writing Up Sensory Notes

Go somewhere that interests you and jot down pell-mell as much as you can record in note fashion of what you see, hear, smell, and touch there. Allow ten to thirty minutes. Don't think yet about what you will make of this; just get down plenty of material for later. Do the same thing at another locale of your choice, or at the same place at different times, if you would like to be sure to have plenty of choice for writing up.

Now look over your notes and see if some fragments especially stand out or if some overall impression, mood, or pattern emerges that would interest some other people. Organize around this. Cut out whatever you think is irrelevant. Add things you may remember but didn't record or that you know about from other sources. Reshape and rephrase what you keep. This could end up as a story, a sketch, a play, an essay, reportage, or a poem.

The Attic
Grant Zimmerman

Above my room is our attic. It is very hot and humid in the summer and very cold and musty in the winter. From it you can hear people throughout the house and hear cars and mowers outside. The air conditioning fan on the roof above the attic doesn't work any more but it doesn't matter. It didn't cool the attic anyway.

The attic is a dusty storehouse for all kinds of old clothes. They are in clothes bags on racks with 500 layers of dust covering them. My mom's wedding gown with the imitation pearls all over it is in a Russel's Dry Cleaning bag on a rack. My dad's army uniform is rigid as a board from heavy starch. There are all kinds of boxes, boxes with everything from wicker picnic baskets to my grandma's old saxophone in them.

The gray insulation sags between the old splintered boards and it seems that it couldn't insulate a shed. There is a hole in the roof near the back where the sunlight comes through in thin golden beams, and you can see the dust particles by thousands floating in the thin beams of light.

The attic is like a family museum that holds many secrets of the past.

The Sights and Sounds of Washington Square
Nicole Ruane

I think that Washington Square Park is fascinating. There are so many people there. Fathers looking for their screaming children, people showing off by roller skating, playing music, dancing, even doing chin-ups on the monkey bars.

Then there are the people who are less fortunate. There is a woman sitting on the ground reading an old newspaper. Another woman is picking things out of the garbage cans. One man is drinking liquor from a bottle and then throwing up.

Some people come to the park just to be here, like me. Others come to take pictures, some to take drugs. Lots of people like to play baseball or throw a ball to their dogs. But I think the best thing about this park is the smell. It's not a pretty smell, but it's a mixture of everything. Hotdogs, pretzels, a slight smell of marijuana and garbage.

Reportage

Visit

Go somewhere that you would like to report on as for a journalistic feature—a locale that's colorful or significant, a place where things important or amusing or typical take place, and so on. Observe, move around, and take notes until you feel you have enough material to do justice to whatever made you choose this place. Use your notes now to render the place according to what it most seems to have to say. You might submit this to a newspaper or magazine.

The Match
Luis Centenera

Sitting high in the wooden bleachers of the Binghampton Tennis Club, I awaited the arrival of the hard-hitting Nako Mashilo from Japan and his arch enemy, the finesse player, Gunthry Todd from Australia. This match was supposed to be a closed event, but I had sneaked in through the bleachers in Gate 14 (a barred gate in the stadium). The screeching of tire rubber was heard in the distance, and out popped the lively five-foot-four Japanese from his crimson red Subaru. Loud rock music filtered through the air with such hard rock groups as the Krazy Kows and the Bubonic Plague. The crazy oriental danced in the parking lot with a bottle of champagne and some seedy-looking broad whose hot pink satin pants were tighter than her skin.

A royal blue Porsche Targa suavely pulled into the barren lot, and out strode the sophisticated Australian equipped with a large bottle of Gatorade and several standard-size graphite glasses. He quickly departed the parking lot, and entered the confines of the playing field. Upon arriving, he methodically rosined his hands, slipped on a pair of dazzling white wrist-bands, wiped his forearms, and meditated silently.

This was only to be broken up by the hysterical laughs of Nako, who was loud-mouthing how he had just locked his "funky woman" in the car's trunk. Some muffled shouts were heard in the distance, but no one minded it. I was too intrigued by such a great match.

The vulgar Nako danced onto the courts with his faded blue jeans and tattered white undershirt and immediately cried, "C'mon! C'mon! Let's get this show on the road." Gunthry glanced up from his seat and gave Nako a look of disapproval. Under his breath, he had coldly muttered, "Disgusting Japanese. Such uncouth tennis players...."

"You ready? You ready yet, Mr. Australianman? Let's go!" he roared again.

"No practice? No volleys? No groundstrokes?" the Australian asked.

"I'm great! No good players need practice. C'mon! C'mon...." retaliated the impatient Japanese man.

"It's quite all right with me, I've already practiced at my private courts," snubbed the nonchalant Gunthry.

"O.K., O.K., cut the chit-chat. Serve first, let's go!"

There they were, two of the nation's up-coming stars preparing for combat. As in the ages of early Rome, two fierce, brave gladiators stood face to face, eye to eye, in the vastness of the arena. Fire burned in their hearts, death in their eyes, and vengeance in their souls!

Suddenly I felt some drops on my head, and I looked up and saw that the sky was all dark and there was sun no more. Down it fell like bullets from hell drenching everything in sight. Yet! The warriors continued playing . . . playing and playing. . . . When it was over, neither lost, for both of them were winners.

There I watched for hours on end seeing what true champions really are. Though they come from different cultures and had their differences, one thing they did share in common was that they both had the heart to go the distance. They both were true athletes.

Interview with a Relative or Friend

Choose someone whom you know and feel at ease with. Find out more about your person's life or about what he or she may be some kind of expert on. Write down some questions in advance and make up others as you go along. Take notes or record and transcribe. Summarize later to emphasize main ideas in your own words. Quote occasionally for flavor and accuracy. Let your subject read this before your final copy so you can make changes according to his or her response.

Submit your interview summary to a newspaper, or include it in a group collection of portraits. Or put together with partners a booklet on a topic for which your interviewee is a good source of information.

Freestyle Frisbee Player Extraordinaire
John Dodelson

My brother Jim is twenty-one years old and rather tall. He works at a bike shop on 14th Street called Stuyvesant Bicycle. When not working, he enjoys playing active sports, riding his bike, and going to concerts. There is one extremely interesting thing that he does (and very well, I might add): he is an outstanding freestyle frisbee player. Freestyle is a two- or three-player exchange or routine limited to five minutes. It is choreographed to music so that the player has a tempo to follow. The titles my brother holds include 1980 Colorado State Champion and 1982 Connecticut State Champion, and he participated in several record-breaking freestyle "stunts."

He has played in ten tournaments, and he says he plans to go for more. I asked him about his worst tournament, and he said that it was in October 1981 in Philadelphia. There was incredible competition, but he says he thrives on pressure. He did badly, however, and it turned out to be his worst tournament, he said with a smile. His best tournament was in Connecticut. He said, "I pounded, which is to say I shredded or slashed. It was a beautiful location, the turf was good, and everything just went right."

Points are scored by judges in two major categories: presentation (variety of moves, execution, artistic expression) and difficulty. Things are based on "how hard it is, and how well you do it." Points are scored for difficult moves presented in a light, easy-seeming way or flow. "The harder the routine is, the easier it looks, the better!"

I asked him how he practices for a tournament. He said that he stretches for 45 minutes and trains on his bike for about 130 miles a week in Central Park. He also does some basic yoga. He said, "If you don't stretch, you'll be lucky not to pull a muscle. Only a statue would consider competing in a tournament without stretching." He also plays freestyle with a partner for 14-20 hours a week. "You can improve your flow, and your partner can give you tips. New things come up." He plays in Central Park's Sheeps Meadow ("nice turf").

Some moves that are essential to playing freestyle are tapping (hitting a spinning/non-spinning frisbee with a finger), delays (balancing a spinning frisbee on your finger), and rolls (spreading out your arms and letting it roll from one hand to the other). I asked him what his hardest move was. He said, "A double-spinning barrel. There are two moments when you can't see the frisbee, timing is important, and it is a contortion move (a jump with one arm under your leg). If you fall you can seriously injure yourself. Some strangely named moves are: gitis (short for flemingitis), indigenous, and a move called psychobash, which is an extremely strange name for a relatively easy move.

I asked him what his most memorable plays were, and he replied, "When you do a great move, and all your friends cheer you on because they're amazed. In Colorado, I got a kick out of seeing myself on video for the first time. I said, 'Can you rewind that? I'll get my partner' (who couldn't have cared less about it)." His worst plays were in the "Octad." He laughed, "My partner played like a pooper scooper; everything hit the ground before he got a chance to catch it!"

In conclusion, I asked him what his future plans were, and he replied with a twinkle in his eye, "I want to be indoor champion of the world!"

Chris Hatfield
Katie Heddens

Chris Hatfield has a brain-damaged cat. But more about that later.

Chris is obviously an athletic person. He plays the hard position of defensive tackle on the Junior Midget Traveling Redskins. He is good at this position, so he's on the first string of this tough football team. Chris also likes swimming. He swam for Hobson West this past summer. He had to quit, though, because he was chosen for the Naperville All-Star Baseball Team. It proved to be a good choice, for Chris's team went to the state playoffs. Chris's seven years of practicing and playing effectively worked in the championship because they won 8-5 and became state champs.

Chris's interest in baseball doesn't stop just with the game. He has collected 3,000 baseball cards so far and intends to keep adding to them. He also likes to play the trumpet. Although he isn't in the school band he has taken lessons for two years at home and says, "I'm pretty good at it." Chris also loves listening to the radio. His favorite group is Van Halen.

Now back to the brain-damaged cat. Chris has given a lot of time and effort to try and help his blind and deaf cat. This tragic event happened four months ago when a careless truck driver hit her. Thanks to Chris, Shadow, the cat, now can find its way around the house and eat by itself.

Interview Sketch

Interview someone in your community outside of your family and write up your notes or recording as a sketch of the person. Choose someone who interests you because of what he or she does or knows or represents. If the person's setting is important—where he/she lives or works—arrange to have the interview there and make some notes on it too. Prepare some questions to get at your interest, but be prepared also to come up with new questions once you've heard some of what the person has to say.

Mix some direct quotations with some of your own restatement of what the person said. Blend summary and quotation without referring to your questions unless you have a special reason. If you want, shift things around to go under certain topics that thread through the interview. At some point describe the person and the place as much as seems worthwhile. A sketch shows what a person or their occupation is like. Give a fitting title.

Your interview sketch might go in a newspaper or into a book about your community. If you choose a person for his or her profession or job, your write-up could go into a book showing what different careers are like.

Dorothy Vismale
Daisy Wright

I interviewed Dorothy Vismale, our school paraprofessional, and asked her a few questions about herself and her job here at Manhattan East.

Before Dorothy came to work at Manhattan East, she was a school aide, and before that, she worked in a hospital collecting hospital records. But here at Manhattan East, Dorothy has many jobs. She assists in the pupils' accounts and attendance records, runs the rexo machine, supervises in study hall, and tutors children in math, science, and very soon, writing.

When I asked Dorothy about what most interested her in coming here to help out at M.E., she said that this was the kind of program that she wanted to be in, and that it was a nice change from elementary school.

I also asked her if she thought she got too much work in the office. She said it's always too much, but she gets it all done because it's all necessary.

Dorothy says that she can't really think of anything that she would change about the school, except for maybe the physical appearance.

Even though Dorothy would like to change the physical appearance of the school, she is still most hoepful that she will be here at Manhattan East next year.

Dorothy was born in Manhattan, then moved to Larchmont, and from the age of six years and up, lived in New York City. She has three children, and her hobbies are gardening, reading, bicycle riding, walking, and listening to modern jazz and classical music.

Journalist
Heather Pitner

The building is made of old brick, and the doors bear the name of a respectable, small-town paper, *The Naperville Sun*. Stairs inside lead up to a bustling room full of desks, papers, and people. This room is known as the newsroom. A typewriter, pens, pencils and stack of papers engulf a busy journalist.

Karen Spalding is this very journalist surrounded by so much clutter, which she would not call clutter at all! These items surrounding her are the tools required to do a writer's job. Karen works for *The Naperville Sun,* and she spends a lot of her time in the newsroom, as she refers to it. Karen writes about events that occur in local women's clubs. She has to attend meetings to find out information. Karen travels around Naperville asking questions and investigating with her curiosity churning.

To become a journalist, certain requirements in education must be fulfilled. Courses that are suggested for high school students are English, modern history, social sciences, and typing. Karen said that it is important to gain experience at a young age. She suggested certain activities in high school. She stated, "It's always good to be on the school newspaper. The school newspaper can develop writing skills." Karen also said, "Newspapers are requiring journalists to take their own photos when they write articles." Photo journalism is an important consideration when making college plans.

There are certain personal qualities that play a big part in the role of the journalist. The ability to speak and write fluently is very important. A journalist is often asked to speak in front of groups. It is also necessary to be able to write articles easily and quickly, as journalists are required to do this every day. Mrs. Spalding remarked, "Journalists must be alert and proofread their writing because mistakes can often turn up."

Working on the job in journalism involves many challenging tasks. When a writer is interviewing a person, being courteous is a good policy. This job requires working with people most of the time. Karen smiled and said, "There is an enjoyable balance between contact with the public and desk work." The journalist usually works in the office at the place of employment.

My interview with Karen Spalding has really stirred my interest in this career. It seems as though it would be challenging and exciting. Writing is something I enjoy, and journalism provides many opportunities to express my talents. Karen told me that one day is never like another. I'd like that change of pace!

Sticking to the Union:
David Livingston Talks About Work and Young People
Allison Joseph

Recently, I visited the main office of District 65, UAW (United Auto Workers Union). The large, brown brick building is home to the union's many different departments. Within this large operation there are dentists' offices, doctors' offices, an organization floor, a senior citizens center, a hiring hall, a college program for adults, and more.

Upon entering the large building, one walks under a prominent marquee and into a tastefully designed art-deco lobby, where a guard asks to see a pass or membership book.

After taking the elevator to the 7th floor, I stepped out and saw a large department, rather bustling, and walked toward the back of the floor along an aisle, where sounds of typewriters, copying machines, and people talking on phones, rang in my ears.

I met Mr. Livingston, the president of the union, a relaxed person in his sixties or so, with a genial personality and a welcoming manner.

As he leaned back in his chair, Livingston told me of the history of the union. I find that many people are ignorant of the importance and even in some cases, the mere existence of unions. I began to question President Livingston on the many faces of a union. What, *exactly*, I wanted to know, *was* a union? Mr. Livingston described it as a "giant cooperative," or, in simpler terms, an organization in which people gather together as a whole to fight for something that's important to them, usually better wages and working conditions. "The union also is always 'there' for the people, providing they're going to put in equal effort," he went on. The organization tries to help people do things for themselves, such as keeping or finding jobs, or getting an education from literacy through college.

When asked how District 65 differs from other unions, Mr. Livingston said, in short, "We care. District 65 treats the people as individuals, *not* as a lump sum."

The union spreads out over about 30 states and the Caribbean. Altogether, it currently holds close to 50,000 members, some of them in different parts of the world. Sixty percent of the members live in the metropolitan area of New York and New Jersey, and the other thirty-five to forty percent of the members live in other areas such as Puerto Rico and Canada. Furthermore, there is a very varied membership throughout the world. Members hold many different jobs and belong to many professions, from lawyers and writers to button-makers, cooks in fast-food restaurants, and workers in factories.

District 65 prides itself on being one of the oldest unions in existence— 52 years—with much experience under its belt.

A question that I feel needs to be answered, is: "Why did people *organize* into a union?" Mr. Livingston stated that during the thirties there were no decent available jobs and no money. People were literally abused, especially those in factories.

When asked how the union benefits its members, Mr. Livingston said rather proudly that the members help themselves *through* the union. Many of the members, being retired, are eligible for social security, medical care when needed, and member benefits. When the facts are added up, it turns out that the retired members receive almost as much money as when they were working!

Regarding pay, I asked Mr. Livingston if all the workers were paid equally, including women and minorities. When the union first organized, they especially wanted minorities and women to join, because they felt that these people would make better and stronger the forces they already had. Yes, he said, management does pay them equally, and that he hopes the women are *not* treated equally. Instead he hopes they are treated in a better way, because they are the ones who have always fought to become better, fought to throw off the housewife stereotype and show the people who say, "It's a man's world" that they are wrong, and that women can do just as well. Livingston says he thinks they are well on their way. With several women vice-presidents, organizers, and department heads around 65, people could say, a woman's place is in the union.

I had been contemplating the political status of the union and wondering how President Reagan's anti-union policies of trying to weaken or break up unions were affecting them. The reply was that though Reagan often gives the union and other organizations like this problems, they are doing all right.

I asked what the union's success and shortcomings were and Pres. Livingston stated simply that he thought that their greatest shortcomings were that members sometimes depend on others within the union, not just for help (since the union's purpose is to help members do things for themselves, and organize), but to have others make decisions *for* them. The union's greatest successes came when the members reached a point when they were able to do things for themselves and make individual decisions.

On the topic of foreign affairs, Livingston said that 65 has pleasant relations with many foreign unions, for example those in Britain. However, there are sometimes small controversies between the union and British companies. For example, a British company owns Gimbels and means to sell it, which they are doing at this present moment. This means laying off many people, and this District 65 greatly resents. To pressure the British corporation not to lay off American workers requires the help of British workers and unions.

I asked Mr. Livingston if there was an approach people could take to help unions gain a better image and attract more positive attention. He replied that the best publicity the union could receive would not be from the newspapers, radio or television, since they have degraded this institution at many times in the past, but from the children and teenagers of the world. Mr. Livingston's final statement went something like this: If our young people, like yourself, would become more aware of unions and what they stand for, and their values become more apparent in the world, we would have a much better chance of keeping unions alive and well and prepared to help new members.

I agree with Mr. Livingston that young people need to widen their horizons and become more aware of not only *unions* but of the important events taking place continually that are linked, in some way, to unions. Besides, today's teens are the future workers and may need the union's help tomorrow.

Family Anecdote

Retell in your own words some incident that is told in your family about one of its members. Ask relatives to recall some story that is passed around because it is comic or dramatic or otherwise memorable. If the story is not already familiar to you, write it down right after you hear it. If it is familiar, write it down from your memory, perhaps reinforced by another's retelling for you.

Exchange one or more of these with others and make a book of them.

Death from Mistaken Identity
Tanya Felkel

In September, 1927, my grandmother's cousin's father, Uncle Jake, and her husband, Uncle Joe, were in Mexico on business. One day, they were driving from Cuernavaca to Mexico City. A little while before, the American ambassador to Mexico had left in a similar car, also with chauffeur, on the same trip, but there was a child in the car, and they stopped for ice cream. When Uncle Jake's car came along, bandits thought he was the ambassador, since he was a very distinguished-looking man. They stopped the car and said they were taking him to hold for ransom. Uncle Joe said to take him instead, but the bandits said they only wanted "the older man." The chauffeur ran after Uncle Jake and gave him his own coat because he knew it was very cold in the mountains.

When the car reached Mexico City, the police were told, and they sent men out on horses with ransom money. They were supposed to be sent by Uncle Joe. But they really messed up the job, because they rode police horses with police saddles. When they reached the place to leave the money and get Uncle Jack back, they found that the bandits had bayoneted him to death and run away.

Eventually, the police hanged a few men, but it was never definite that they were the real criminals.

Some Family Highlights
Jonathan Lipsky

How the Name Wellman Came to Be

My mother's maiden name is Wellman, and many years ago my great-grandfather's brother came to America from Russia.

It was a long hard voyage across the Atlantic, but when he got to the immigration office he was feeling very excited.

When the man at the desk found out his name was Wholenceck he had a hard time pronouncing it so he asked what my great-great uncle wanted to be when he settled in America. He then replied, "A good and healthy man." Therefore it was changed to Wellman (Well-Man).

A World War II Shootout

It was World War II, and the fighting was intense. My great-uncle Gerald was a U.S. pilot.

Story has it that he was captured while traveling through Poland in a car. He was brought back to a German prison camp (not concentration camp) and was supposed to have escaped in a German plane.

While he was heading home the Americans took him for a German pilot and shot the plane down.

Note: What really happened is not clear, but parts of this story are true.

Founder of a Nation

My grandfather Luie Lipsky was one of the founders of Israel. He helped Golda Meir in giving Israel her own state. (He started before Golda Meir was in these talks.) He and Golda were very good friends and continued to work together.

After he died, in honor of him they named a street after him, which is called Luie Lipsky Street.

Courage
Robert E. Whitacre

This is a true story about my grandfather, James C. Lynch.

On July 10, 1943 at about five p.m. three miles southeast of Palma di Montechiaro, Sicily, my grandfather's platoon encountered a strong enemy roadblock and was being forced to withdraw. His platoon sergeant was seriously wounded in this action and fell in an open field some two hundred yards from the enemy pillbox and immediately became an exposed target. Disregarding furious enemy fire, my grandfather voluntarily left his covered position and raced across two hundred yards of open field, swept by enemy machine gun fire, to rescue the wounded sergeant. His sudden gallant action inspired two other members of the squad to rush to his assistance. Together they were able to remove the wounded man to cover and render first aid which was instrumental in saving his life. Because of my grandfather's gallant conduct and his coolness under fire, he was awarded the Silver Star for valor.

Civil War Story
Carolyn I. Shull

My dad once told me a story that his grandparents told him. His grandparents lived on a farm in the South.

One day my great-grandparents were doing their daily work when a neighbor came and said that Sherman's troops were coming and asking all the farmers for any food they had. How could they save their food? They needed it. They quickly went out to the smokehouse, where all their meat was hanging, took it out, put flour all over it, and threw it out on the ground in the yard. Sure enough, Sherman's troops came and asked them for any food they had.

My great-grandparents said, "We heard y'all were coming so we poisoned our meat."

Sherman's troops said, "Let us see it anyway."

My great-grandparents showed them the meat and they thought it was really poisoned and left. My great-grandparents had meat to last them the winter.

How It Used to Be

Interview an older person about what life was like and how things were done when he or she was young. Prepare some questions about things you are curious about, but let your person ramble some too. Record in some way what they say and write this up afterwards in your own words. You can move some things around for better organization if desirable.

Do this several times alone or with others and make a collection. You might try to cover a certain ethnic community this way or interview mixed ethnic groups in the same community. For such a collection you might write some commentary about what you see in the responses. This could be an introduction to the whole or headnotes between interviews.

The Land of Milk and Honey
Mary Stevenson

The land of milk and honey is where Anna Zeglen thought she was going to. In the year 1905, Anna traveled from Poland to America on her own. She was twelve.

She traveled steerage, along with the animals, the most inexpensive and uncomfortable way to travel. While on the boat, she met a friend, a blessing, who spoke the same language and felt the way she did. Because of lack of money her friend had to be sent back to Poland. Anna was alone and frightened.

When Anna arrived in the foreign land, her heart fell. Instead of seeing streets paved with gold, she saw the poor city of New York.

She was to meet her sister, who had sent the money for her trip, in Chicago, another foreign city.

Anna married and raised a family. She delivered all of her seven children.

When one of her many children started school, she used one of their school books to teach herself English

Later, life was spent farming, mostly in Illinois and Indiana. On her farms, she had many animals on which she operated when they were ill. She lived her life without being hospitalized until she was in her eighty-third year. She was suffering from cataracts. Now, at the age of ninety, Anna Zeglen is the head of a five-generation family. Even though she says her life has been hard work, she is grateful to God for letting her live long enough to retire to Southern California, her Heaven on Earth.

My Grandfather's Marriage
Wesleyan Hsu

Did you know that if someone was going to get married in old China the parents had to pick who their child would marry?

Well, when my grandfather was growing up his parents had to choose who he had to marry. My grandfather had bad eyes at the time, so his parents wanted him to marry before he died, while his next door neighbors had two daughters who were ready to marry also. So my grandfather's parents said to their neighbors, "Let my son pick one of your daughters to marry." Then they agreed. So one day my grandfather went to the neighbor's garden to pick one of the two. He looked and looked, then he picked the younger girl.

On the wedding day, nobody is allowed to see the bride's face, so my grandfather's neighbor switched the bride with their older daughter because they thought she wasn't pretty enough and nobody would marry her.

After the wedding the switched bride took off her veil, and was my grandfather surprised, because he didn't marry the girl he wanted!

At first my grandfather didn't really like her, but now my grandparents are very happy and they really like each other.

Highlights of a Coffin Maker
Maria Dunberg

In England fifty-five years ago, when my grandfather was about sixteen, he started working as a coffin maker. He worked as a coffin maker until he was twenty-five.

One time when he went to the mortuary to measure a lady, the first thing he saw when he came into the room was a man's head cut off at the neck. Then he saw the police checking the rest of the body for identification. He later found out that the man had committed suicide by putting his neck on the railroad track and having a train run over it.

Another time he was putting a lady in a coffin and she groaned. He wasn't scared because he knew it was just wind from the intestines.

The very first time he ever had to put a lady in a coffin it was pitch black outside. He and his boss had already taken the lady and the coffin to where it needed to go on a handcart. The boss told my grandfather he could put the handcart down at the other end of the yard, then leave. Since my grandfather was only sixteen and this was his first time he was scared. He was so scared that he waited outside the mortuary until his boss came out to go home. When my grandfather's boss saw he was still there he asked him what he was doing there. So my grandfather said, "I thought I'd wait for you." After he and his boss had put the handcart away my grandfather got on his bicycle and rode home with the feeling that the dead person was behind him.

Folk Ways

Ask older people how something is traditionally done or made according to how they were taught. This can cover arts and crafts, care and maintenance. Note down what your informants tell you and put this later into your own words. You might identify them, if they don't object. Take photos or make drawings if either seems indicated.

Or choose one thing you want to know about—quilting or carpentry, for example—and survey a number of older people. Write up what different informants say, and make a booklet on that subject. [Among the following samples are some folk cures collected by a seventh-grade class.]

Folk Cures

A Rash
Jennifer Foertsch

A long time ago, for a rash they used to use a pretty tasty-sounding remedy. You would mix one tablespoon of baking soda, one tablespoon of cream, and one half a tablespoon of honey. Use more or less depending on how big or small the rash is. Spread the mixture on the rash. It's too bad you can't have a lick!

Sore Throat
Christine Surges

When my grandmother was a girl, goose grease was a sure cure for a sore throat. After you cooked a goose you saved the grease left in the pan. Then when someone got a sore throat you saturated a wool cloth with the grease and wrapped it around their neck. Boy, that wool must have itched!

A Sick Stomach
Jennie Sharp

If you have a sick stomach and a peach tree, you are luckier than you think! The cure my stepfather gave me will surely get you feeling better! (Or sicker.)

Take two cups of water and boil it. Add half a cup of shredded peach tree bark and inspect it for bugs. Add it slowly. Let it boil for ten minutes then strain it. Drink the water, then pick the splinters out of your tongue and between your teeth. And spit out the centipede!

A Sprain
Barna De

This is a cure for a sprain which my mother gave to me from *her* mother. It is quite a variation from a modern medical cast. All you need is some lime, tumeric powder, and a stove. Sounds pretty interesting so far, right? Depending on the size of the sprain, you take a chunk of lime, then you take some tumeric powder (about as much as it would take to equal three-quarters of the lime). Then you must take the two ingredients and work them into a paste. You then warm it up, well below boiling. Smear the mixture on the sprain, and keep it there for a couple of days, or until your sprain heals.

A Backache
Carol Kantayya

Are you suffering from a painful, aggravating backache? Try this cure and end your excruciating pain.

Take a piece of a deer's antler (a piece measuring about two to five inches long), and pound it thoroughly by using a hammer or any other hard substance. Then, take just enough water to make a paste with the crushed antler until the mixture is smooth and without any lumps.

Have someone spread and massage the paste onto the sore and painful parts of the back. Leave the paste on the back for about two hours.

I got this folk cure from my uncle, Dr. Prabhakar.

Canker Sores
Ben Sander

My mom uses alum to heal our canker sores. This cure is doubly effective. Firstly, the alum has some kind of healing power. And secondly, once you've tried this cure, never again will you get a canker sore. You see, alum tastes like bad lemonade. It's too sour, and it makes your mouth pucker up.

To use this cure, either lick your pinkie and put it in the alum, or wet a popsicle stick and put it in the alum. Then apply it to the affected area.

If you survive (fifty-fifty chance) your sore will be gone in no time flat.

Badly Bleeding Cuts
Steve Satrim

In the old days, when someone was cut and had badly bleeding cuts, they were not always able to get to a doctor to have stitches. Many people used a folk remedy. They washed the cut as well as they could. Then they soaked two or three tea bags in warm water and placed them on the cut. If it was really bleeding they would use more tea bags. The tea bags were held in place with a dry cloth that was tied or pinned on. It was believed something in the tea closed down the blood vessels and helped stop the bleeding.

Badly Bleeding Cuts
Heather Hayhurst

If your sister just bit you and blood is gushing out of your arm, you're in luck because this is a cure for badly bleeding cuts. First, for this cure, you have to have some spider webs. You'll probably have some under your bed! Next, you take the spider webs you just found and be sure there are not any spiders on them. If there aren't any spiders, then take the spider webs and apply them to your cut. You should apply enough spider webs so they cover the cut thoroughly.

I got this cure from my grandma, Irene Hayhurst.

Korean Soup
Ami Shin

I learned how to make the Korean soup from my mother. The soup is seaweed soup. I know it sounds sick, but when you taste it, it really tastes good. My mother learned it from her mother and so on. It's an old recipe from Korea.

First, you put sliced steak into a half pot of water. Put that on the stove with medium flame. But I almost forgot, before you do anything else you have to put the seaweed that you buy at the store into a pot of water and keep it there until it gets soft. Because they usually dry it in the sun, it's hard. After the water boils and the meat is brown, you put the seaweed into the pot, but first drain the water out of the seaweed. Then you put some salt and soy sauce and taste it to see if it tastes good. Then half-way close the top and cook it for about half an hour. Our family has been putting in some other secret seasonings. I can't say what because then it wouldn't be secret any more.

When I followed the instructions and made the soup for the first time I put in too much salt and soy sauce and ruined the whole soup. So I suggest you put in a little at a time. But my second time I made it perfect.

Biography and Chronicle

Biography: Phase

Narrate some experience another person went through during several months or years that amounted to a phase of that person's life having something of a beginning, middle, and end of its own. The person may be from the past or the present. Draw from fresh sources such as interviews with the person or diaries, letters, or memoirs by the person, and perhaps indicate in some way appropriate to your presentation what these sources are. Bring out the nature of the experience that makes for the phase, and keep in mind an audience that might be interested in the person or that experience.

A Stunning Senior Year
Melisa Levitt

Tom had flown through his final year at high school in a daze. It wasn't a negative daze, in which you are so bored and apathetic that you finally become completely dulled to the world around you, seeing it through a thick, dividing fog—when you care to look, which in this condition isn't often.

No, Tom hadn't been dulled to the world that year because he was bored. He had finally just been dizzied by the importance and fervor of finishing activities of that year.

All of the old family friends talking to him in elevators, or on the street, the men maybe even slapping him lightly, in a jocular way, on the shoulder, exclaiming heartily, "*Well*, well, son/boy/Thomas/Tom [how he was addressed varied according to how long his parents had known the man, and how friendly Tom had been with them] you've made it at last to that final senior year, eh?" (By this time, Tom's eyes would be glazed over—which they had started to do by the first "well"—and his head would start to gradually tilt so that he really wasn't looking at his aggressor.) "So, have you any ideas about college? Want to go to your dad's old Yale? Good school, Yale." (This last statement would be said with widely varying amounts of enthusiasm. Tom experienced a flash combination of admiration, pity, and apprehension through his stupefaction when someone really worked up a lather. Was this what college did to you?) Both sexes would ask for the list of places to which he had applied, with more men asking about possible majors and careers. (The career question Tom never answered the same way twice, as he really wasn't sure.) The women, however, would lead up to the whole question indirectly, having first asked about his parents—especially his mother—and after having repeated a less hearty version of the men's speech, with maybe a cheek pinch or pat instead of the shoulder slap (and asking and reminiscing about his *mother's* college) would remind him about cute little ("Well, actually, she isn't so little any more, is she?") Carrie (his sister) in her sophomore year coming up with her nose to his heels.

He first realized what the full significance of what he was in for while being a counselor at a camp during the summer before. The dizziness started as the two months drew to a close and he and the rest of the staff his age began to be drawn together by their nervous joking about the coming school year. Then he actually entered school, with all the other excited students and the teachers telling them that now they were the seniors, the oldest, the examples. That sort of thing really got to them after a while—it sank in by the first interview, with his mother squeezing his hand comfortingly, hopefully, before he uneasily slid it away from her in embarrassment, and finally became a faint persistent worry while waiting for the returns in a daze.

His stupefaction did make him slip behind for a month or two in German and chemistry, but it soon enabled him to become a homework machine, his memory constantly inhaling and exhaling as he got assignments and fulfilled them promptly with his memory. He had done well on his SAT's and did well on his Regents and all other tests except for those for which his memory hadn't been properly briefed. His teachers were ecstatic (he had always been an average student), calling it a perfect year—Thomas at his best—consistently outstanding work—students like Thomas make teaching worth it—he proves that a good career as a student only takes work, for inspiration will follow.

He smiled occasionally, ironically, at his parents' and teachers' assumption that his stupendous improvement in his studies was due to some intellectual and creative awakening, at a time when he was feeling his most stolid and mechanical.

Tom dated a fair amount of girls, as quite a few were fascinated by the sudden sprouting of his apparently hidden genius. He enjoyed (as much as his dulled nerves could feel enjoyment) these breaks from his involuntary, unreasoning routine. With one or two he had a faint feeling that he really could have something, if this were not his "Robot Year," as he came to call it. And so they all passed on into the yearbook.

He genuinely did enjoy being with his friends. He related with them, and his metal memory bank would melt slightly back into living cells under the heat of their camaraderie. Aside from his sudden storm of industry, they noticed no differences between Tom-the-Junior and Tom-the-Senior, which faintly comforted him in an offbeat way.

The metamorphosis from a mechanical tadpole began with his acceptance at Cornell, the college of his choice, and took a great leap as he remembered this with relief at his graduation ceremony, his indistinct worry finally exterminated. But the metamorphosis finally culminated when Tom fell in love, at his job as an orthopedic surgeon's receptionist, with Judy, the surgeon's apprentice. It had continued as he had met others of his age from last summer who hadn't gotten into their favorite colleges, and he realized how lucky he was that he had had only a tiny worry and had gotten into Cornell.

The full-faceted, sonorous-voiced bullfrog now has long-term marriage plans, and Tom is now rather ashamed of his "Robot Year," and is glad that he and Judy never met during it. He is still amazed that it could and did happen, but I think that he has begun to accept that he was only an instinctive and defensive shell that he put up around himself, and that he was only bettered in both study habits and personality by his "Robot Year."

Oral History Plus Book Research

Interview someone who lived through some history that you would like to know more about. Combine what that person has to say with information you obtain from some books, articles,

or documents related to that subject. That is, printed sources
may supply background for what your informant tells you or
may fill in gaps not covered by his or her experience.
   Include this in collections of other oral history, or make part
of a family or community history.

The Spanish Civil War
and My Grandmother's Experiences in It
Amanda Tobier

The Spanish Civil War began in 1936 and ended in 1939. It was a battle
between the Fascists, led by Francisco Franco, and the Loyalists. Franco
wanted to overthrow the Loyalists and take power, whereupon the Loyalists
fought back.

The First Republic, proclaimed in 1931 after the fall of the monarchy,
included Socialists and Communists, called Loyalists. Franco, a Spanish
general, revolted against this Republic and proclaimed the Second Republic.

The Loyalists were in favor of democracy and freedom, while the Fascists
wanted a dictatorship. The Fascists had the help of two other countries also
under dictators, Hitler's Germany and Mussolini's Italy. The Loyalists were
aided by the Russians, and by volunteers from France, England and the United
States. The volunteers from the U.S. called themselves the "Abraham Lincoln
Brigade."

The Fascists won this war and ruled Spain for forty years, until General
Franco's death. Then a new system of government was formed.

My grandmother's story starts like this: She spent three months on the
island of Majorca in a small fishing village. My grandmother went to Majorca
to work on the translation of a book (from Danish to English), and she
deliberately chose a place to work where she didn't know the language and so
would not have to have any contact with her surroundings, except to get the
bare daily necessities.

Her parents (my great-grandparents) moved to Barcelona later that year to
escape the oppressive life in Nazi Germany. When my grandmother visited her
parents there, she decided she really liked the country and the Spaniards. Then
she heard that under duress, all able-bodied men and women were going to be
drafted into the defending army (against Franco), leaving only children and old
people behind. She felt great concern and compassion for them.

In France, there were other people concerned for these unfortunate
Spaniards. These people were untrained for combat or in nursing professions,
and they organized themselves into committees to do what they could to
rescue the helpless. The rescue group, which included my grandmother,

received large sums of money to carry out their mission, and also French hospitals offered to accept the wounded. The rescuers were told that the children suffered from malnutrition and possibly various diseases.

After a while, my grandmother and others set out in large cars with food, blankets, and first aid kits. They didn't have to drive very far into Spain when they came upon the first groups of children roaming the roads. There was usually an older child of ten or twelve years who served as leader over many smaller children. The children were shy, suspicious, and naturally unfriendly towards the strangers. One of the people in the rescue group spoke very good Spanish and patiently attempted to explain what they were there for. The sight of food usually made them more responsive to my grandmother and the other rescuers. None of the children knew where their parents were. They all resented being left alone and generally were quite unwilling to talk about it.

"Having obtained permission from the French government prior to our departure to bring in an unlimited amount of children," my grandmother says, "we had no difficulty in getting back into France. Our charges were more than happy to ride in a car after having had some food at last."

During a period of four to five months, around the summer of 1937, my grandmother's group alone collected several hundred children. At the hospitals, after the first couple of days of good food and nursing care, the children became more approachable. Some even spoke of their parents, brothers and sisters, and worried if they would ever be able to find them. Of course, people tried to find out their names and the names of the villages they came from, but that was not an easy task. The children were assured by everyone that as soon as the fighting stopped, they would be brought back to Spain. My grandmother and others tried to teach them French, in order to make it possible for them to go to school until the war was over. This way they could lead more normal lives. However, most of the children refused. They also refused to be separated from each other. Foster families were an impossible dream; they had to remain together. After a while, couples or single people began to appear, searching for their children. They always felt rejected when their children said, "They are *not* my parents," or, "We are not related to them," etc. The younger children could not remember their parents. The older ones usually did but blocked the memory out.

By 1939, after the outbreak of World War II, all the children had returned to Spain, which at that time had begun to settle down after a dreadful civil war.

Bibliography

Goldston, Robert. *The Civil War in Spain.* Bobbs-Merrill Company, Inc., New York, 1966.

Payne, Robert. *The Civil War in Spain, 1936-1939.* G. P. Putnam's Sons, New York, 1962.

The Columbia Encyclopedia. The Columbia University Press, New York, 1950.

Chronicle: Recent

Tell a story of what some group did. Members of a team or staff might have collaborated in some organized action, or some individuals might have chanced to undergo some experience together or to weave a web of action through independent behavior. Draw on accounts by participants and witnesses, fusing these in your own words while indicating sources in a way appropriate for your manner of presentation. Many newspaper and magazine true stories are such accounts.

Ildfjeld

Pia Bom

In 1973 a volcano eruption happened on Heimaey, Iceland.

It had been a normal work day. Now it was 1:40 in the morning between the 22nd and the 23rd of January, 1973.

There was a small earthquake. The people on Heimaey thought it came from the mainland, but shortly after that a volcano erupted.

"It was five or six minutes to two when I saw some fire through the bedroom window. I had gotten up to get a cup of water," said an Icelandic friend of mine, who lived in Heimaey when the eruption took place. "I jumped out of bed, put on my clothes and ran out of the house into the street. When I looked westward it seemed like the earth was burning, and there was a tumbling sound."

He took his car and drove around the back of the old volcano "Helgafjeld" to see what was happening, but he was stopped by a big flamewall that rose as high as a hundred meters straight up. The noise was deafening. Boiling hot stones flew in all directions. Warm, bright red lava flowed from the crack in the ground out over the fields.

He took a few snapshots then turned the car around and drove to a farm on the other side of the crack. Here he saw the fire-sputtering crack getting longer and wider from minute to minute. Ash was falling all over him.

When he was back in the town again children and grown-ups were in the streets. It was weird to see the whole town alive in the middle of the night.

After a couple of hours the crack had reached the length of about 1,500 meters. Toward the north the lava reached the sea. Tons of ash were thrown many hundred meters in the air. Luckily the wind was blowing away from the city, so only five to ten cm. of ash covered it. The big portion of lava streamed out of the crack and tumbled in the beginning toward the west and northwest of the island, away from the city. The citizens, therefore, got a while to flee down to the ocean to get away from the island.

When the eruption began, 60 to 70 fishing boats were in the harbor. They had come to stay in calm waters from the storm the day before. So the citizens went as quickly as possible down to the boats when the eruption began. Just before 3 o'clock a.m. the first boat sailed to the mainland. At 7 o'clock a.m. about 5,000 people and many animals were evacuated. Sick and elders were flown away in W.H.O. helicopters.

The day after the eruption began, there was a western wind blowing, but by night time it had changed to a southwestern wind. Then a lot of ash rained over the city. It got hard to stay outdoors. The ash was lying in high piles in the streets and on the routes.

Those who had not left started to move the ash from the houses with flat roofs and from the important streets.

They were working 24 hours so that they would save as much as possible of the city, but the ash made it uncomfortable to work outside. Once in a while there came a very strong smell of sulphur and different kinds of other gases. Sometimes chunks of lava fell, stones called "bombs."

The following days the crack disappeared, and the ash, lava, and gases came from the new volcano, "Ildfjeld," meaning "firemountain" (a name which it got very quickly). From there a new lava stream crept downwards to the city and covered one house after the other. After a week the whole eastern part was under a thick cover of lava. The lava stream just crept along, minding its own business, toward the harbor.

On the 12th of February all ships and boats were told to leave the harbor. A lava wall 40 meters high stood then only 80 meters from the pier. If the lava reached the harbor and therefore closed it for ships, it would limit those that stayed from getting food.

The harbor was Iceland's most important fishing harbor with many big factories for packing and exporting fish. It wouldn't be possible to have another harbor like it on Heimaey. Therefore the Icelanders began to fight against the lava. They had to stop the lava flow that threatened the harbor, for the lava came 30 meters closer every day!

First they tried to stop the lava by throwing water on it, then they even tried using fire extinguishers but with no positive result. Cooling the lava worked. The lava stopped. The front part was hard enough so that it could hold back the rest of it, but people were still afraid that it should break because the inside was still hot and molten rock. It stayed where it had stopped, luckily. If you go to Heimaey some day you will be able to see it in the back of the fishing factory and the pier.

At the end of March the lava made some enormous flows to the city. The largest one happened the 22nd of March and destroyed 70 houses. In April the volcano began to slow down. The last part of lava came out the 28th of June.

From the beginning of June people began coming back. There was only 30-50 cm. of ash on the streets. About 500 houses were destroyed. One-third of the people didn't return to Heimaey, either because their house was under lava or ash or they were too afraid of another eruption; many said the latter.

When the eruption ended one-third of the island was totally destroyed. One-third was more or less covered with ashes, but the last one-third was nearly undestroyed.

The damage to the houses, factories, and other kinds of houses was estimated to be about 400 million Danish kroner ($4 billion) in 1973.

Before the eruption very few tourists came to the island, but the eruption has had a big influence on tourists. Many just come for a one-day trip. They arrive in the airport, a bus picks them up, they drive around the island, stop at some places, and get a bag to put pieces of lava in, get driven back to the airport, and leave.

Twenty meters under the top of the lava, there is still floating lava and it is about 900°C. Scientists think it will stay like that for ten or more years, at least until 1991, and even longer under the volcano. People are planning to use the lava to heat up their houses.

Chronicle: Historical

Tell the story of what some group or community did far enough back in the past that you must rely on documents such as first-person accounts from the period and from public accounts. Weigh the reliability of these various sources and piece together a narrative doing as much justice as possible to what they offer.

Submit your article to a regional publication if it deals with an aspect of that region. If the story centers on a certain issue or topic, think of an audience interested in that issue or topic.

Civil Liberties and the McCarthy Era
Ayanna Lee

The McCarthy era started long before anybody had heard of Joseph McCarthy. The combination of the communist victory in Russia in 1917, the increasing power of the unions in the United States, and the pressure of the social reformers made Big Business fearful of losing their power. However, no organized action was taken until 1938, when the House UnAmerican Activities Committee (otherwise known as HUAC) was formed. Although it was formed to investigate both the Nazis and the communists in the United States, it soon decided to only investigate the communists (even though the Second World War had started and we were about to enter it to fight with Russians against the Germans).

After the war, the international communist party began getting more and more power in the world. In 1948 the Communist Party in Czechoslovakia overthrew the non-Communist government and established communist rule. In 1949 there was a communist victory in China, and Russia exploded its first atomic bomb. Then in 1950 the Korean War started.[1] All of these events were portrayed to the American public as signs of a world communist "conspiracy." Even earlier in March 1947, President Truman issued Executive Order 9835, initiating a program to search out any "infiltration of disloyal persons" in the U.S. government.[2] Therefore, when Senator Joseph McCarthy became known, it did not take much to get the public started.

This paper is going to look at how basic civil liberties were sacrificed because of anti-communist hysteria.

The Constitution gave certain civil liberties (rights) to Americans. Some of the civil liberties it established are: freedom of speech, freedom of the press, freedom of association, the right to due process under the law, and protection against unreasonable search and seizure. These civil liberties were denied to many Americans during the frenzy of the McCarthy era.

The McCarthy era touched almost everybody's life. He accused people from almost all the different fields of work. His main targets were people in the government, the military and the entertainment business. Others investigated teachers, intellectuals and union members. These investigations were not usually based on concrete facts but on rumors, hearsay, and misrepresentations. They also assumed that the persons were guilty just because they were accused. (Normally, people are considered innocent until proven guilty.) When Eisenhower was President, he issued a security order that said if any charge, no matter how foolish or unsupported by facts, was brought against a government employee, he or she would be suspended until proven innocent. These kinds of false accusations ruined the lives of many people. A person I talked with told the story of how her father was fired from his job when he was elected union president at the factory where he had worked for 17 years. First, the owners put up "Wanted" posters, saying he was a communist. Then, the National Guard came with the owners and surrounded him and marched him through the factory, past all the other workers. When they were outside in the parking lot, they let him go and told him he was fired because he was a communist or a communist "dupe."

There were two main agencies formed to get communist "subversives." The first one was called the House UnAmerican Activities Committee (HUAC), which I mentioned before. HUAC was an agency formed to stop the communists. It was allowed to bring in and question suspected communists and "fellow travelers" about their communist connections. If they used the 5th Amendment (not having to give evidence that might incriminate them), or if they refused to testify, the members of HUAC could hold them in contempt. They could lose their jobs or go to jail because of this. HUAC also distributed millions of anti-communist pamphlets, warning the American public about the dangers of the communists.

The other group was called the Subversive Activities Control Board (SACB). SACB made all known communist organizations and suspected communist fronts register with them. Since it had become illegal to be a communist, many groups did not report themselves. The SACB contacted groups that it considered to be communist or "pinko" to make them register. The SACB registration required the name and address of every member and officer of the organization. Once an organization had registered with the SACB, they could not send communications through the mail or broadcast over the radio or television to more than two people, unless their material was labeled "communist propaganda."[3]

People who were brought up on charges in front of HUAC or the SACB included: real communists (members of the Communist Party, USA, whose leaders were put in jail), communist sympathizers or fellow travelers (people who knew or associated with suspected communists), intellectuals, and people who disagreed with the U.S. policies about communists both inside and outside the United States.

The Internal Security Act of 1950, which set up SACB, also set up detention centers (concentration-like camps) for suspected subversives. When the President declared an "internal security emergency," these subversives would be rounded up and held in the detention centers without bail.[4] The Immigration and Nationality Act of 1952 also took away the right of people to bail and to trial. It said that the 2.5 million aliens who resided in the United States could be arrested without a warrant, held without bail, and deported for an action that was legal when committed. These actions included membership in any of the subversive organizations. These actions could be reported by anonymous people, and the person who was arrested did not always have the right to question that person or demand proof of the charges.[5]

All of these laws came from the ideas of the Smith Act, which made it "a crime to advocate, advise, or teach the duty, necessity or desirability of overthrowing the government of the United States or any of its states by force and violence."[6] These acts were set up on the idea that there was a "clear and present danger" that threatened the existence of democracy and the United States.

Anti-communist activities went on all over the country. In some areas committees looked at the books in the libraries and the lesson plans of the teachers in order to find communist propaganda. Senator McCarthy also investigated the overseas libraries of the federal government. There were over 40 books taken off the shelves wherever they were found. Two of these were *The Children's Hour* by Lillian Hellman and the *Selected Works of Thomas Jefferson,* edited by Philip Foner. They also forced teachers to stop using the Rugg Textbooks.

> This country is being systematically communized, perhaps unconsciously, through its educational institutions.
>
> These institutions are instruments through which left-wing

theories and philosophies may be and are taught to large groups of young Americans by persons whom they respect and trust—their instructors.[7]

The same kinds of things were said about the universities. Many teachers and professors were called up before the Committees and lost their jobs because they were accused of being communists.

Entertainment was another area where many people were accused of being communists, especially in the film industry. Many people were called up to testify and to identify others who were subversives. A person who was accused of communist activities was immediately blacklisted. The blacklist was a list of people who could not be hired to do any work. If someone hired someone on the blacklist, then they were suspected of being a communist too. Hundreds of people could not get any work because of these lists. If a person confessed and said they had been wrong to be a communist and then named others who were communists, however, they could often go back to work. Naming others proved they were really no longer communists. But if someone refused to inform on others, it was "interpreted as the ultimate evidence of conspiracy."[8]

Of all the trials and hearings, one of the most important was the trial of the Rosenbergs. Ethel and Julius Rosenberg were charged with espionage. All of the evidence in their trial was supplied by a few people who had already confessed to being spies and were either in prison or under indictment. The key witness was David Greenglass, Ethel Rosenberg's brother, who was a machinist at the Manhattan Project when the atomic bomb was being made. He said he made sketches from memory for Julius to give to the Russians. He said he gave the information to Harry Gold, who also testified against the Rosenbergs.

They were found guilty and sentenced to die in the electric chair, which they did even though many famous people appealed for them. There is a lot of controversy about this case. People wonder if Gold cooperated in return for an early release (he only served 15 of his 30 years when he was suddenly released). It is known that Gold and Greenglass did not have the same story before the trial but they were placed on the same floor of the jail so they could talk to each other. It is also known that Gold was prepared for the trial by 400 hours of interviews with the FBI. These sorts of things were not uncommon in the trials during the McCarthy era. People were often accused rather than proven guilty.

Television and the media, which helped McCarthy to get his point across to the American public, are what finally caused his downfall. The army accused McCarthy of seeking special treatment for an aide who had been drafted. The hearings were televised and they enabled the American public to see what McCarthy was really like.

And over the following months, as 20 million watched, McCarthy interrupted constantly with his made-up points of order. He treated witnesses rudely and showed himself an unscrupulous bully.[9]

The downfall of McCarthy in 1954 ended the worst violations of civil liberties. Although some things continued, like loyalty oaths and subversives lists, everything was toned down, and the subversive trials just about stopped.

The McCarthy era was not the only era in American history that violated people's civil liberties. The Anti-Masonic and anti-Catholic movements did too. The McCarthy era is also often compared to the Salem Witch hunts because of the way people were accused and tried. Each time people thought they were protecting America. In this paper I have tried to show how, to protect democracy, people's civil liberties were taken away.

Footnotes

1. Howard Zinn, *A People's History of the United States,* New York: Harper & Row, 1985.
2. Ibid., p. 420.
3. Victor Navasky, *Naming Names,* Dallas: Penguin, 1980, pp. 22-23.
4. Zinn, p. 424.
5. Navasky, pp. 22-23.
6. David Davis, *Fear of Conspiracy,* Ithaca, NY: Cornell University Press, 1971, p. 289.
7. Ibid., p. 299.
8. Navasky, p. 34.
9. Daniel Boorstin and Brooks Kelly, *A History of the United States,* Lexington, MA: Ginn, 1981, p. 610.

Bibliography and Other Sources

Boorstin, D., and Kelly, B. (1981). *A History of the United States.* Lexington, MA: Ginn.
Encyclopaedia Britannica. Chicago.
Davis, D. (1971). *The Fear of Conspiracy.* Ithaca, NY: Cornell University Press.
Fried, R. (1976). *Men Against McCarthy.* New York: Columbia University Press.
Herbert, M. Personal discussion.
Hofstadter, R. (1967). *The Paranoid Style in American Politics.* New York: Vintage.
Lee, J.G. Personal discussion.
Navasky, V. (1980). *Naming Names.* Dallas: Penguin.
Zinn, H. (1985). *A People's History of the United States.* New York: Harper & Row.

Other Research

Survey

Select a subject that you want to know what other people think about. Write this out as a question or as a set of questions. Then ask whatever people you want responses from—maybe a particular group, or maybe a mixture of people for comparison. Record answers.

Pull the answers together and write up the results. Part of your summary might be in the form of numbers and percentages, maybe charts or graphs. Some quotations might be good for illustration. Summarize also in your own words the gist of what people said. Weave this together with any figures or quotations. Describe the kind of people you polled.

Post this up, or put it in a newspaper. Or make it part of a bigger project like consumer research on a product.

Insight
Chandra Taylor

I asked four eighth graders, "What is the point or goal in your life that you would have to reach to make you feel that your life was worthwhile?" From these four people—Jeremy Fader, Kim Brown, Damian Eckstein, and Njameh Samuels—I got surprisingly honest, serious, and interesting answers.

Jeremy Fader:

Jeremy hesitated for several seconds before answering. When he did answer me, he said, "The goal that I would have to reach would be to be able to win, or to actually win, an important tournament, such as Wimbledon or Forest Hills."

Kim Brown:

Kim had some trouble answering me also because she said that she had never really thought about the matter. After four or five minutes of thinking, she said, "The goal that I would have to achieve would be to become rich and famous and simultaneously to feel that my 'fame and fortune' were helping others."

Damian Eckstein:

Damian didn't hesitate at all. He was completely serious when he said, "The goal that I would have to reach in my life would be to be the pilot of a 767 airliner jet." When I asked him why, he said, "No particular reason. I guess that's just what I want to be."

Njameh Samuels:

Njameh had three goals that she felt would make her life worthwhile if she achieved them. She said, "My main goals are to go to college, to become a good pediatrician, and while I'm studying for my doctorate, to share an apartment with a close friend."

Success in School
Remi Adegbile and Cassandra Thorne

Students who succeed in school have certain qualities in common. A group of 97 students from Isaac Newton were questioned to determine what qualities led to success. Success was defined as having a grade average over 80%.

It was found that, of the students surveyed, 94% of the students who do well in school spend more than 3 nights per week studying. Only 65% of students who have poor grades, or are failing, study for this amount of time.

Thirty-five per cent of the students who do not do well are absent more than 5 days per marking period, while only fifteen percent of the honor students are absent as frequently.

Parents also play a role in the success of their children. Only 46% of the parents of poor students go over the homework with their children, while 60% of the parents of successful students go over their homework. The students said their parents go over their homework with them when they do not understand the subject very well.

From the survey it was ascertained that students whose study habits are consistent, who have a good attendance record, and who receive assistance from their parents are the students who are most likely to do well in their school performance.

News and Views on Homework
Lorraine R. Mazelis

Homework! Too much? Too little? Just enough? Why on the weekend? This is an interesting issue discussed by students and teachers alike. Why have homework at all? Everyone seems to be asking these questions, so I decided I would try to find some answers.

I asked teachers and students from second grade to college level what they thought about homework and why. I asked a total of forty people and got these answers: 12.5% wanted no homework, 60.0% wanted a moderate amount of homework, and 27.5% wanted a lot of homework. I wasn't surprised. Although many students say they hate homework, when the question is asked seriously they all know they need to have some homework.

I also got some interesting reasons. I had one seventh-grade student tell me that school was the time for work, and home was the time to relax, while another seventh-grader from the same school told me that students should get a lot of homework because we need education. "A lot so I learn," says a P.S. 163 second-grader.

"I hate homework!" A lot of people seem to say that, but only one person I asked gave me that reply. "We should have it, but I hate it!" said one sensible seventh-grader. Some said that we should get only a little because some people have after-school classes.

I had one teacher tell me, "A lot, because it's good exercise for the index finger." While another teacher gave me a more serious answer: he thought a little bit every day. "It should be meaningful, so they can understand the concepts the teacher is trying to get across."

One college student told me that students should get a lot of homework because it takes that long to get to know the work well. Another said, "Because you study and practice a lot so when a test comes you know what's going on."

A typical answer I got from all levels was that with no homework you don't learn anything; with a lot you're too pressured. So a little is just right.

Not everybody seems to feel that the amount of homework is an important issue. There was one college student who said she didn't know, started giggling, and mumbled, "Crazy kid."

Some said that homework keeps the mind going and makes the student more interested. Some said that a medium amount was good, but if they wanted more that should be an option. Another told me that the correct amount was "enough to pass."

One college teacher told me that students should have a lot of homework because it makes them think about their work and do it on their own.

And that is what many students and teachers think about homework.

A Poll on Nuclear Energy
Gemma DiGrazia

This poll was conducted mainly among middle-class New Yorkers. Almost all of the adults had a college education. The majority of them live on the Upper West Side. There was an equal amount of females and males. Most people who answered were over forty or under twenty.

The questions asked were:

1. Do you think nuclear energy is necessary as an alternative energy source. If no: What are the alternatives?
   36% thought nuclear energy was necessary. All of them mentioned that other energy sources would run out.
   64% said it wasn't necessary. Energy alternatives they listed were: coal, solar, waterpower, and conservation of existing energy.
2. Describe what you think the effects of radioactivity on humans are.
   All people mentioned some physical symptoms as effects of radiation and radioactivity. These are:

symptoms	% of people who mentioned each symptom
death	60%
genetic damage	58%
radiation sickness	56%
general sickness	52%
cancer	36%
sterility	12%

3. Do you think the public is fully informed about nuclear hazards and safety? All said no, the public wasn't fully informed. 25% said no because they think most people aren't educated enough to understand the problems of nuclear energy.

   50% said no, because they think information is deliberately withheld in lies and coverups by the government and nuclear energy people.

   5% said they think nuclear energy is too technical and complex for almost everybody to understand.

   20% said the public is not told everything because there is no reason to panic them when they can't do anything about it.

4. Would you know what to do in case of a nuclear disaster (i.e. melt-down) in your area?

   55% said no.

   45% said yes. Those who don't feel nuclear energy is dangerous had faith in the authorities to tell them how to avoid harm. Everyone else was afraid of dying and said they would run or hide, listen to T.V./radio but not believe everything they heard, or hold their loved ones and pets.

5. Do you think that children should be educated to the benefits and dangers of nuclear energy. Why or why not?

   2% said no, people at that age shouldn't be burdened with such things. 98% said yes, they are our future. Future decisions depend on them. Yes, so they are more fully informed about the world we live in. Some people wrote yes, though wait until they're old enough.

6. Do you think you can do anything to educate others about nuclear energy?

   18% said no, they were not educated enough themselves to teach about it.

   12% said yes, educate people to its benefits.

   60% said yes, they would tell people the facts and were sure that these would convince them of their dangers.

7. Are you in favor of using nuclear energy?

   12% said yes only if for medical purposes or if safety is drastically improved.

   48% said yes, either now or in the future. Most of these people thought it was necessary to have nuclear energy and it was just a matter of making it safer.

   40% said no, because of obvious dangers and lack of possible safety ever.

8. Do you think we can have safe nuclear energy?

42% said no because of either total unsafeness of any nuclear energy or because those in control will push it on us before it can be made safe.

30% said maybe. They said this because of lack of information or belief that it *can* be safe, but it might be safe long after it is in use.

28% said yes. These people believe either that nuclear energy is safe now or will be very soon.

The people who were for nuclear energy contradicted themselves a bit on the question that asked if you think the public is fully informed on nuclear energy. All of them thought that not all the information about nuclear energy was available to the public, yet they all thought that they had enough information to feel safe and in favor.

The people who were unsure felt they didn't know enough.

The people against nuclear energy also felt that information was kept from them. One of the issues everyone agreed upon was the issue of the public's awareness of the information about nuclear energy. They all seem to think we need to know more.

Everyone thought that a nuclear energy accident would be harmful to people, and yet some people felt nuclear energy was safe or will be soon. And these people were in favor of using nuclear energy as an energy source.

Before I took the poll I had some ideas of what kinds of answers would be given back to me. I had hoped that most of the people would have been against nuclear energy, but the majority of people were for nuclear energy. Another thing that surprised me was the amount of people who were uninformed or unsure. I had hoped that people would be surer on an issue like this.

From this poll I have learned a lot. I have learned how people have such different opinions from each other and how rigid some people are. The most surprising thing is that people have such opposite opinions while using the same information to get their opinions.

Profile of an Enterprise

Choose an activity or enterprise that interests you, like a factory, business, laboratory, farm, government agency, etc., and arrange to interview a key person there and to tour as you talk. Record or take notes on the interview, and jot down notes also on the activity and the place. Prepare some questions to satisfy whatever curiosity you have about the activity.

Pull your information together later into an account of what goes on at that place. Quote from the interview occasionally and mention details to give flavor and back up things you want to show. Your write-up can follow the order of your visit or be organized around features of the enterprise or around stages in the activity run there

Sometimes the activity may be complicated enough to require more than one visit or interviews with more than one person. Alone or with a partner, visit at different times that afford different information, and interview several people knowing different things about the operation. The enterprise may, for example, have different phases occurring at different times and areas and involving different people. To help you, the organization may have a booklet to hand out which you can draw some information from (mentioning the source). You can also discuss with others how best to put together all that you have found out into a smooth description of the activity that shows your reader what it consists of.

Your feature article can go into a newspaper or magazine or be included in a booklet about community enterprises. Or just print and distribute it.

An Inside Look at AT&T
Richelle Rowe

Potted plants, wall hangings, security guards, modern architecture—these are a few first impressions I received as I entered the visitor's center at AT&T's Bell Labs. There to greet me was my cousin Pat Lacka, who is a technical supervisor of software.

We then walked down the hall to Pat's office. I was surprised at how small the office was. I expected a person in management to have more space given to her. The room was filled with typical office equipment—chairs, desks, a blackboard, shelves, etc. Pat told me a little bit about her job. Her main responsibilities are to supervise her staff, see that assigned work gets done on time, be personally interested in the people she works with, and be available to help with problems that might come up. She has to know all about the products made in her department.

Pat invited me to tour the rest of the building with her. It was nice to see a lot of women employed in important positions at the labs. Pat took me to a room where all the switching systems are. When someone calls someone else this switching system connects their call. I found this room fascinating. We also toured the secretarial offices. I was looking forward to seeing the main computer room with over two hundred computers in it, but unfortunately when we arrived there the door was locked.

The atmosphere at Bell Labs was friendly and relaxed. The people seemed happy to be there and happy in their work. I think as an adult I would enjoy being a part of that.

After spending an hour and a half with Pat at Bell Labs' main facility, I boarded a shuttle bus to AT&T's Information Systems building, where I was met by Pat's husband John, who is a telecommunications person there.

Sitting at his desk tinkering with his microchips and circuits, trying to put together and design a new computer, John realizes he is having some trouble. "Okay, that does it," John said, "I'm going down to the lab and if I can't get it to work then I'm going to go to Paul's office and ask him for help."

Ten minutes later John is in "Pac Rat's" office. Paul's office is so jammed with paper and paraphernalia that everyone on his work team calls him a "pac rat." After figuring out what he's done wrong, John is on his way back.

Each office in this building is shared between two people. There are two or three computers per office. John's office consists of two bookcases, two desks, a blackboard, swivel chairs, a white inflatable airplane (fun thing), a volcano lamp (old college fun thing), humorous photos taped to the door, drawer of floppy disk games, circuit and microchip boards scattered everywhere, shelves filled with books and catalogs, a cup of pretzel sticks (energy), and no room to move around. His partner, or rather, roommate, Dennis, wanders from place to place so no one knows where he is—kind of an absent-minded professor type.

John showed me different labs where he works with all sorts of computer testing equipment as well as the actual computers he and his fellow team members have put together. He also took me in some of his friend's offices just for a brief peek at what they were doing.

I was in an inventor's environment. John and his co-workers are members of the technical staff microcomputer exploratory group computer systems, information systems of AT&T—so their ID cards read. Surrounding me were all the technical equipment and ideas that make up this field of work.

Research Article

Choose a subject you want to know more about. Make a list of questions about the subject you want to find answers to. Write each question on a 5" x 8" card, and write notes on it about what you find out toward answering that question. Include also the sources of information. Get help from your teacher or librarian about how to find books and magazines or other sources of information on that subject. Interviewing an expert is one way of getting informed. If the subject is something that is rapidly developing, like some things in science and tech-

nology, try to get the most up-to-date information, which is found usually in periodicals—magazines, newspapers, newsletters, and specialized journals.

After you've gathered your information, organize your notes and decide which points about your subject should come before others and which should go under others. An outline might help to fix in your mind this sequence of topics and the ranking within a topic. Try your article as a talk to some group. Speak from your notes and outline. Ask for a response from your audience to help do your next draft. If you tape your talk, you can revise that into your article, taking the audience commentary into account. Try this draft out on some readers to see if it needs further improvement. Look at a book or article that cites sources in footnotes and lists them in a bibliography. Follow that form for your own.

Print copies to distribute and submit for publication. If there is a particular group, like a club, that deals with your subject, you might read your talk to them as a lecture.

Women in Colonial America
Ia Robinson

Introduction

Everyone knows about the women's rights movement. Even today American women are still fighting for rights equal to men's. But have you ever wondered how these traditions started? You would have to go way back in time, back to the early days of colonial America, when a woman had to obey every word of her husband, and when wife beating was legal. There you will find the starting point for women's standing in America. From this report I hope you will understand what women then had to go through and how the line in the Declaration of Independence, "all men are created equal" was not true for women.

Home and Family Life

Marriage

A young girl in colonial America would be married before she was out of her teens mainly because it was thought that if you married after the age of 25 you were an old maid. Old maids were thought of as good-for-nothing women who were jealous of married women. They were treated so poorly that it almost was thought of as total humiliation not to be married by 25.

Girls of wealthy families were given some share of the family fortune when they came of age or were married—usually both at the same time! Because of the high death rate, colonial women usually married more than once. It was thought that a man or woman who had more experience with marriage was most likely to be chosen for another marriage. Once some young women asked the governor if he would prevent any young man from marrying any widow until they got a chance first!

A woman without a husband and children was considered an unnatural creature. Women who refused to marry were looked upon with horror. Young girls were supposed to think about marriage before they were 13 or 14, perhaps even get married at age 12!

Marriage then was done frequently, as I said, because of the high death rate. Widows were supposed to marry for money or any practical reasons rather than true love or passion.

Role in Family

The women's role in the family was a clear one. The women had to follow the husband through thick and thin. The husband was boss or "master" to the wife or "mistress," as she was called. The mistress had the job of taking care of the family, several other important responsibilities that I will explain later, and to obey the master's every word. She was to make him happy and had no other reason to be put on this earth in "God's eyes."

Child Rearing

Having a child, as well as being one, wasn't easy. Many women had extremely large families, maybe as many as 20 children. Imagine having 20 children running around your house, and a small house at that! Many families never had the chance to grow any bigger than about 13 children because of the amount of deaths in childbirth and the deaths of young infants.

Those who did live weren't much better off. The childhood they led wasn't a pleasant one. Not only did they have to do laborious chores, but the women of colonial times were often abusive to their children, not only mentally but physically as well. Mothers would whip, starve, and beat their children, thinking it was for the child's own good. Mothers would also threaten the child with ghosts and monsters and would try to toughen their children by making them take cold baths in freezing weather. Young infants were beaten and whipped with sticks before they were able to talk! Children would be starved to discourage overeating, and strapped to boards to encourage them to grow up straight. Mothers viewed play suspiciously, not wanting children to follow their own animal instincts.

It was a hard childhood for those who survived it but was thought of as normal upbringing, and when young girls got married and had children, they often repeated the treatment.

Caring for the Sick

One of the women's important responsibilities, and one they took very seriously, was their medicine. Death was a familiar face in the colonies, and women did their best to prevent any disease from hitting someone in their family. There were few university trained doctors in colonial America, which may have been a blessing because the doctor's cures and remedies were more dangerous than the diseases at times. Cures were based on the writings of the ancient Greeks, which consisted of painful concoctions that were so crazy you could understand why everyone relied on and preferred remedies of women.

Some of these weird cures were sent in from the mother country (England). Doctors there recommended such strange things as putting cobwebs on a cut to stop the bleeding and putting hedgehog fat in the ear and covering it with black wool to prevent deafness.

Since doctors has such bad cures and were hard to find, women had to take charge of the problem. Young girls, before they were able to take on a house of their own, had to know all the cures that their mothers knew. Women studied medical books and made remedies out of things they had in their gardens. The mother would know how to make palsy drops and pokeberry plaster and how to brew tea from herbs. All these medicines were passed down mother to daughter.

Cleaning

Cleaning was one of the jobs set aside for women. With this job came many others such as washing the silverware, washing the children, and washing the clothes.

The women had to make their own soap, which was made of lye and animal fat. This was first done by collecting ashes and mixing them with water, creating lye, and then gathering animal fat, putting that all together in a large kettle, and stirring it up on an open fire. The method was passed from mother to daughter. The soap was put into large barrels and stored somewhere for bath day.

Bath day only came once or twice a year for colonists. It was thought that people as well as animals should smell! In fact too much bathing was considered unhealthy, which is probably why a number of colonists got sick and died. Even though all of this may sound disgusting to us, it was helpful to colonial women. It meant they didn't have to bathe and wash the children or the house as often, which saved them a lot of time. Because of their demanding schedules, time is what they had little of.

Cooking and Food

Tending the kitchen garden was women's work, and so was picking the vegetables and slaughtering barnyard animals. This was all preparation for a daily meal which women were in charge of.

Cooking a meal was not one of the areas where colonial women were most creative. Families did not expect something interesting or delicious but expected to eat whatever "mama" made. Meals were the same every day because the wife usually had too much to do other than preparing a different dish every night. A typical meal usually consisted of salted meat and corn cakes, with some sort of drink like whiskey or water.

In order to make this type of meal or any other dish, the woman had to use huge kettles, weighing over 40 to 70 pounds, a lot to carry if you were always pregnant. A woman would spend hours stirring a hot boiling kettle full of stew or soup.

Harvest time was the busiest time for women and men. While men went hunting for meat and brought in their fall harvest, women had to preserve all of the vegetables, salt all meat, and store them in barrels. The method of preserving meat was like many things passed down from mother to daughter.

Making Clothing

It may be hard to believe but there was one job that women actually liked. This job was making clothing. Women would sit in the parlor stitching away, enjoying the company of friends. To women this was the most leisurely activity. Girls were taught how to sew and embroider.

The process of making cloth was a long and laborious one. The hardest cloth to make was linen, which was made from flax and took at least sixteen weeks to produce. Wool was slightly easier to produce, but it too was difficult. A popular combination of both linen and wool called linsey-woolsey was used commonly.

Although cloth-making was a long and tedious job, sewing the cloth to make clothing was fun for the women. With colored cloth, which they dyed with special coloring recipes handed down mother to daughter, they created patchwork quilts and men's suits (that took over a year to make and were worn only on special occasions). Making clothing was something that again men held women responsible for.

Because of the slow job of sewing, families did not have many clothes. Once the clothing was too small for one member of the family, it was passed down to someone younger until it became worn and finally turned into patchwork, because colonial families could not waste anything.

Making Other Items for the Home

To make her home more comfortable, a woman would make decorative items. These items were made with much effort, thought and creativity. Their hand work was beautiful as well as practical.

Knitting was one of the ways that women made accessories. All stockings, mittens, and caps were knitted. Knitting, like sewing, was a continuous female occupation. Young girls carried their little knitting baskets everywhere. As soon as little girls could hold the needles, they were taught how to make stockings and mittens for themselves. Elderly people, such as grandmothers who were too old to do any kind of regular women's work, kept their hands busy with knitting needles.

With skills that they learned, girls and women were able to make decorative bed hangings, petticoats, and maybe even pictures for the wall. Upper-class women always had something on hand that they could pick up and do on social occasions.

Patchwork done as social activity was called a quilting bee. This was done by several women sewing together pieces of scrap cloth. Usually tea and cakes were served while women gossiped about the day's events.

Last but not least was another job of women, providing light for their dark colonial homes. This was candle-making. At first women had the hard job of dipping a string into a pot of wax, but later candle molds were invented so the candle wax could be poured into the molds. These candles were considered top priority.

Women's Clothes

Being in style was not something that the poor could afford. Therefore only the rich women dressed in the expensive wigs and dresses from Europe. These dresses had sleeves cut short at the elbows and were surrounded by ruffles and sashes. The European wigs all had to be powdered and fixed up before they were worn. A woman who spent money on such a masterpiece treated it very carefully. When she slept she laid her head on a wooden block so as not to disturb the perfect hairdo. Sometimes a wire cage was worn over it at night so the mice in the house would not crawl into it. These wigs not only attracted mice but vermin as well!

The rich women of colonial America tried hard to copy the styles of Europe. Because there were no fashion magazines to follow, women turned to dolls made in England called "fashion babies." These dolls were dressed in the latest fashions from Europe and were exhibited in shops in Philadelphia and Boston and soon copied by colonists.

The poorer women wore long dresses called petticoats. Most of the time they would wear one petticoat over another, with some sort of apron caught up in the front or back.

A bodice, which is a laced top that looks like an outside corset, was worn for more than a century by women but first started in colonial times. These bodices were worn tightly. They were stiffened with whalebone and were open slightly down the front.

Hoods were worn at all times by women. Even when a hat was worn a hood went over it.

Shoes were patterned to many women's preference. Shoes were dainty, and some were made of silk with heels a couple of inches high and narrow thin soles. Those shoes obviously belonged to the rich. The poor had sturdy shoes, but none had high heels.

European styles soon went out because of the Revolution. Any woman who was spotted wearing a European wig was thought to be siding with England, and so ended European styles.

Political Life

Property Rights

Owning land was something that women weren't supposed to do. Many widows were allowed to own land while they were still widows, but once they got married again, which they usually did, all land-owning rights then went to the husband, who also paid taxes on the land. Girls of wealthy families were able to own land once they came of age, but the girls were usually married by then and the property went to the husband. Because of this few women owned land.

Few widows could support themselves without a husband, and wealthy or poor girls were almost always married. Because you had to pay taxes to vote and women's husbands paid the taxes, married women had no right to vote.

Many times when the husband died, the widow could claim only one-third of the property, and the rest went to the children or relatives. With only a small piece of land left, the widows were almost pushed into poverty.

Voting

Since only taxpayers could vote and most women didn't own land to pay taxes, many of them weren't allowed to vote. But there were a few women who did meet voting requirements. Unfortunately these women didn't exercise their voting rights.

Women didn't even bother thinking about voting, leaving it the man's responsibility. Most women weren't even aware that voting was their legal right. Of course some women did. These women owned small amounts of land and were unmarried. Those wealthy widows who did know that they could qualify as voters stayed away from the polling places to protect their ladylike images. Books written by men and imported from England called "Ladies' Books" didn't describe women as voters.

So though most women were married and couldn't vote, there was a small group of women in the colonies that could vote but rarely did.

In 1790 a New Jersey legislature adopted a new election law. This law referred to voters as "he and she," meaning that both men *and* women could vote. Unmarried women soon started going to the polls. Unfortunately the law was abused and the New Jersey legislature was forced to repeal it in 1807.

Other Women's Rights

Divorce and Beatings

Once a girl said her sacred wedding vows, that was it. She and her land became total possessions of her husband. Whether her master was a good husband or not was a matter of luck. Many times a woman could find a good husband who would take care of her and treat her nicely, but there were husbands who beat their wives. Some beatings went as far as murder. The law premitted beatings but not murder. A man who murdered his wife was hanged. A woman who murdered her husband was burned alive! The law made the husband responsible for the woman's conduct, so if he should feel that she was misbehaving he could discipline her. Unless she was permanently crippled by the beatings, the law considered the beatings to be "moderate punishment."

The worst part about this wife abuse was that a wife could not separate from her husband without his consent, and none of the courts in New England and the South granted absolute divorces before the Revolution. Marriages were to continue until one of them died. This was a disgusting way to live. Many murders occurred during this time. A clergyman attempted to murder his wife by "ty'g her up by the leggs to the bed and cut'g her in a cruel man'r with knifes."[1] As long as this man's wife wasn't cripple, it was considered legal.

Education

The main reason young girls went to school (where they learned only the basic schooling) was so they could teach their children what they had learned. Learning to read the Bible was another reason young female students went to school. After finishing school, boys went to a college (if they were rich) and girls had to get married. Some women pursued their education after they were married.

"Ladies' Books" teased women who were educated by calling them "bluestocking" or "learned lady." A woman who was as well educated as a man was thought unnatural. It was also thought that a female with true intellectual equality to a man was not only unattractive but must have a damaged brain!

Even a college education was not impossible to acquire. The only problem for one female student who was highly qualified was the large amount of men with only one woman. Because of this, the university president took her in as his private student, and she continued her education under his supervision. John Adams gave advice to his ten-year-old daughter when he learned his wife was teaching her the basics of Latin grammar. "I learned in a letter from your mama, that you was learning the accidence. This will do you no hurt, my dear, though you must not tell many people of it, for it is scarcely reputable for young ladies to understand Latin and Greek."[2]

Witches

In 1692 there was mass hysteria in the Massachusetts Bay Colony. The neighboring Indians were becoming more aggressive, there was a smallpox plague, taxes were being raised on the colonies, and many other terrible things

1. From *Founding Mothers*, p. 54.
2. From *Founding Mothers*, p. 209.

were affecting this colony. Many Puritans blamed it on the devil. It wasn't long before some men and women were being accused of taking instructions from the devil.

It all started with some girls who were listening to stories from their servant. Some sort of excitement made the girls hysterical. Witchcraft was suggested as the cause for the girls' fits and visions, and soon everyone was believing that the devil was in Salem. The girls, enjoying their new attention, were asked to name those who were possessing them. The witch hunt began. It lasted four months, killing 13 women and 7 men, all believed to be witches. The growing number of girls who thought they were subject to fits of hysteria, blindness, etc. would accuse innocent women and men, who were brought to court.

The witch hunts ended when Rebecca Nurse, a respected community member, was hanged. She was testified against by 39 of her own neighbors, who said that she had to be a witch because of her piety, good works, and Christian conduct. This shocked Salem and the clergy into taking a more realistic view of the situation. The Reverend Increase Mather criticized the kind of evidence the court in Salem admitted by saying, "Better that ten suspected witches should escape than one honest person should be condemned."[3]

Soon people started admitting their false accusations, and on January 14, 1697 a fast day was declared for the whole community in honor of their neighbors who were killed.

Economic Life

Typical Work Outside of Home

It was quite common for a widow to carry on a business after her husband's death. Because of this, there were few occupations from which women were excluded. Many jobs done by men were occasionally done by women.

Opening a shop was one of the things women did other than running a home. In their shops women would sell some items made by themselves or things that they picked from their gardens such as melons and vegetables. Some women were able to get items imported from Europe. A shopkeeper in Boston advertised during the Revolution that she had "every sort of beauties, just received from France."[4]

Running a plantation was commonly done by women after their husbands died and they had to take over. One Englishman, who was staying at the home of a female plantation owner, described her as "a very acute, ingenious lady."[5] Yes, these women were very ingenious. They grew tobacco, raised cattle, and

3. From *A Pictorial History of Women in America*, p. 34-36.
4. From *Founding Mothers*, p. 36.
5. From *Founding Mothers*, p. 26.

bought and sold slaves just as well as men did. Some women ran the family business better than men!

Another job that many women did was running a tavern. A tavern was like a fast-food restaurant and bar all in one. Some taverns had rooms for rent like a hotel. One-third of the taverns were run by women alone. The rest were run by husband and wife teams. All a woman had to do to start a tavern was apply for a license and hang out a sign. In addition to lodging for strangers, taverns also became the meeting place for local businessmen, lottery drawings, and cock fights.

With taverns, plantations, and stores women were able to hold a part in the business world of colonial America.

Unusual Work Outside of Home

There were always exceptions for some women. As I mentioned before, a widow carried on her husband's business when he died, or started one of her own.

Occasionally there would be women blacksmiths around. In 1754 the just-widowed Mary Salmon of Boston announced that she would "carry on the business of horse-shoeing, as theretofore, where all gentlemen may have their horses shod in the best manner."[6] These women clearly had a lot of muscle power. They learned to stand the heat and were highly trained. They must have participated in the work while their husbands were still alive.

Women barbers were not uncommon. Many men who traveled mentioned that they were "shaved by the barber's wife."[7]

In the shipping business, Mary Butler of Maryland supplied her customers with blocks and pumps for ships, and Temperance Grant of Rhode Island carried on the family shipping business for 22 years after she was widowed in 1744. These women did so-called men's work and were very successful.

Conclusion

Women of colonial America, as you have read, had a very hard life, but luckily times have changed. In writing this report I learned a lot about colonial women and now try not to take anything for granted. I hope we never repeat this chapter in history and learn from it. Unfortunately many women in other countries are still fighting for their basic rights. But I'm glad American women can pursue life, liberty, and the pursuit of happiness!

Bibliography

Books

De Pauw, L.G. (1975). *Founding Mothers*. Boston: Houghton Mifflin.

6. From *Founding Mothers*, p. 33.
7. From *Founding Mothers*, p. 32.

Speare, E.G. (1963). *Life in Colonial America*. New York: Random House.
Tunis, E. (1975). *Colonial Living*. New York: T.Y. Crowell.
Warren, R. (1975). *A Pictorial History of Women in America*. New York: Crown.

Non-Book Sources

The Museum of the City of New York.
The Metropolitan Museum of Art.
Speaker from The Sleepy Hollow Restoration at Phillips Manor, Tarrytown, New York.

Thinking Up
(Imagination)

Dreams

Jot down a dream soon after you have it so you'll remember it better, or record your dreams regularly in your general journal. Tell the dream to a partner or group until you have it well in mind, listen to what they have to say about it, then write it as a story or poem. You don't have to stick completely to the original but can change it or add to it.

Read your dream to a group and talk about whether others have had similar dreams. Or include it in a booklet of stories or poems by you or others. If the dream features dialogue, write it as a script and arrange to perform it.

Haunted by Homework
Marcus Watkins

One night when I was up in my house alone at night I heard a tapping. It was like someone was trying to get in. When I went up there I looked out. In the fog there were two people—it was Mrs. Oliver and Mr. Mollahan. They kept on saying, "You owe us homework, Marcus, and we want it." They were talking like and looked like zombies. I ran downstairs, and there they were saying, "We want our homework, Marcus, and we want it now. We are tired of sending letters home. We want it now." They were saying this holding a whole lot of papers except mine.

I knocked them both down and ran upstairs again. I tried to call my mother, but when I picked up the phone all I heard was, "You owe us homework, Marcus, and we want it." They were all over—in the bathroom, in the kitchen, closet, living room, balcony, behind the door, etc. Then when they did catch me, Mr. Mollahan grabbed, and I yelled, and then I woke up. My mother was grabbing me. Boy, was I scared.

Nightmare
Jennifer Rosen

It happened one night
around half-past four
and gave me a fright
when it knocked down my door.

I tried to decide
whether to fight or to flee,
but when I ran,
it grabbed onto me.

I yelled "Let me go!"
with a kick and a scream,
and then held my breath,
as I longed to be free.

It bounced me around
on what I think was its knee,
then threw me down
and buzzed off like a bee.

All of a sudden I heard a ring
and woke with the joy there was no one around.
"It was all a dream," I started to sing
and then collapsed with exhaustion onto the ground.

Not Only the Lonely Night
Susannah Kaplan

One night I looked out of my window,
Pressing my nose against the glass
That shut the darkness out.
The restless trees out in the courtyard
Ruffled their leaves like the feathers of a bird.
I heard someone whistle.
It was only the wind
Calling to me in its lonely voice.
The sound of soft footsteps echoed quietly.
I went to bed

Thinking it was only the lonely night tormenting.
Delicious sleep engulfed me.
But soon I awoke.
His horrible face was peering in the window.
I pulled down the shade.
He broke the glass.
I pushed him and he fell
Screaming, screaming
Into the night.

Nightmares
Diana Schlesinger

Crystallized scones hung
   in her bedroom;
she called them her
        edibles.
His bedroom was as large
   although the frozen pond
took up the center space.
She always had nightmares about his pond.
     Why was it always frozen?
He said
    that
ice was naturally projected
into his room.
    She claimed it was his frozen heart.
He laughed,
    looking disgusted.
She took his frozen heart.
    All of his motion stopped
As she laid him down
    on his pond—
       which was slowly melting.
Feeling free now,
     she pranced into her room.
She laid down with his heart.
NO MORE NIGHTMARES.
    Her scones tinkled.
His hand rose slowly
     out of the melted pond,
grabbing a scone and piercing it into
   her head.
She laughed slowly.

I Have This Dream

Cree Snyder

Every year, over and over,
I have this dream.

The plane leaves, we crash.
There's blackness and no survivors

except for my brother and me.
We walk and walk, trying to find him.

Over and over,
I have this dream.

A bus, my mom, Tasha,
a place to sit.

We stop, get out of the bus,
only my brother and me.

Over and over,
I have this dream.

My mom says buy some food,
but hurry, the bus might leave.

We run into the store,
come back out, and the bus is gone.

We walk and walk
trying to find him.

Over and over,
I have this dream.

We get to his city and I
see him, up on his hill.

I cry, I'm happy,
but not for long.

I keep walking,
but he is always the same distance away.

Walking, walking, Daddy please stay.
He waves and beckons me on,
laughing, smiling.

Daddy, I'm tired.
Over and over I have this dream.

Jokes

Write down some jokes that you have heard. Make up a new joke or two. Alone or with others, put together this way a book of jokes and exchange it with another person or group who did the same thing.

Moral Jokes
Merritt Johns

There once was a bunny who always beat up a poor little chicken. One day a fairy godmother told the bunny if he touched the chicken once more she'd turn him into a goon. The bunny, not knowing what a goon was, beat up the chicken again. The bunny then turned into a goon.
Moral: Hare today, goon tomorrow.

Two men were painting the Sistine Chapel. They slowly were running out of paint so they began thinning it out. Suddenly a loud voice shook the Chapel and said, "Repaint and thin no more."

In a certain kingdom, there was a king and a jester who always were fighting. One day the jester stole the king's throne and placed it in his glass house. Because the house was glass, the king's army could see the throne and arrested the jester.
Moral: People in glass houses shouldn't stow thrones.

A horse appeared to a man and said he would grant him three wishes. The man told the horse he was happy with the way things were and to just go away. However, the horse kept pestering him to make the three wishes. So the man walked up face to face to the horse and said he wished the horse would die. The horse instead of dying bit the man's head off.
Moral: Don't ever look a gift horse in the mouth.

There was a boy born with just a head—no body. He was taken to school one day and set on top of a desk. He rolled off the desk and because of his embarrassment, he rolled home. On the way he met a gypsy, and she said she'd grant him a wish. He asked to be turned into a grape. So the next day he turned into a grape on his way to school. A fat woman then stepped on him, and he splattered all over the sidewalk.
Moral: Quit while you're a head.

Question Jokes
7th-Grade Newspaper Class of Olivia Lynch

Q: Where do you put a boy's valentine?
A: In the male box.

Q: How do you stop a bull from charging?
A: Take away his credit card.

Q: Why didn't the skeleton cross the road?
A: He didn't have any guts.

Q: A man was locked in a room for one month. In the room there was only a piano, a bed and a calendar. How did he eat, drink and get out of the room?
A: He ate the dates off the calendar, drank from the springs from the bed, and took the keys from the piano to get out.

Just Jokes
Evan Sallustro, Ruby Lawrence, and Julie Brams

What do you call a country where all the cars are colored pink?
A pink carnation.

If a seagull flies over the sea, what flies over the bay?
A bagel.

You can fill a glass, you can fill a jar, but you can't Philadelphia.

There were three men stranded on a desert, and they were each allowed one item. The first one wanted a fan, the second one wanted a bucket of ice, and the third one a car door. The first and second asked the third, "Why a car door?" He replied, "To roll down the window if it gets hot."

A man with a truck full of penguins was riding on a highway, and a traffic policeman stopped him, saying, "Bring those penguins to the zoo!" The driver said, "O.K."
The next day the driver came back with all the penguins wearing sunglasses. The traffic policeman said, "I thought I told you to take them to the zoo." The driver said, "I did. They had so much fun that today I'm bringing them to the beach."

Riddles

Write a Who-Am-I? or What-Am-I? poem by imagining an object or creature describing itself—what it has and does. Or just describe it in your own words in a riddlesome way. No names; just hint. Try several.

Read them to others and let them guess. Make a book or bulletin board of riddles.

Heed Me
Nava Fader

My face wears no smile,
My limbs, I have but two (an injury from birth).
One shoulder raised to shorten
My ever whirling arm.
I control your every move
And declare all I know
In trembling tones that echo
Through the halls.

Clock

Powerful
Tishuanda Cunningham

I'm like a nightmare that you never wake up from.
Once you use me I haunt you forever.
Once I'm born I never die.
I am very dangerous and very strong,
I have the strength to destroy anything.
I serve my purpose and stick around for more.

I am the powerful lie.

The Last Poem
David Bock

I am the end of every road.
I am the last stop on the train.
The top rung on every ladder.
The power failure of all life.
The final round of the last fight.
The bottom of the ninth, two outs.
I am the final flame of life.
The sign-off of eternity.

I am death.

My Gold Eyes
Mercedes Jacinda Verdejo

I sit in the grass,
camouflaged with its color.
My skin with splotches
which show the years I have
lived.
My gold eyes, that once sparkled with
life,
now show the things I have seen.
Filled with dark circles, they are
old.
The grass all around me
protects me
from all the world's problems.

Being Something Else

*Imagine you are an object and make up a story told from that
object's point of view about some predicament or typical
situation it got into. (How about a kitchen blender or a flower*

vase?) Or do the same thing for an animal or plant. Try to feel and talk as it would.

You might agree with partners to pretend to be the same thing and compare your stories afterwards, post them up together, or make them into a booklet titled for that object or creature.

Owl
Corin See

As the world darkens
I awake, ready for the night's catch.
I open my eyes, seeing a world
invisible to most, but normal for me.
I ruffle my brown-black feathers
and smell the night wind.
From my high fortress I
silently glide, dark against the stars.
I sense that I will do well tonight,
and, as if to start it off, I see a
furry brown form run through the
pine needles.
I majestically swoop on it,
my steely talons grasping at the
air then touching and puncturing
its feeble brown furry skin.
I feel its warm insides
as I return to my aerie,
and I quickly chew and swallow
it, though it is still barely alive.
I glide through the darkness
looking for my next meal.
I am the owl, revered,
wisest of the birds.

The Life of a Potato
Adine Kernberg

I was born some place in Idaho.
Life was simple, days went slow,

But then when I finally started to grow
What I wanted to be is what I did not know.
My friend Tater wanted a wife and tots.
I exclaimed, "I'm going to be a big potato."
Well, at least that's what I thought.
But then one day a big truck came.
From then on life wasn't the same.
I was set for money, power, and above all fame!
Who was to know that "Chip" was to be my new name!
I was gathered with some chemicals, I proceeded to mingle.
"Hey, old chum, we're brothers now! Pringle and Pringle!"
So that's how I was brought into this new family.
Just to think, these flat chips were once a part of me!
Now I am the cuisine of the tall, short, sweet and rude.
I guess it's a way of life.... I am junk food!

Concrete and Acrostic Poems

*Write a poem by placing the words and letters to form a shape
related to the subject of the poem. This is a "concrete poem,"
which looks like what it says.*

*Or write a poem in which the first letter of the lines spells
out something vertically (an acrostic poem).*

Ripoff
John Maida

Right across the street from us
Is the deli.
Peter is the name of the owner.
Overcharging is his specialty.
For instance, a five dollar bill gets you two lbs. of sugar with
Five cents change!

A Drop of Water
Julie Lefkowitz

A
drop
of water
falling down
towards the earth,
glimmering in the light
of the glowing, golden orb
crystal   clear,   descending
towards   its   death   and   the
creation of smaller, inferior droplets.
It speeds up like a race car which
was stopped but is now accelerating,
heading   towards   a   possible   collision   or
self-destruction. Ping! It collides with a lone
blade of grass, slowly sliding down toward
the soil, where it will be absorbed
into its final burial place. Its faint
and frightened voice cries out
as it feels the earth and
itself become as one.
Destruction.

Still Manhattan
Agustina Rodriguez

Many people can never have
Attention because it's always
Noisy.
Half of the time people
Always go somewhere far
To get away from
Today.
Another bit of advice:
Never go out after 10:00.

The Coral Tea Rose

Yael Ptachewich

Fragrantly, growing
Single and sweet
complementing
superbly
adored

T
H
O
R
N
Y
G
L
I
S
T
E
N
I
N
G
A
N
D
P
E
T
I
T
E

Good and Bad Sides
Miles Chatain

Good   and   Bad
  sides make up the human mind.

The good side   The bad side
is a Dr. Jekyll,   is a Mr. Hyde,
a lover of beauty,   one who shuts
people, and kindness, himself away
one who gladly   from the world,
accepts the world   lurking silently in
for what it is.   the dark, loathing
The good side   people, holding malice
thinks about   in the heart,
Life.   welcoming death.

There would not be a
  good side   without a   bad side.

See-Saw
Roxanne Glass

I am a see-saw.
            I am very unstable.
I never know what I am
            or what I feel.
I think one way
            then I change
and look at things
            from a different angle.
I get involved with someone
            who's not for me,
Then I shift
            to the other side.

Stories

Story Starter
Get an unfinished sentence or an intriguing sentence from someone else and take it from there. Invent a story starting with this sentence or using it as your title. If some classmates use the same story starter, you can compare stories afterwards. Make a booklet of stories begun with the same sentence, which you can make the title of the booklet.

The story starter of the first story below is the title. In the second story, it's the opening sentence.

That Was the Morning
When the Thing Appeared!
Ann Donovan

The sun had just started spreading it's sunny glow on the fluffy white blanket of snow on our lawn when I woke up with a yawn. It was Christmas morning, and no one else was awake yet. So I decided to doze off until I felt like investigating what presents lay underneath the Christmas tree. I plumped up my pillow, straightened my covers, and snuggled deep into my warm bed.

Unexpectedly something bumped into my bed with such suddenness I woke up with a start. I still felt like I was the only one awake, but something was in the room with me! Quietly I whispered out my sister's name, "Laurie," but she didn't answer. Instead I heard a soft whine and a growl. I was really scared now! Maybe I could sneak out. Slowly but quickly I crawled off my bed and inched across the floor to the light switch. A soft thing hit me in the ankle and started to nip my toes. Terrified I fell onto my beanbag chair and closed my eyes, hoping that the Thing would go away. Something (mostly the Thing) jumped on top of me and started to lick my face with a hot rough tongue. But "Things" don't have tongues, or at least I didn't think they did. Carefully I opened one eye and pulled a yellow blanket off from on top of me before opening the other eye. And there, sitting on my stomach, was a bright-eyed, sandy-furred, brand-new puppy!

Immediately he started running in circles and chewing anything he could get his jaws on. I had never seen a puppy with such spunk! I read the tag twice to make sure I was seeing right. It read, "To Claire. . . . . Love, Santa." And after that wonderful Santa I named my puppy. As I hugged my puppy so early in the morning I whispered, "Merry Christmas, Santa."

Case No. 865207
Sara Martin

Suddenly, as Henrietta looked up the street for the bus she was waiting for, she saw approaching the face that she feared, so she ducked into the nearest store.

As soon as she was sure he had passed, she went back outside cautiously, looking around before letting herself be seen.

About ten minutes later, she boarded the bus which would take her home.

She was never seen alive again.

Police Report 6/25/81
Filed by: Sanlau and Gingham
Case No. 865207
Homicide: Fischer, Henrietta S.
Residence: 117 Ave. B, New York City, New York 10009
Age: 27
Birthdate: 12/18/54
Height: 5 feet, 5½ inches
Weight: 135 lbs.
Hair Color: Sandy brown
Eye Color: Dark brown
Distinguishing Marks: mole under right ear
Found: in alley between 117 and 118 Ave. B. Stabbed 5 to 6 times in chest with what is believed to be a kitchen knife. Will know more when autopsy comes in.
Other: Neighbors claim to have neither seen nor heard anything helpful. However, landlord said she and boyfriend had been fighting and she threw him out. He could not tell us boyfriend's name, but gave description: tall, 6 feet 4 or 5, shortish dark brown hair and brown eyes, rugged face, late 30's.

. . .

"Well, what do you think?"
"Jealous boyfriend kills girl."
"I don't know. I just have a funny feeling about this."
Police Report 6/30/81
Case No. 865207
Transcript of interview with Roberts, Kenneth E.
Roberts: You can't arrest me. I know my rights. I didn't do nuttin' anyway.
Interviewer: We're not arresting you, Mr. Roberts. We just want to ask you a few questions about Henrietta Fischer.

Roberts: Oh, yeah, tragic thing, eh? So, ah, what's the verdict? Suicide?

Interviewer: Homicide, first degree.

R.: Don't look at me. I haven't seen her for two weeks, at least. She told me to get out, so I did.

I.: Why were you in her apartment earlier this week?

R.: I had to get some of my stuff. Before, she wouldn't let me get any of it, but then she called me and said I could come over any time to get my stuff.

I.: Why did you look around before entering the building?

R.: She—ah—she told me not to—ah—let her landlord see me.

I.: Why?

R.: How am I supposed to know?

I.: That's why you looked around?

R.: Why else?

I.: What did you do inside?

R.: I walked up the stairs, opened her door, got some of my things, and left, like I told you before.

I.: Was Ms. Fischer there? Did you see her?

R.: No, like I said, I haven't seen her for more than two weeks, when she threw me out.

I.: Why did she throw you out?

R.: We had a fight, we both got real mad, and she threw me out . . . just told me to shove off.

I.: How did you get into her apartment?

R.: It was open, but even if it wasn't, I have the keys, from before, when I lived there. I forgot to give them back to her. I guess it don't matter much now.

I.: Was she friendly to you when she called?

R.: Yeah. Yeah, she was real nice, like she wanted us to get back together or something. She said she wanted me to come over that day, but I said I didn't think I could handle it. She said ok, and I said I'd drop by sometime this week.

I.: Her phone was out of order when we searched her apartment. Would she have used another phone, like a neighbor's or the landlord's?

R.: What does it matter?

I.: Answer the question, please.

R.: I don't know. Maybe. Maybe not. She might have mentioned something, but I'm just not sure.

I.: Thank you for your time, Mr. Roberts. You may go. We'll get back to you if we need any further information. We would appreciate it, therefore, if you didn't leave the city, until the case is closed.

R.: I got no place to go anyway.

. . .

"What do you think now?"

"Same."

"I still don't know. You got nothin' on him, you know. He says he hadn't seen her for more'n two weeks."

"So he says."

"This autopsy report tells us nothing we don't know, Captain."

"I know."

"It says she was stabbed six times in the chest with a long, thin knife."

"I know."

"What have we got to go on? I'll tell you what we've got. Nothing. Absolutely nothing."

"I know."

"I hate cases like this. A meaningless murder, no witnesses, nothing to go on. It's cases like this when I get to wondering what we're really here for."

"I know, I know."

Photo Story

Cut out several photos from magazines, sift through them a number of times, think about the story possibilities of each, then choose one you want to make up a story about. If you do this with partners, you can exchange and have a greater variety to choose from. A photo of a place may suggest a setting for a certain action; a story of people talking, some characters and dialog; an action shot, some plot. Write what the picture seems to say to you about what is going on or what the circumstances are. From such hints make up the rest. Pair stories and photos side by side on a bulletin board or in a booklet. Or surround each photo with several versions if partners have chosen the same photo.

(It was not technically possible to reproduce the photos on which the following stories were based. The first was a head-on shot of an armadillo in mid-leap. The second showed a young man and woman drifting romantically downstream in a row-boat.)

The Ugly Armadillo
Jackie Miller

Deep in the forest, there lived an armadillo named Al. He lived a very easy life. In the morning, he searched through the damp earth for roots, which he ate for breakfast. Afterwards, he would crawl back to his home, which was really a cozy hole under the ground, and go back to sleep, as armadillos despise the daylight. Later in the everning, after the sun had set, Al would go visiting his other animal friends. All the animals enjoyed Al's good-natured sense of humor. Nothing could make him happier. Well, one thing could.

Early one day, while Al was searching for his breakfast, he happened to overhear a conversation between two of his friends.

"Al came to visit me last night," said the first.

The second replied," He's such a great guy. I love his jokes."

This first interchange caused Al to beam. The second, however, did not.

"Yeah, he's really super. Except he's *so* ugly."

"You said a mouthful. If he could just improve his looks, he would be perfect."

Poor Al gloomily waddled back to his hole. He couldn't believe what he had just heard. Sadly, he cried himself to sleep.

That night, he set out to improve his looks. After a few minutes of wandering amilessly around, Al ran into his friend Robin.

"Robin," he asked, "what do you think would make me better looking?"

The bird thought for a while. "Well, one thing you don't have is feathers. I personally am of the opinion that no animal is truly beautiful without feathers."

"Thank you so much," cried Al as he scurried away, anxious to begin his makeover.

While Al was pondering how he could acquire feathers, he ran into another one of his friends, Della Deer.

"Della, how could I make myself more attractive?"

"Well," said Della thoughtfully, "I always think large antlers are handsome."

Al couldn't get over his excitement. Now he had two ways to improve his looks.

He spent the next morning gathering scattered feathers from under trees in which various birds lived. Al proceeded to break two large twigs off of a dead tree. These items he carried back with him to his hole. When he arrived at a mud patch, he began to roll around. Then he threw the feathers all over his back. As a final touch, he stuck the twigs in his ears.

The next night, Al thought he would visit some of his friends. He was anxious to hear what they thought of his new image.

First, he went to see Robin. But when Al came close, Robin suddenly stopped singing and flew away, chirping with fright.

A little bit disappointed but still unabashed, Al went to see Della. However, the minute she set eyes on Al, she ran away as fast as her legs would take her.

Sobbing, Al crawled back to his hole. He couldn't understand what had happened. He had taken all of his friends' advice, but now they seemed to think him even uglier than before.

The next night, Al decided he owed his friends an apology for frightening them the night before. But, prior to going out to meet them, Al removed the twigs from his ears and washed off the feathers from his back.

The night before, after conversing for a while, Robin and Della decided that the "monster" must have been Al. So while Al was cleaning up, they came over to greet him.

"Hi, Al," they said together, "we're sorry about last night. We just didn't recognize you."

"I was just trying to do what you told me to," Al complained.

"Oh, Al, you shouldn't go changing to please us," explained Robin.

"Yes," agreed Della, "We like you the way you are."

"But I thought you believed me to be ugly."

Della tittered, "Oh, Al, if you are a nice person with a good sense of humor you can never be ugly."

From that day forward, Al decided just to be himself. He made more and more friends in the forest with his kind words, and lived happily ever after.

River Dance
Lesley Parent

Marianne unlocked the door for me, then walked around to her side of the car and got in. I stuffed all my shopping bags full of bright new spring clothes into the back of Marianne's red Chevette. She started the car, and as I pulled on my seat belt, she asked, "You never answered me before . . . have your heard from Jeff lately? I thought he was coming home in time for you to take him to the senior prom."

We passed a couple of subdivisions and some stores. I finally said, "I think he forgot about the prom. He hasn't written me in a long time. Maybe he has some big exam or something." I didn't want to say what I really felt: Jeff and I are over. I hadn't seen him since spring break, when he came home from college for a week. He spent most of his time at my house. We didn't go out once—he said that he was sorry, but he was saving his money for school. Personally, I think he spent it all on some secret girl at college. It's not that I don't trust him. I just don't feel very secure with him hundreds of miles away in a college full of older, more beautiful girls.

"What about your gorgeous dress?" Marianne interrupted my thoughts. "It's such a shame to waste it." She didn't sound too upset. After all, she's totally secure in her lifelong relationship with Tom, her guy.

"I'll talk to you later, okay?" I called as she dropped me off at my house. She was depressing me too much to invite her in. The rain, which had started while we were in the mall, had stopped, and the sun was shining on the rain-soaked earth. It smelled like spring—damp earth and rain. My long auburn hair blew gently about my face as I walked up the stony path to my house.

The sound of the vacuum greeted me as I walked through the entrance hall. Kicking off my tennis shoes, I padded through the dark hallway into the soft rose-colored kitchen. Mom smiled a hello, and excitedly nodded toward the kitchen table as she maneuvered a chair around to vacuum under. I glanced at the old wooden table and my stomach flopped. An envelope with Jeff's familiar scrawl on it. I grabbed it and dashed upstairs, blowing a kiss to Mom and tripping over Rover, my dog.

Once in my room, I flopped on my bed and stared at the envelope. It was too special to open right away. It must have gotten lost in the mail, because it was postmarked over two weeks ago. I slowly opened the precious envelope, praying that it didn't tell me that Jeff didn't love me anymore.

"Dear Denise," it said. "I know I haven't written or called, but I've had some major tests, and other things came up." I figured these "other things" were blond girls with perfect measurements and tans year-round. "I have some bad news. I'm not going to be able to make it for the prom." Tears filled my eyes, blurring his words. "However, I'll be in town on the 18th. Could we go out and celebrate our own Senior Prom? I know it couldn't compare, but I want to see you, and I have to make up for ruining your plans. Unless you call me and tell me otherwise, I'll pick you up at quarter to eight. Love, Jeff."

The 18th! Oh my God! That's today! I checked the time—5:58. I slid down over furry, carpeted stairs in my stocking feet, hurdled Rover, and ran to show Mom. When she read it her black-violet eyes sparkled with excitement. I think she knew how I'd been mourning over Jeff for so long. "Well," she said, "you have a prom to get ready for. I'd get going if I were you!" I hugged her and scrambled upstairs.

It's lucky I had my prom outfit ready early, so I could wear it tonight. I showered, shampooing my hair three times and splashing on shower gel at least twice. Once I had carefully applied my face and curled my hair for about an hour, I was ready to dress. I gingerly pulled on my stockings, afraid to get a run before I even stepped out of the bathroom. My dress was beautiful ivory satin and lace all swirling together in a beautiful mass. It fit me perfectly—narrow at my waist and gradually pleating out into gentle flounces. I looked in the mirror as my mom came in. "Oh, hon, you look really terrific! Stunning! Jeff'll be glad he's back!" I wondered about that. I hoped I'd look as good as he remembered.

It seemed like eternity before the doorbell rang. But it was exactly 7:45. I opened the door to a gorgeous blond in a black tux towering over me. I smiled. He smiled. He handed me a rose, looking me over with green and gold flecked eyes. "You look beautiful," he said softly, as if I would melt or blow away if he spoke too loudly.

Once in his silver Corvette he said, "I'm taking you to our old place in the woods. Is that okay?" I was surprised—why get all dressed up to go sit on our rock by the bubbling brook that passed through the town? As it turns out Jeff had rented a caterer to serve us an elegant dinner in the beautiful little boat Jeff rented. I loved him so much. How could a guy away at college have planned all this?

As we drifted along the water, we talked and everything was perfect. Our beautiful clothes, the late evening sun glinting through the trees, and my fingers trailing through the cool water, the wonderful meal of steak and a huge salad and potatoes. We drifted into a little pond and sort of floated for a while. I leaned against Jeff and listened to the night sounds—the crickets, the birds, and no cars or people to disturb us. We didn't need to talk, I thought. But Jeff said, "Ummm, Denise?"

"What?" I asked, looking at him. In the moonlight I could see his strong face flush. He fumbled in his pocket.

"You know how I never spent money or took you anywhere over spring break? Well, I was kind of saving my money for this." Out of his pocket came a black box, looking minute in his big hands. I gasped in astonishment. How could I have thought he'd been spending it on blondes?

My hands trembled as I opened it. In the moonlight there sparkled a gold diamond ring. Tears spilled down my cheeks, I was so happy!

I know you're only eighteen, and I know I didn't write much, but—."

"Yes! Oh, yes, Jeff!" I hugged him as hard as I could, but tenderly. The prom could never have compared to this beautiful magical night.

Fictional Correspondence

Make up an exchange of letters as a way to tell a story. Why are these particular people writing to each other? Date the letters. Try to make the style of each correspondent's letters fit his or her personality. The correspondents may be telling each other about events happening where they are, but the letters themselves can be events—requests, threats, suggestions, congratulations, flattery, thanks, etc.

Just Three Weeks
Sue Abernathy

July 1,

Mom,

I hate it here. Please come bring me back home, Okay? Thanks a lot.
Miserably,
David

July 4,

Dear David,

What's wrong, honey? I'm sorry that you don't like where you are, but I can't come up to Camp Christmas Tree and get you now. Just try to concentrate on having a good time and before you know it, the three weeks will be over and you'll be back home with Dad, Mark, Pepper, and me. Now be good and don't forget to brush your teeth.
Lots of love,
Mom

July 9,

Mom,

I tried having a good time like you said, but it's kind of hard when nobody here even knows I'm alive, and that's not all. There's no night light in the tent and it's awful dark at night. Crickets chirp outside and they won't let me sleep. And guess what else? They're going to make me swim! You never told me I'd have to learn to swim. Could you please write a letter to my counselor and tell him I'm allergic to water? During my horseback riding lesson, Ziggy, my horse, got spooked and almost bucked me off his back. I was so scared! Are you sure you can't take me home?
Unhappily,
David

July 13,

Dear David,

I understand exactly how you feel. The same things happened to me at my first summer camp, and I lived, so you will too. I'm sorry about not telling you that you would be taking swimming lessons. I suppose I forgot to mention it somehow. Don't worry, though. Only one more week to go! Have fun and we all miss you.
With hugs and kisses,
Mom

July 17,

Mom,

I made a friend! His name is Tom and he's in my swimming group. Since we both stink at swimming we help each other out a lot. You might not believe this, but he gets scared at night too, so we stay up all night together and talk so no wild animals will attack us. Today he fell asleep during our pottery class. Maybe we could use a little sleep after all. My horse still hates me, but it's not so bad now because I can talk to Tom about it.

> Love,
> David

July 20,

Dear David,

I am so happy to hear that you're making friends and having some fun. I can hardly wait to see you again. I'll see you in four days.

> All my love,
> Mom

July 23,

Mom,

Could I stay another three weeks, please? Tom is asking his mom too. We want to be in the same tent again and use our same horses. Guess what! The swimming teacher says we're good enough to be intermediate swimmers now instead of beginners! Isn't that great? Please send my rock collection. Tom collects them too and we're going to trade. See you in three weeks!

> Love,
> David

In Response
Sheshonya Rivero

In response to your letter,
I guess you want a thank-you
or some kind words
for seeing through my hidden realities,
and I guess you really think
I succeeded.
Who are you trying to fool?
Most definitely not me.
Sure they pushed me around,
and you wanted me to rise,
but how could I?

It was you that encouraged me,
but it was also you that led me astray.
You told me about the powers that I had,
but you didn't show me how to use them.
You told me I had a jewel,
and that I will have it for the rest of my life.
Well, I don't want it any more,
and do you know why?
Because you left me.
I was confused and afraid.

I decided to try and achieve success without you.
I did all that striving and conquering,
but it didn't work,
and success didn't come.
I kept trying and trying,
and after five years of trying
what do I have to show?
Nothing, I don't have anything at all.

You said, take the challenges in spite of the problems.
Well, guess what,
that didn't work either.
You made me believe those things,
knowing that it was only you
who could keep them going.
You knew I was weak,
and when I started to get stronger,
you decided to move out.

You want to know one more thing?
Well, I'm not giving up yet,
I'm going to come back knowing
I achieved success all by myself.

And one more thing—
it was your words that told me,
but it was me that held on and on.

Just one more thing—
Thanks.

Woman to Woman
Joanna Santiesteban

Dear Mom,

It's hard to believe my first semester in college is over! I don't know about my exams, but I don't plan on worrying about it! Break will be awesome! Sue Marney—you met her—and I plan on spending this week-end in New York, or Nu Yawk as the Easterners say it. Georgetown U. is gorgeous! The snow drapes over the campus like a lacy tablecloth, and everyone wears big fisherman-knit sweaters instead of coats. Our roommates left today; Carol to UA and Cathy to New York. When we go to New York, we plan to stay at Cathy's, and even Carol's taking the train in. But now, the dorm is so empty! For once our dorm actually seems big. The house-mother is a total rag! "Keep those rooms clean or demerits for you two!" Oh brother. I'm working part-time at a boutique and I get great discounts. In our co-ed dorm, there are D&D games every Friday night now. They get pretty involved, but I'm not into it. Write me, Mom. You haven't lately. Is something wrong?

Love ya,
Joanna

Dear Joanna,

Sorry I haven't written you. Have fun in New York, but be careful! You better worry about your exams, or you are in big trouble!

Life here in Chicago isn't peachy. Joe's moved out for a few days, due to a "personal" problem. He refuses to tell me. But I'm beginning to get a hand on my feelings. It's rather difficult.

Sorry it's short, dear. Got to run.

Love,
Mom

Dear Mom,

I'm sorry, but Joe has never had personal problems before. It's definitely not like him. I know how your mind works, Mom. You are probably blaming yourself, jumping to anything as the solution to your problems. DON'T. Mom, you're perfect for Joe, no matter what the circumstances are. If the densest person in the world can see that, I'm sure you can. You have to be there for him, but don't neglect yourself. Your key is counselling. I've got to go.

Love,
Joanna

Dear Mom,

WOW! I never knew people could fight like that! Has that ever happened before, I mean fighting over the phone like that? Amazing. I talked to Joe (kill me later). That fight must have let a lot of steam off. Honestly, tell me if everything's o.k. as you made it sound in your last letter? Sue Narney is an expert on divorce; her mom's gone through six, and she says that maybe Joe's problem is something's threatening his masculinity or he's facing a mid-life crisis. Joe is seeking counselling, but now I think you need it. Go. I don't believe Joe's staying at the YMCA! Couldn't he have stayed at a friend's or something? Mom, take control of your life. I love you.

                                                                Joanna

Dear Joanna,
     Counselling was a good idea, but the nerds in those therapy sessions. They keep rehashing over their divorces, but I'm not getting a divorce! Joe and I are talking every other night, and we get into some pretty deep stuff. I'm so busy trying to sort out my life with Joe, and our office is opening up a new advertising agency in New York. You'll probably see some commercials. You surprise me sometimes. I am supposedly more experienced in life than you are, but.... How much aren't you telling me?
     Thanks, Joanna. I love you.
                                                                Mom

---

Fictional Journal

Tell a story through a journal you make up as if one of the characters in your story is keeping it. All the reader sees is this character's journal. So everything has to come through it. Indicate where the entries begin and end. Write in the style this character would use. What series of events is this person writing about from day to day or time to time in his or her journal?

Present this to others as you might any other story. Reading aloud might be especially good if you or someone else wants to act the voice of such a character.

Grow Up Already
Lisina Russo

                                                                April 4
Dear Diary,
     That counselor says I have to write down my feelings every day. She made me buy a diary. It's stupid anyway. She says anything I tell her will be kept confidential, but I don't believe her. I think she's lying. She wants to see me

more than once a week. She says she likes to talk. But I know it's because she doesn't want me to run away again. She thinks if she keeps an eye on me I can't do anything. HA!!!!

April 5

Dear Diary,

I saw Jim today. I told him about the counselor and this dumb diary. He agrees with me, he thinks I should stop going to her. Her—the counselor— Ms. Bozan, she keeps asking me about my feelings. Who the hell cares about my feelings? The only one who cares about me is Jim.

April 6

Dear Diary,

My mother is trying to be nice to me, it is so annoying. She thinks I'm going to run away too. But I'm not, Jim promised me we could go to his house this weekend, and I wouldn't miss that for anything.

April 7

Dear Diary,

My mother is an ass. I hate her. If I disagree, she cries. And she watches my every move. That stupid counselor said it would be better if I stayed with my mother this weekend. I shouldn't have told her.

April 9

Dear Diary,

I'm not going to Jim's. He says he understands, but that lady is ruining our relationship.

My father came home today, it's about time. He goes for weeks sometimes, and then pops in when he feels it's convenient. That's when I start to feel bad for my mother. I know she's trying to help me, but she tries too hard.

It's terrible when my father comes home. He always yells. He did today when he found out about the counselor. He doesn't want me to go. He says it's a waste of money. My mother said it will help me, he says I don't need any help. That's when my mother started another crying fit. Why don't they just get divorced, it would make my life a lot easier.

The worst part is when he blows his top. Sometimes he throws glasses, other times he hits my mother. He used to hit me until I threatened to call the police. He only hits me sometimes, meaning only when he can catch me. He's usually drunk when he hits, and the next day he's gone and we don't see him for a week or two. It doesn't matter anyway so why think about it.

April 15

Dear Diary,

My mother got a job, she works at a museum. My father left, he said he's not coming back. Good Riddance!!!!

April 25

Dear Diary,

Ms. Bozan is mad because I don't write down stuff every day. So I'm writing to calm her down.

My mother says we don't have to be on welfare any more. I have to say I'm very proud of her. She's very brave. But she still doesn't understand me. I'm sixteen, but she still babies me.

April 28

Dear Diary,

Mom just got her first paycheck. She's really doing well. She bought a new pair of jeans and a sweatshirt.

My only problem is—well, Jim wants me to stop going to Ms. Bozan, he asked me to go on a trip with him. I think two weeks ago I might have because of my thoughts of running away and all. But I think my mother needs some support now. Besides, since my so-called father is gone, I'm not as scared of being home as before.

April 29

Dear Diary,

My mother and I get along pretty well. Last night she wanted to braid my hair, that's when I told her that I wanted to be treated like an adult. She sort of understands. But I know it will be hard for her.

Jim is different. All he wants to do is take me away. I know what he wants to do. Well—I want to go sometimes, but I don't feel that he wants to be with me for just me any more.

May 3

Dear Diary,

Jim said it straight out, he said that if I didn't leave home with him, he was leaving. He sounded mad, he scared me like my father used to. I just realized it, Jim is just like my father. He only married my mother because he got her pregnant. He didn't even love her, just like Jim. I always regretted that. Even *that* I haven't told to Ms. Bozan. I don't want to end up like my mother did. I'm going to be better, I just know it.

May 7

Dear Diary,

Now I've started to wonder if I ever loved my father. Every time I think of one nice thing he did, I remember a night that he come home drunk or hit my mother. Maybe there was a time that I loved him, but not enough to miss him.

May 10

Dear Diary,

We're moving, we're moving out of the project. My aunt is giving us some money, we will live in her building.

I had thought over and over about leaving with Jim. Well—it's not like I need Jim to survive. I think I'm handling it fine by myself.

May 14

Dear Diary,

Ms. Bozan is driving me crazy, all she is doing is making me remember all the bad things from the past. She keeps bringing out all of my bad memories. I hate her. I have to stop going to her. I don't want to remember my father, or Jim, or that time that I ran away or thought of suicide. I want to live in the present, I don't want my father's memories to be held against me when I get older.

June 1

Dear Diary,

I know it's been a while but my mother had a breakdown. She had been worked too hard. I got scared, I don't want anything to happen to her, she brought me this far. I don't think I could make it the rest of the way by myself.

Anyway, she's fine now and we are on our way to Gimbels. I think we are also on our way in life. I will end this diary now. I know it was a short one, but it helped me grow. Now I think I just want my mom to help me do that. Maybe I'll even let her braid my hair.

First-Person Fiction

If your story material and intention are of certain kinds, you may want to pretend that one of your characters is telling the story. Since an "I" would recur during the narration, this general method consists of telling the story "in the first person." But within this framework there are still choices about point of view. Where is "I" in relation to the events? Besides such choices as Exterior and Interior Monolog, and Fictional Correspondence or Journal, you could present your story as:

- *a reminiscence by the central character (as if it were auto-biography)*
- *a reminiscence by a minor character who is more witness than participant (as if it were memoir)*

Fit your choice to your main purpose for the material you have.

Getting Ready for School

Felicia Allen

I just woke up and it's so quiet! Only Sandra and I are up. I better use the bathroom before the rest of them get up.

Now Sheila, Silvia and Ma are up, and I'm half-way dressed. Silvia is in the kitchen, ironing her pants, and Sheila is waiting for Ma to comb her hair.

"Sandra, do you ever go to your first period class?" Ma always wondered how Sandra could leave from Manhattan at 8:00, and make it to her first period class up in the Bronx, when it starts at 8:00.

"Yeah," Sandra said, in a very loud and nasty voice. "You don't have to worry about it, anyway."

"Well, if that's the way you feel, I won't. And if you can't talk to me in a nicer tone of voice, don't talk at all."

"Ah, shut up!"

"I'm the only one who tells anyone to shut up around here. I'm the only one who's grown! You ain't grown yet!"

"Don't tell me what to do!"

Ma grabbed Sandra's arm, and Sandra pulled away from her. Ma smacked Sandra and Sandra hit her back.

"Who do you think you're hitting?"

"Don't nobody hit me and get away with it!"

Ma has Sandra on the bed, and Sandra is fighting back.

I went into the kitchen just as Silvia dropped the iron, ran into the living room, sat on the couch, and started crying. I tried to calm her down, telling her to stop crying.

Once Silvia is calmed down, I go into the bedroom and finish Sheila's hair. Then I go back into the kitchen and finish Silvia's pants for her, while she combs her hair.

Ma is screaming at Sandra: "Get out and don't come back! I gave her too many chances. Nobody takes advantage of me like that—her time is up!" Grabbing Sandra's key from off of the dresser, she shouts, "Get out, and I mean now!"

I tell Sheila, "If Sandra comes back before me, don't let her in."

Just One Joint
Zach Chassler

I smoked a joint laced with angel dust that morning. Of course I didn't know it. I was just into pot, but I would have never taken the heavy stuff like angel dust had I known it.

After a drag on the joint I instantly felt paralyzed. I just could not move. Here I was in my own house just off St. Mark's Place in my own bed with my roomie Mike just a room away, and I couldn't move a muscle. I tried to call Mike, but my lips couldn't move. I felt as if I would never move again. Just then Mike walked into my room.

"Hey Sid," he said to me, "you should really stop taking drugs, you look awful."

And I was sure I did, for I was suddenly on the ceiling of my room looking down on myself. I lay sprawled across the bed, the joint I was smoking still in my hand. But soon I was back in my body and Mike was shaking me frantically. He was yelling things like "Sid, wake up!" and "Don't die on me now, buddy!!!"

But I was far from dead, paralyzed maybe, but dead? Never. I looked up, and Mike was still shaking me, but the thing shaking me was not Mike but a creature from Hell. This revelation shocked me out of my paralysis, and I began fighting what was once Mike.

"Calm down, Sid!" said the Mike-demon in a soothing tone.

But that couldn't fool me. I continued to throw vicious blows at the Mike-demon's head until I was sure it was dead. But as the Mike-demon dropped to the floor limp and unmoving it transformed back into Mike, the same Mike who had roomed with me in college, the same Mike who had just yesterday saved me from being hit by a car. Oh my God, what had I done?

I took another drag on the joint and ran out of the house. I had to tell the police what I had done.

The street was a vibrant whirlwind of colors, and I could feel the sidewalk pulsating under me. I began walking up to people and asking them to get a police officer, but all that came out of my mouth was a slurring noise. It was as if I had no control over my tongue. I felt foam and bile begin to spill out of my mouth. Then people began looking at me. They became very ominous like shadows just around a corner. They formed a wall around me. Why were they doing this, and how could I escape? I had to get out, so I went charging through the human wall. I started to walk quickly, but the wall of people kept following me. I began to run. Right out into the street I ran. I didn't think of stopping until a cab rounding the corner hit me, and everything went black.

I awoke in the hospital with a doctor standing above me.

"Well, I see we've come to our senses and woken up, haven't we?" the doctor said. "Yeah, I see we have," I said and to my joy realized I could once again speak. I tried to move my hand and couldn't, but to my relief I looked over and found it in a cast.

"You gave your friend a minor concussion, but he's okay. In fact he's waiting to see you. Would you like him to come in?"

I nodded my head.

When Mike came into my room I felt a great sense of joy. We embraced.

"Do you forgive me?" I asked.

"On one condition," he said. "You give up drugs altogether. Deal?"

"Deal." I replied

She's Only Fifteen
Janette Linde

I heard a car coming up our hill, and the headlights cast their lights onto my bedroom wall, making shadows. It stopped in front of our house, and I knew it was Vickie coming home. I was still mad at her, and even though Mom told me I was being stubborn I still thought Vickie could have taken me along with her. She knew how much I wanted to see the movie. After all, haven't I been pestering Mom and Dad to take me to see it? The car door slammed, and I thought of how lately Vickie's been getting extra privileges.

Like today when Julie called up and asked Vickie if she could go to see *Star Struck.* Vickie didn't want to ask Mom because Mom's told us a thousand times if she's told us once that we can't just go somewhere on spur-of-the-moment plans. But Julie kept at it, and Vickie finally asked. And Mom said, "Yes!" I asked Vickie if I could come along and she said that she couldn't just bring me along, it wouldn't be fair to Julie. I got mad so I started to bug Mom about the principle of the matter, "Hey, whatever happened to your no spur-of-the-moment plans campaign?"

"It's not as if Julie is a stranger, they're best friends. And Anne, Vickie *is* older than you."

"But she's only fifteen!!!"

But the case was closed. Dad drove Vickie to Julie's house, and I got stuck home.

Now it was four hours later and I was lying in bed, sadistically letting Vickie bump into all the things she couldn't see since she had left the lights out, thinking I was asleep. She finally got to her desk and switched on her little table lamp (I have one too, but hers is in better shape). She turned and saw me looking at her.

Immediately she began apologizing. "Anne, I really wanted to take you along, but I don't think it would have been right. And anyway it wasn't that good."

I just turned over and put the pillow over my head. I heard her muffled voice, "Aw, come on, Anne, don't be like that."

When I didn't answer she gave up trying and just got ready for bed. About five minutes later she was asking me something else, "Anne, do you mind if I leave the light on for a while?"

I did mind, but I wouldn't give her the satisfaction of knowing, and if I left the pillow over my head I wouldn't be able to see the difference. I heard her sigh, and then I heard a chair scraping. I knew she'd be sitting at her desk, writing in her diary. I didn't have a diary, because, personally, I didn't have the need for one. I confided in Vickie and she confided in me. That's why I was so mad when she got a diary from Mom for her thirteenth birthday. Vickie kept writing in it, and I was worried that she would forget about me.

So I started looking for the keys to the diary (they always give you two), and when I found them I took one and hid it. I figured Vickie would just think she had lost it. But to this day I have never used that key because I found that Vickie still talked to me: about all the guys that honked and whistled at her in the street (and she's only fifteen!), about all the guys she had crushes on, and everything I could possibly want to know. But tonight I was curious, and I didn't want to ask Vickie, so I decided tonight would be the night I peek (but only at tonight's entry!).

It only took her fifteen minutes to finish whatever she was writing. But, tonight, the night I wanted her to fall asleep fast, she seemed to be thinking about something because it took almost an hour for her to go to sleep. When I heard her breathing deeply (she's told me hundreds of times that she doesn't snore) I got out of my bed and went over to my lamp, lifted it up, and got the key. Then I went over to her desk and got the diary out from the second drawer, left-hand side, under the book on knitting. I don't know why she keeps that book, she should throw it out: she tried to knit a simple scarf and she turned it into a total disaster. She's hopeless. I went back to my desk because if I put her light on she would probably wake up. I then sat down on my chair and unlocked the diary. Uneasily I looked over at Vickie. She was still asleep. I convinced myself that she would never know and at the same time my curiosity would be satisfied. Well, here goes.

I opened it up to the last entry and immediately I saw that I should have let it alone:

June 18, 1980
   I keep trying to decide if it's better or worse that the doctor told me the truth. I can't handle it as well as he probably wanted me to, and sometimes I just want to break down and cry. Mom and Dad

haven't told Anne yet, and I wish they would. I almost told her tonight, but I can't do that. She shouldn't have to worry about me, and she'll find out soon enough anyway. She's mad at me now, and you don't know how much it hurts when she won't talk to me. I always think that I don't have much time left. Mom and Dad don't talk about it with me. That's another reason why I want to tell Anne, so I can talk to her. I've always been able to talk to her and now, when I need her most, I can't. I've had to go to the hospital, for tests, twice this week already. I go during school time so Anne won't know. Mom is letting me do a lot of things that I wouldn't have been able to before, and I guess Anne is jealous. I just wish she wouldn't get so mad at me. I love her so much. There's so much I want to say, but I can't so I have to write it. Grandma and Grandpa don't know yet, but I think Mom and Dad are going to tell them this weekend. I'm not sure if I want them to know because they'll pity me, and I don't think I can take that. I'm getting tired now (the doctor said I'll get tired more easily now and not to push myself) so I'll stop now.

In shock I lowered the diary to my lap and turned to look at Vickie. She looked so peaceful and healthy. But she was dying. And she was only fifteen. . . .

Third-Person Fiction

Assuming that you already have story material in mind but are wondering how to proceed, consider if you should tell it "in the third person," that is, narrate events from entirely outside the story, with no "I" involved. If you do, you need to decide which characters' thoughts and viewpoint you'll give. It will make a lot of difference to the story whether you:

- *Enter the minds and give the viewpoints of* **none** *of the characters.*
- *Rotate the point of view among* **many** *characters, letting us glimpse some thoughts and feelings of each.*
- *Alternate between perceptions of* **two** *characters.*
- *Limit point of view to the perceptions of* **one** *character.*

If you do not want your story narrated by one of the characters, then write it in the third person and select which character or characters we are to see events through, if indeed through any. Before deciding, you may want to consider **First-Person Fiction.**

The Conflict
Sarah Wood

Patricia scowled at her mother. Mothers just don't understand. It's almost as if she was never a fifteen-year-old. No sympathy at all! They're always saying how they were young once, too, but it's all just a load of crap. When it comes to the important things, like boys, they turn into staid old fogeys.

"Mo-other, this is a once-in-a-lifetime opportunity!"

Mrs. Dubree stared unyielding at her daughter, wondering why she was always so disagreeable. "Why is it that you don't know what's good or bad for you?" she thought with a tired sigh. She was tired of fighting her daughter about the same things every weekend. Patricia had developed an angry, defiant, challenging stance with one hand on her hip, which she now relaxed into. She remained passively negative.

"Mother," Patricia complained again, standing purposefully in what she hoped would be a more adult position, resting one hand on her hip. "It's not like it's *any* rock group, it's Duran Duran! And it's not like I'd be with *anybody*, I'd be with Steve."

"*That's* the *problem*," Mrs. Dubree drawled, wanting to sound reasonable but inflexible so her daughter would know not to push it.

Patricia frowned. Her mother was *so* unreasonable, but perhaps she could be persuaded to change her mind. "He's a nice boy, Mom." She hoped her light voice would pacify her mother so the bargaining could begin.

Mrs. Dubree seethed with anger but kept it under control. Her own daughter wheedling like a beggar on the street! "Patricia, you are *not* going to the Duran Duran concert, period," she said firmly, keeping her anger under control.

"Why're you yelling at me? You're always so damn superior! I bet *you* went to concerts when *you* were fifteen! Or maybe," she added slyly, "they didn't *have* concerts that long ago." She hoped that cutting remark would come as a slap across the face and show her mother what she thought of her.

Mrs. Dubree suppressed a laugh and tried to keep her mouth from twitching. She remembered having said something similar to *her* mother, too. "It's not unreasonable, Patricia; Duran Duran concerts are dangerous. I wouldn't trust Steven to take care of you." She hoped Patricia would mature a little and understand her concern.

"*You* wouldn't trust a police squad to take care of me!" Patricia considered stamping her feet with anger at her mother's distrustful tone.

"Why's she so frustrated?" Mrs. Dubree thought. "Why can't she understand?"

"Why's she such a prude?" Patricia thought. "Why can't she understand?"

There was a moment of impassivity when mother and daughter stared at each other.

"Patricia, you're not going." It wasn't an unreasonable, unjustified statement. It was fair. Mrs. Dubree turned way to leave, argument over. She would not allow Patricia to go to a dangerous concert where she could be hurt. She could hear it on the radio anyway.

Patricia slouched against the wall, desolated. Life was over, thanks to her dear supporting mother. *Everyone* would be at that concert, except her! It wasn't fair. Her mother had *no* right to tell her no. It was unreasonable. Mothers tend to be.

The two had reached an impasse.

Laid to Rest
Vicki Koerper

The sky was gray as the long procession of cars made its way through the streets. In the back seat of a silver limousine a girl with long brown hair and a sad face sighed and turned to stare out the tinted window, seeing the outside world but not registering any feeling. That was the way she wanted it because it hurt too much to think about. It was easier to ignore it. Sometimes, she could imagine it never happened. But it had.

The flowing stream of cars turned into a small cemetery. Solemn people stood around a coffin covered with bright, happy flowers. Happy? How could anything be happy at a time like this? The Reverend started the obsequies. The drone of his deep voice was becoming fainter and further away as Karen's thoughts turned to days gone by.

"Where's mommy?" asked an excited little girl back from her first day of school.

"She's resting," replied a masculine voice. "She can't be disturbed."

"She's always 'resting,' she can't be that tired!" retorted the little girl logically. "I bet she's just pretending."

With that, a young Karen bounded up the steps to see if her mother was feigning sleep. Exasperated, her father followed and stopped her part way up the flight of stairs.

"Karen, we've talked about this before. Remember?"

She remembered. She just didn't want to. Her father assumed she had forgotten.

"Your mommy is a sick person. She needs lots of rest," her father went on.

"But she's in bed all day," whined Karen. "She just doesn't want to play with me."

"That's not true," sighed her dad. "She can't."

"Why not?"

"She's sick."

"Why? What's wrong?" Karen bombarded her dad with questions.

"Your mom has a heart murmur."

"Does it talk to her?"

"No, silly, it doesn't talk, but it makes her feel yucky." Her dad simplified a serious disorder for Karen.

"Oh." Karen's interest was aroused. "How did she get it?"

"She's always had it, but after you were born it got worse."

Karen pondered this for a moment and then chirped, "Can we go see if she's fake sleeping?"

"Only if you're very, very quiet," her dad whispered.

"OK."

Hand in hand, Karen and her father ascended the steps. Karen poked her head through the doorway of her mom's room cautiously, as if there were something frightening in there. Instead, she saw her mother's thin, pale face resting on a pillow with her eyes shut.

"She's sleeping," Karen whispered loudly.

"No, I'm not." The soft voice startled Karen. "Come on in."

Karen slowly made her way through the plush expanse of blue carpet to the side of her mother's bed. She was frightened that her mother might get sicker if she were there. After all, wasn't she the one who made her sick in the first place?

Karen came back from her reverie when the Reverend's voice stopped. She listened for a moment and slipped into the past again.

It was her sixteenth birthday. Everyone at her party was having fun, except her. How could she when her mother had gone into the hospital for emergency surgery the day before? Karen made her way through crazed dancers and happy people, feeling a hundred years older than her friends, to the quiet kitchen where she could be alone. Her best friend followed her.

"Cheer up," said Tracy. "After all, it's your sweet sixteen."

Karen turned around to face her friend, her face nervous and drawn. "I'm scared. What if she never comes home?"

"She will, don't worry. She's had this operation before. It'll work." Tracy was a compassionate friend, but she wasn't following Karen's train of thought.

"That's what I'm afraid of," Karen choked out. "She had it before, and it didn't work."

"Oh," said Tracy simply.

The two girls looked at each other, reading the other's eyes.

"What if . . . ."

"No. She can't."

Karen came back to the present when she heard the Reverend ending his lengthy prayer. She felt the strange sensation of being watched. She looked up. All eyes were on her. Startled and confused she quickly turned, her vision blurred, and half-stumbled, half-ran through the crowd. Free from its cloistering grasp she ran blindly.

"Karen!" her father's shout barely penetrated the noise of the wind in her ears.

The ground moved, causing Karen to stumble. The grass rushed up to meet her solidly.

"Karen, are you all right?" her dad's breathless voice asked worriedly.

"It's my fault!" she sobbed incoherently.

"What are you talking about?" asked her father confused.

"She died because of me!"

"No."

"Yes, It's my fault she had that heart condition!" hiccupped Karen.

"Karen, you listen to me and you listen hard. Your mother had a heart murmur all her life. The doctor warned that a pregnancy might be too much. She ignored him. She was so happy when she found out we would be having you." Trying to fight tears, her father continued. "She never regretted having you. You were her life. She would hate to hear you blaming yourself for her death. She loved you!"

"Oh, Dad!" Karen cried, "What are we going to do without her?"

"It will be hard, but I know that we will make it."

They slowly made their way towards the grave. Karen picked up a rose from one of the many bouquets on her mother's grave.

"We'll make it," she thought, "somehow."

The Martyrdom of Frank
Randall Peterson

All heads lurched forward as the bus driver threw the bus into a higher gear. The babbling voices of kids mingled together into a high-pitched, indiscernible muddle of sounds. Tangled locks of hair were all that were visible over the tall backs of the seats.

The bus squeaked to a halt in front of a flat-roofed building. Most of the bricks were beginning to crack and chip away. The walls were discolored in vertical stripes. Years of rainfall had left its mark as it trickled off the roof.

Streaming out of the bus, the kids headed to their respective classrooms. The only fifth-graders to ride that bus, Sean and Aaron, were reminiscing about a football game they had played that weekend.

Sean wore perfectly fitting, fashionable clothes. His wardrobe consisted of a variety of name brands selected with impeccable taste, but they were usually rashly donned and colors often clashed. Spots of dry mud were caked on his knees. Aaron's clothes, though not as attractive or popular, were always clean and pressed and complemented each other. His hair, short and blond, was always neatly arranged on his head.

Once inside their room, Aaron and Sean passed Frank's desk. After a quick surveillance they determined that Frank was not in sight. Sean grabbed Frank's math book and dropped it into the garbage can. The whole class watched as Frank returned and began searching frantically for it. Bursts of uncontrollable laughter escaped, and Frank discontinued his search, realizing that he was being mocked.

Frank was the mechanism through which the fifth-graders released their frustrations. He was tall and gangling. Upon a small nose perched glasses with wide plastic frames. The lenses, thick and strong, shrank the area around his eyes and gave his head the appearance of an hourglass. Upon his head rested a divot of red hair.

The day proceeded in a similar manner. When adding fractions became dull, Aaron would lean and mock, "Frankie, how often do you wash your hair?" in a tone as if he were addressing a two-year-old. Muffled giggles were prevalent around him and he sank lower into his seat.

During a particularly long lecture about adverbs, Sean would twist his face into a weird expression. He would take his right arm, stretch it over the crown of his head, and scratch behind his left ear with it. The class, realizing that this was one of Sean's more polished imitations of Frank, exploded into a half-checked snicker. This continued until a stern glance from the teacher brought it all to a halt.

Frank's eyes never left his scuffed cowboy boots. Weeks of torment had subjugated his dignity. His self-esteem was dead.

On the way home from the bus stop, Aaron and Sean practiced their daily ritual of hurling stones at various types of birds. Aaron successfully provoked a mother robin to flee from its nest to the security of a tall willow.

As was customary, Sean went home with Aaron. After extracting some tantalizing morsels of food from the refrigerator, they slumped into some well worn beanbags. Between segments of Heathcliff, Aaron lifted the lid off of his brother's gerbil cage. The smell of fresh cedar wafted into the room. Catching the spry rodent was a difficult task. Only after cedar chips and sunflower seeds were strewn all over did Aaron pin the gerbil's tail to the bottom of the cage.

"Watch this!" exclaimed Aaron. He held the struggling creature upside down and let go, giving him a little spin. The gerbil plummetted down, turning over and over. It reached the beanbag and landed perfectly, feet down. A faint thud was emitted as a small crater formed around the trembling creature. Sean laughed gleefully at the rare spectacle.

The trick was repeated several more times before Sean was convinced that it wasn't just luck. Sean flipped the pet over in his hands to examine its soft white underside. The fragile creature twisted and squirmed to be free of his inverted position and the hot anaconda hands.

The two boys faced each other and placed the gerbil between them. When it darted toward the safety of the bookshelf, they would roll it back into the middle. The undaunted rodent made many more futile attempts. Exhausted, it crouched, tense and trembling. Sean nudged it in the side with his finger. It lashed out.

Sean expelled a cry of pain. He lifted his hand. From it a brown figure dangled. He shook his arm violently, but the limp body wouldn't release its deathgrip. With one rapid movement, he flung the creature off. It glided through the air, collided with the oak paneling, and dropped to the ground. The little creature didn't land on its feet this time, however, but rather on its back.

The drooping body lay motionless, its life gone. Deep red blood boiled out of Sean's fingers, but all eyes remained on the still form. The two boys sat in silent reverence, struck with the gravity of their actions. The gerbil was dead.

The next morning was brisk and cheerful, but Sean and Aaron were silent and solemn as they trudged to the bus stop. The chirping birds perched on a fencepost were left alone today, for the two boys finally realized—life is fragile. They had bought themselves pleasure at the cost of a life.

The clamor on the bus did much to revive the boys' spirits, and they were soon busy rehashing tales of last week's football game. Sean began explaining how Aaron had caught a kick-off and returned it eighty yards to score the winning touchdown.

As the two boys bounded down the school bus stairs, they could see Frank leaning against the slide. His orange, unkempt hair seemed almost aflame as the morning sun streamed through it. A pile of books rested in the glistening, dew-covered grass. Upon this foundation perched a brown paper lunchbag, its contents overflowing.

The two friends glanced at each other, knowing what the other was thinking. A grin spread across their faces as they broke into a trot. When they closed in on him, Frank tensed like an animal.

When Sean reached Frank, Aaron was already far ahead of him. Sean's laces met the lunch, sending it flying toward Aaron. It spun end over end and was almost to Aaron's arms when the brown protective covering was rent to pieces. Sandwiches, cookies, and fruit in cellophane bags were scattered in a cluttered array. Frank collapsed in a sobbing pile, just one more gerbil in Sean's life.

Sean and Aaron gazed at each other, bewildered and disgusted. They were shocked that anyone could be so maudlin and react so strongly to a little game or joke. Obviously, all the fears and emotions of the previous night had long since been forgotten.

Horror Story

Write a story whose main purpose is to scare and horrify. Do this by plunging the characters and the reader into some circumstances and atmosphere that are menacing and bewildering. Then reveal the horror or series of horrors involved in the unanswered questions.

Collect yours and others' stories into a book of mystery and horror.

The Horror
Peter Freedberger

DEDICATION:
This story is dedicated to Howard Phillips Lovecraft (1890-1939) the greatest horror fiction author of the 20th Century.

This story could not have been possible without a little help from old H.P. himself. I used his brainchildren: the Necronomicon, the Deep Ones, and the other creepy crawlies mentioned.

"Ph-nglui mglw'nafh Cthulu R'lyeh wgah'nagl fhtagn"
"In his house at R'lyeh dead Cthulu waits dreaming"

The Call of Cthulu, by H.P. Lovecraft (1926)

October 22, 1871

There was no way I could have foretold things would happen so rapidly as they did. My only warning came in dreams, which I tried not to recall. Oh, I wish I had never laid eyes upon the accursed house. But that would be no comfort, for they'll kill us all anyway.

On the chilly dark morn of October 7th, I moved into Fireside Manor with Calvin McLeod, my personal secretary and long-time friend. We had been to the Manor only once before, and it had looked much more welcoming in the August sun. I shrugged off my vague uneasiness and proceeded up the front steps with Calvin. He fumbled with the keys for a moment and then the door was open. I hoped our furniture had been delivered without damage.

A bit later, after we had arranged our things in their proper order, we prepared a late luncheon of fresh salmon and a loaf of hard bread. Cal ate heartily but I was on edge, so I put my portion on the block of ice in the kitchen, so it would keep.

We explored the main floor of the house, as well as the top floor. However, try as we might, we found no trace of the door to the basement. This didn't deter Calvin, whose love for mystery made him suggest a hidden door. I humored him. In these houses, anything was possible, after all, so we searched for a portal that would lead to the lower portion of the house. Luck apparently was with us, because we found a downward spiraling staircase behind the mahogany bookcase in the living-room, and we agreed to venture down come the morrow.

I threw some logs into the giant brick hearth and started a blazing fire. But strangely enough, the warmth was not comforting. It was more repressing, and I felt a tingling and, dare I say, a FEAR? Something in the flames...an undefined shape. Dancing, writhing, mocking. I rushed forth from my chair and doused the flames with a bucket of ashes. Calvin looked at me from his easy chair, his expression puzzled.

"What the devil, John? Why did you—?"

I held up my hand to silence him. "Calvin, I am in a state of unrest. Call me a fool if you like, but the fire ... the fire...."

My friend said nothing. I felt a bit ashamed, being frightened like a schoolboy.

We trekked upstairs to retire for the night.

Calvin went to his room, and I to mine. I put on a sleeping gown and crawled into bed. I am not exactly sure how long I slept, but I dreamt a particularly terrifying dream.

In this vision of sleep, Calvin and I were floating down a river in a small dinghy. I held a candle aloft. The river, I think, was underground, so save for the candle, we had no other light. I looked over the side of the boat and saw the water had turned a dark crimson. Blood, I realized calmly. I turned to Calvin to remark upon this, only it wasn't Cal any more. In his place was a hideous reptilian fish creature wrapped in a seaweed shawl. It was looking right into my eyes and it held my gaze. As I peered at the creature's ancient eyes, I noticed the monster smelled like decay. Of *what* decay I cannot even begin to describe. We continued staring at each other, and a name became clear to me. This thing was a Deep One .... Suddenly we were no longer in the boat but whirling round and round, in a swirl of blood, and the thing clutched at my feet. It croaked, "Jowakup, Jowakup, Jowakup!"

"John, wake up!"

I opened my eyes. Calvin stood over me, concern easy to see in his face.

"John," he asked, "What's wrong? You were screaming loud enough to wake the dead!"

I hoped not.

I told Cal my dream, and he nodded. "I can understand now what you were screaming about." I asked what I had cried out. He looked at me. "Deep Ones. Where is poor Calvin? My God, the blood!" I shuddered. Needless to say, I did not sleep again that night.

After breakfast downstairs in the kitchen, Cal was very eager to go down the hidden stairs, so we descended slowly. I was wary. The cellar was dark, even with the candles we carried. We moved our candles forward. The light revealed nothing but six wooden crates of enormous proportions. Calvin and I inspected them closely and they were found to contain rotting and mouldy books, most dealing with arcane magic and the occult. Must've belonged to the previous owners, but we both were a bit shaken. One book caught my scrupulous eye. It was big and bound in cracked leather. The title? THE NECRONOMICON. It was written in ancient times by a mad Arab named Abdul Alhazred. As a professor of Arabic studies I knew what it was at once. *This* rare copy was in English. I knew what it told of: fantastic and terrible monsters from beyond space who lived on earth underground and under the sea. Cthulu was an example. Supposedly he was an Elder God who slumbered deep under the Pacific in a sunken city called R'lyeh, awaiting the time when the stars were right. Then he would ravage over the world.

Of course, I believed none of that. It *was* written by a lunatic, to be sure. I told Cal of the book's history. He smiled along with me as I reached for it.

Can I explain how that hellish book felt to the touch? Dry, yet membranous and slippery. And ... it seemed to pulse in my hand! The terror of the previous night's dream rushed back, and I hurled the volume back into the crate with a cry. Calvin probably thought me a madman at that moment, but he said not a word, and he remained my loyal friend as long as he lived.

During the next few days, we did not again enter the basement. Cal's sleep was untroubled, while my horrific visions increased their graphic gore. Deep Ones killed me every time my head touched the pillow. There was something else, too. A huge, evil creature, vaguely anthropoid in form, but with a mass of octopoid legs protruding from its face. It had wings resembling those of a bat. And I knew, *knew!* that this was Cthulu.

We finally went back down to the cellar to throw away all those books. I felt pure *terror* at the thought of going down there again. Calvin prodded me along good-naturedly. "Confront your fears, John, whatever they may be." Then he gasped. I followed his eyes down to the floor. I saw the trap door for the first time.

We climbed down the ladder and waved our candles, our eyes straining.

I gagged. It was here. A presence. A stench. I knew at once that Deep Ones were not things of mere mightmares, but horribly and hideously *real.* And when I heard the pulpy wet cracking sounds from behind me, where Calvin had been, I knew a Deep One had crushed my friend Calvin McLeod to a warm jelly, not giving him time to scream and realize the full horror of his situation.

I turned and saw the grinning creature shove Calvin's heart into its bloody jaws and bite down, spraying me with Cal's life.

I think that was when I went mad.

I burst past the fiend, flew up the ladder, and ran from the basement and the house forever.

But as I fled, shrieking, I heard the terrible thing croak in a disembodied voice: Ph-nglui mglw'nafh Cthulu R'lyeh wgah'nagl fhtagn. Yog-Sothoth. Cthulu. Shub Niggurath. Ai'y-ee'h ogthrod Gn'Gahn'gb'le. The stars are in alignment!

And now I sit in my little rented flat, waiting for something to scratch on the door, chanting, CTHULU! I know the end of human life has finally come.

Love Always
Isabella Stern

She walked into work quite happy because today was a day of love, Valentine's Day.

She had no one special of her own, but she liked studying others as they received their valentines.

When she got to her desk, which she decorated all in red for this occasion, there was a little white envelope on the corner of her desk. She couldn't wait to open it. "Who could it be?" kept going throught her mind. When she opened it, it read

Dear Nancy,
    I can't live much longer without seeing you face to face. As you read this I will be watching you, so don't break my heart and throw it away.

Love always,
X

She took it and ripped it to shreds. Of course she knew it was a joke, but it made her so angry. She was really excited. She thought for a moment that someone might care about her.

"It's so annoying when someone does that," she kept complaining to everyone.

She decided to forget about it, but when she returned from lunch, there was now a large box wrapped in silver paper with red hearts in the same place as the card had been. She knew it was only a stupid game that someone was playing, but her curiosity got the best of her. She had to open it.

Slowly she undid the paper, making sure she didn't rip any of it. She opened the lid, reminding herself over and over that it wasn't real. When she opened it, she let out a loud scream, making everyone run to see what had happened. Inside was a human heart that was no longer beating. Scattered around it was shredded paper. The note said:

To Nancy My Love,
    Ripping that letter was like tearing my heart out and I want you to have a memory of both.

Love always,
X

Murder Mystery

Murder mysteries are based on detection by deduction—on figuring out from clues "who done it." So tell your murder story by gradually revealing facts. Give yourself some room for this; it's hard to plant or disclose clues successfully in a very brief story. Try a version out on friends or partners and see how satisfied they are with the clues and the final unravelling.

To Alfred Hitchcock.
May he rest in peace.

One man turned a losing baseball team into a first-place team. The local
sports reporter loved it (for a change) until the night they found that they
had ...

The Dead Center Fielder
David Douek

I cover our city's major league baseball team, the Mustangs. As long as
anyone can remember they have been in what we reporters call "the lower
division" of the standings. The Mustangs were and will probably always be a
fourth-rate team.

My name is Willie Nelson, and I'm a sports writer for the *Tribune*. What I
want to be is a sports columnist. The difference between the two is that a
sports writer is confined to a particular team whose sport is in season; a sports
columnist, on the other hand, is free to write about any sports topic he
chooses.

If a columnist is good, other papers will buy his articles. If I became a
columnist I'd have money, fame, and another step up the ladder of success. As
a sports writer I sit here giving away free tickets and betting tips. But as a
columnist I could pick my own story. For instance: Max Brenstein—how he
went from rags to riches and owner of the Mustangs.

Max was a poor research chemist. He joined with two other chemists and
formed sort of a corporation. They developed this plastic that's supposed to be
perfect for artificial organs. They should have become rich, but only Max did.
The patent was taken out in Max's name. He became a millionaire, and the
partners became Max's employees.

Max runs the Mustangs the way he does his plastics company. He figures
that with all the money baseball players make in the way of commercials and
other ads, a team's salaries just have to be minimally competitive to keep up
attendance. Max's perfect team would be a bunch of underpaid players with a
couple of underpaid stars that would work hard at staying in last place. He
would get the most money that way. I think he fears a championship; it would
mean raises for the players. Of course he has to humor the fans by telling them
that the team is trying to improve and is going to get better. Some people
believed it, but to the majority's astonishment it came true.

Melvin McClay was the difference. He was the best center fielder I'd ever
seen. How the Mustangs got him I'll never know.

When I first saw him he looked like the perfect athlete—skinny and tall
with reflexes like Ali's. He was nice too. He never refused an autograph or an

interview or questions about his diabetes. He did a lot of commercials for the Diabetes Research Foundation and raised quite a bit of money. He was the type that could do it.

Brenstein kept him at a pretty low salary, considering his value. For three years he had a low salary. Then an agent offered him everything, and Max got hot. He kept Mel out for half a season and attendance dropped 40 percent, and so did the Mustangs. Max gave in and signed him to a $9 million contract for six years. The fans were happy he got it. Most fans usually get jealous, but not the Mustang fans.

He earned it. In half a season he batted .347 and hit 26 homeruns. Three were grand slams. The following season the team shaped up considerably. The bumbling idiots Max called players were becoming players, and Mel led the way.

It was the last game before the All-Star break. We trailed first place by only half a game. We were at home, the stadium was full, and Jake Johnson was pitching for us. The game was against Boston, who were on a streak. The score was 1-0 Boston in the bottom of the 8th. I went back to the empty hallway to get some water before the ninth. From the owner's private booth, which was next to the pressbox, came Max Brenstein, wearing a hat and pulling up gloves.

"Giving up already?" I teased him. "They've still got an inning, you know. Even the fans are staying to see it."

He said something rude and passed by. I let it go. It was typical of him.

It was bottom of the ninth. The shortstop was thrown out, and our catcher got a double and Melvin McClay stepped up to bat. The crowd stood up and roared. Boston took out their pitcher and put in a man named Sipen, a fast-ball thrower clocked at 98.6. He was the best relief pitcher in both leagues.

McClay hit the first pitch into the center field stands. We won 2-1. The Mustangs were in first place.

We reporters went down to the locker room. We surrounded McClay, asking him the usual questions. He answered them all patiently and thoroughly. Then he said, "Pardon me, fellas," and he reached into the locker and pulled out his insulin kit. The reporters were used to the injection and looked at it with less interest than they would a wall. Then moments later Mel became quite ill. An ambulance was called and he was dead on arrival. I won't even go into how the fans felt. Doctors told us it was insulin shock. The new center fielder was Ron Meyer.

City police searched Mel's locker. The insulin kit was gone. Jerry, the locker room attendant for 15 years, had been arrested under suspicion of murder but freed after witnesses stated that he was elsewhere. He passed the lie detector and was sent home.

The police next got to Luis Reed, the Mustang's trainer, who kept a supply of insulin in his office refrigerator. He accounted for his activities with witnesses, passed a lie detector test, and was sent home.

The coroner's report said there was cyanide in the body; Mel had been murdered.

Four days later the funeral was held.

Publishers all over the place were trying to buy rights to "The Melvin McClay Story."

The police were baffled, but they promised everything. They didn't do much because they had no clues.

Ten days after the murder Max agreed to meet with me about the team's future, but I had other questions to ask.

He began by telling me something about financial loss.

"I checked with your ticket manager," I contradicted him. "Your sales are up 10% since the murder. The team's still in first place, and you're racking up on Mel's memory. So cut the crap, okay?"

"Well, remember, my payroll. Athletes cost—"

"Cut it, Max. You have the lowest paid team in the league. You're paying your catcher half of what he's worth. Meyer is getting minimum wage, and with McClay dead you've eliminated 1.5 million a year. You're cleaning up."

"You can get the hell out of here. You're not going to cover my team with that attitude. Why, I play golf with the publisher of the *Tribune* and I'll have him—."

"No, you won't, because I know who killed McClay."

He sat there with an innocent look and said, "Good, let me be the first to thank you and. . . ."

"I thought we weren't going to play games." He stared at nothing silently with a guilty look on his face.

"That's better," I said. "Now let's consider a few things. First, you were mad at him for holding out for the salary he deserved."

"So we had our differences."

"Well, his death saves you a few million."

"So I benefited," he said. "That doesn't make me a murderer."

"Mel gave himself an insulin shot before and after each game. He didn't feel ill during his game, and he died of cyanide poisoning. So we assume it was put there during the game."

"So?" said Max.

"In the last inning the locker room staff was watching the Mustangs bat. That would give the killer time to do the deed."

"How does that involve me?" he asked angrily.

"Well, you had Meyer promoted the next morning. You could have discussed it with the scouts and manager like most teams. And because of the All-Star break you had time. Makes a person think you planned it."

"Bull!"

"True, those are just embarrassing incidents and are quite harmless. But, when tied in with a few facts, the case becomes interesting."

He said nothing.

"For instance. It seems your plastics use a substance that's a product of hydrogen cyanide. Your lab uses it in bulk. Your knowledge of a lab and access to the cyanide could make you a good poisoner. Finally we come to the interesting part. During the last inning of Mel's last game, when I assumed the poison was added, you weren't in your seat. And I alone saw you heading down the back stairs. You were wearing gloves. To hide finger prints maybe?''

An innocent man would have thrown me out, or something like that. But not Max. He closed his eyes in defeat and then quietly asked, ''Why haven't you told the police? Is this blackmail? What do you want—money?''

I was sick of being a reporter. I wanted to be a columnist. I wanted national recognition.

''You,'' I said, ''can give me an inside source. You can give me details about secret trades and other league talks. One step in front of everyone else, that's what I want.''

''That's all?'' he asked as if I were stupid.

''That's all,'' I said. ''Let's begin with that secret owner's meeting. . . .''

My career took off, thanks to Brenstein. The Mustangs were back in fourth place, but that didn't hurt me. Brenstein also owned our city's basketball team, and he helped me the same way he did with the Mustangs.

Six weeks after Mel's death, my editor gave me a column. A month later I was in forty newspapers. I was writing scoop after scoop.

One day I came home and found my dog dead next to his food dish. I bought a new one, and a few days later he was dead by his food. It smelled of wild cherries. I hear cyanide smells like wild cherries.

I asked Brenstein about it. He said with a smile, ''Anything a body eats could turn out to be, heh, spoiled.''

I started to answer, but he cut me off. ''Don't think about going to the police. You're an accomplice to the McClay murder. I'd have the best lawyer money could buy. Our score, so to speak, is settled.''

I can't eat much nowadays. I lost 20 pounds and I smell wild cherries everywhere. I got the column, and my by-line is known. It's in papers coast to coast. But will it be in the obituary tomorrow?

Spoof

Do a comic imitation—a spoof—of some familiar writer or type of writing. Consider fairy tales, soap and space operas, animal or sports stories, romances, and so on. What are the traits of your target that your readers will recognize when you imitate them? Make fun of them by overdoing them, by going farther in the direction they're already heading.

Make collections of such parodies or mix them into collections of the type they spoof.

Spam Sade, Private Investigator
The Cookie Crumbled
Christie Opal Eileen McNeill

It was a typical foggy evening in downtown Toledo. It was Sunday. I sat alone in my office. It was dark. I like the dark. I gazed at the reflection of the blinking neon sign of the Waldorf Towers Drive-In Motel, dimmed by the mist, a mist that seemed painted there, solidified, like peanut butter. That's what it was like. Mom's peanut butter cookies, packed in a tin for me every weekend when I visited her at the Uptown Toledo Correctional Institute. I glanced around the room, thinking about all the crummy years and all the crummy cases that cluttered my file cabinets. From outside the door, the crummy gilt letters sneered back at me.

SPAM SADE
PRIVATE INVESTIGATOR

I tipped back my stained Fedora and reached for the ash tray I never use. Mom said cigarettes were bad for me. I liked the image, though. Sometimes I would watch myself in the mirror, cigarette dangling from a curled lip, practicing a nonchalant snarl. It looked good. Spam Sade, Private Investigator. Then my eyes would smart, my tongue would burn, and I needed a band-aid. I gulped my glass of milk and enjoyed. "Why aren't I married and working only part-time like every one else?" I asked myself. I know the answer. For my line of work it had to be Solo Spam, in a can by himself. Then she walked into my life.

I saw her through the shadows. She was the opposite of every woman I had ever known. She wore a tight hat and a large dress. Her hair was knee length and wispy, all two of them. "Spam Sade, Private Investigator?" she whispered softly, huskily, like a dust storm on the 3rd Avenue El. I didn't hear her, I was so mesmerized by the sunshine she sent into the room. Then I realized she carried a flashlight because the bulb in the hall had burned out seven years before. When I opened the door I saw her true beauty. The hat and dress were fluorescent yellow, and she wore fluorescent pink gloves and shoes. She had light skin, pink cheeks and blue lips. "Punk?" I asked.

"No," she replied, "I feel fine." I asked her to take a chair anyway. Gratefully, she took a chair, and folded it away in her tote bag. She had a sense of humor. I liked that.

"So, what can I do for you?" I asked.

"Well, Mr. Sade . . .". and pulled out a handkerchief and blew her nose. It echoed for a while, like a trumpet blown under water. I reached for the red cookie tin. "Here, have a cookie, cookie," I said. I had never seen anyone eat like that, except in the zoo. Mom would be pleased.

"I'm looking for a friend, my friend, Kathy Klutz." She raised her handkerchief, now soaking wet. I handed her mine, she blew her nose in it and handed it back to me. "So what about Ms. Klutz?"

"She was my best friend, I had lunch with her on Thursday—a health salad, two granola bars and a box of Ayds, and I haven't heard from her since."

"Have you tried to call?" "No." "Have you tried her apartment?" "No." "Then how do you know she is missing?" "I just have a feeling."

"I understand. Just one of those things. But let's get it straight from the beginning, cookie. I don't come cheap. $2.50 a day, plus bus fare." Without a blink she gave me a check and a discount coupon at McDonald's. I dialed her friend's number. No answer. "You're right so far," I said. "No answer." I took her friend's address and told her to go home. This was a man's job.

"Oh, Mr. Sade, it's so reassuring to know this is a man's job," she said. I watched her leave through the window and hail a cab.

Time was of the essence, so I roller-skated to the apartment. The door was open. I found Ms. Klutz, all right. She was in the bathtub, cold, submerged three inches beneath the water, a rope around her neck, clutching a matchbook from Jack's Club. I took a wild guess. She was dead.

It was a familiar story, one from the books. It's not unusual for someone to drown in their bathtub with a rope around their neck, clutching a matchbook from Jack's Club. But it looked too much like an accident, murderers always try to make a murder look like an accident, but then again it looked too much like a murder that looked like an accident. It had to be an accident that looked too much like a murder that looked too much like and accident. Therefore it had to be an accident. No one can fool Spam Sade, Private Investigator.

I walked out, leaving Ms. Klutz in a clutch. I had to think. My bus pass had expired, so I strolled down the street. The light ahead of me welcomed, Jack's Club.

Jack and I went back a long way, and I needed a friend. Tinker, tailor, soldier, sailor, rich man, poor man, beggarman, thief, Jack had been there. I flipped my calling card, a peanut buttter cookie, across the bar. "Hi, Spam, the usual?" Instantly my chocolate shake was in front of me. The juke box moaned a bluesy tune, and I thought of her. How was I going to tell her that her best friend had drowned in a bathtub, wearing nothing but a rope around her neck? It would kill her. She was so child-like, innocent. She would have a nervous breakdown. They must have been so close for her to sense that something was wrong in so short a time, only days after they had shared a health salad, two granola bars and a box of Ayds.

I went back to the office and stared at the telephone. I would be straight with her. "Ms. Klutz, your friend was a real klutz, she's dead." "She can't meet you tomorrow, she's way over her head, she has a sore throat . . . ." As I placed my hand on the phone, it rang. "Spam Sade, Private Investigator." Instinctively I knew what the voice was going to say. "Spam Sade, Private Investigator? This is Jack." The voice was not familiar. "Jack who?" "Jack, of Jack's Club, stupid." "What can I do for you, Mr. Club?" "I'm looking for a girl. She owes me five thou. I've got her picture." "Where do we meet?" I asked. "Jack's Club, stupid. Three o'clock tomorrow." "Who do I ask for?" I asked. He hung up. Strange sort of guy, that Jack.

Without hanging up, I dialed her number. "Hello Mr. Sade," she said. "This is Spam Sade, Private Investigator. What are you doing at this number?"

"I live here, stupid, that's why you have the number." I hadn't counted on that. She was more clever than I thought. Carefully I arranged a meeting for the following afternoon, at the fountain near the downtown Toledo Ironworks.

I didn't sleep that night, despite warm milk and Mom's cookies. I thought about Jack's phone call; I would have to see that picture. I thought about her, and our meeting tomorrow, and how inconspicuous I would be, in my Ralph Lauren tennis shorts and racquet. Maybe a scuba diving suit, hiding in the fountain. No, too fishy. Maybe I'd dress like a woman. No, I'd look like my mother. I crumbled my cookie in my hand and went to sleep.

As I stepped off my bike I saw her looking at me, strangely. "A raincoat?" she asked, startled. "It's Bill Blass," I said, "I wanted to look inconspicuous." "In July, in a heat wave?" "It's part of my job." "Aren't you hot?" "No, I have nothing on underneath. Can we walk?" As we strolled I tried to control my nerves and the bicycle. "Your friend. I found her, in her apartment. She's way over her head in things, and has a sore throat." Her eyes riveted mine. "You found her dead under three inches of water in her bathtub, with a rope around her neck, clutching a matchbook from Jack's club," she said. "How did you know?" "I can take a hint. Do you think it was murder?" "No, it looked too much like a murder disguised as an accient to be a murder, so it had to be an accident." I tried to be kind and promised to meet her later. She kissed me on the lips. Unsanitary, Mom always said, I might go blind, and I still had to see Jack's picture.

I walked into Jack's Club, flipped my cookie on the bar, and played a bluesy tune on the juke box. Jack approached. I knew it was Jack, because I didn't recognize him. He shoved a picture in front of me. It was her. I didn't say anything, I was choking on my chocolate shake. I needed my wheels, I needed to get out of there, fast.

Back in the office I hung up my skateboard. She was waiting for me. She had brought lunch, but I preferred Mom's cookies. As least they were predictable. I confronted her with the picture Jack had given me. "Please understand," she pleaded. "I was young, innocent, only 54 years old. He promised me a future. He sold me land in Florida that wasn't any good. He sold me orthopedic shoes on time, and I couldn't pay him back. He kept urging me to dance, but I couldn't, because the shoes wore out. Kathy Klutz was my step-sister. I killed her to get the money to pay Jack back. I just had to keep dancing, tap dancing, in my orthopedic shoes."

Suddenly, Jack burst in, brandishing a loaded zucchini. In a flash, it came to me. Jack's Club ... the club of Jack ... a loaded zucchini. Quickly I exploded in a rash of activity ... hives, poison ivy, chicken pox. All my reflexes came to the fore, as Jack crumbled under the weight of the skateboard, Bill Blass raincoat, Ralph Lauren tennis attire, three quarts of milk, and Mom's peanut butter cookies. The police would later determine that Jack had died of natural causes.

She turned to me in relief, for solace. But I had known her type before. Just another dame, misled, on her way to the slammer. She tried to kiss me goodbye. Mom said it was unsanitary, so I brushed her aside.

It was dark again, on a foggy Sunday evening in downtown Toledo. I was alone in my office. I gazed at the reflection of the blinking neon sign of the Waldorf Towers Drive-In Motel, dimmed by the mist, a mist that seemed painted there, solidified, like peanut butter. That's what it was like. Mom's peanut butter cookies.

Fantasy

Make up a story that takes place in the real world but that also takes off from it into some events and situations that don't normally happen. In other words, mix fantasy with reality. You can use fantastic elements to bring out some truths about everyday life.

A Dream of Darkness: Help Me
Wynne Bickhaus

Prophecy Holder

The doorbell rang. It maliciously echoed through the shallow house. I went to answer it. When I opened the door, I found a plain box. In it were some eyeglasses, just about as ordinary as the wrapping they came in.

There was a card in the box. "From me." Who's "me"?

Full of curiosity, I put on the glasses. Out of nowhere, I saw a helpless, threatened girl. She was tightly cuddled in a corner.

What was happening?

On her face was a wide-eyed expression. She looked so familiar. I wanted to reach out and help her. Quivering, rosy lips made me realize the girl was I.

A shiver went down my spine. I could feel the vibrations as a cold, musty sweat broke out all over. Breathing heavily, I whispered, "Help me!"

I slowly took off the glasses, placed them carefully in their box, and gently closed the door.

Shocked, I ran upstairs, each step remotely away. Hoping the visions would be gone, I quickly paced to my room. There, on my pillow, lay the prophecy holder. A sudden darkness closed in. Effigies hung on the wall.

Once more I couldn't resist curiosity. Drawing toward the glasses, my hands were unstoppable. Shaking, I placed the frames in front of my eyes. The picture came. I trembled. Something . . . I could not pick out the word . . . held me.

I was older. The malice had not prevailed. Was serenity there? Where was I? Who was I with? Something bad was there with me. The word I could not think of before came to me. The something was evil. It trapped me, caught me, engulfed me.

NO!

The glasses fell off and broke.

The word "relief" became a new word to me. It was just my imagination! I know it was. Picking up the treacherous glasses, I threw them into my Superman wastebasket.

"Anyone home?" The sound of my sister's voice was soothing.

"I'm up here, Trace." I turned away from the wastebasket.

Her healthy face appeared in the doorway.

As I caught a glimpse of her, I turned away to wipe from my face the tears I had unknowingly shed.

"Hi, kid," she said. There was a pause and then, "What have you been up to?"

I turned back to face her but said nothing.

"Al, what's wrong? You look pale."

"I'm fine," I managed to say. "Just fine."

Delusion or Illusions

It was close to midnight and I still lay totally awake in my bed. At least I thought I was. My heavy eyelids were half-way closed. I could easily have fallen asleep; yet, I was afraid to. I was frightened of my imagination. Suddenly, too heavy to stay open, my ponderous eye-covers dropped.

Help me!

What?

Help me!

Who are you?

It's me. Oh, no! Help me!

Who's me?

Please hurry! He's coming.

The girl who I thought was I had her back against a closed door. Her shaggy auburn hair tangled and twisted about her thin, bruised face.

"Let me in!" bellowed a rugged man's voice.

The frightened girl shrieked and, suddenly, the door burst open. Slouched in the doorway, the enormous man closed his hands into fists. The girl was nowhere in sight.

A flannel shirt strained over his muscles, and his strong jawbone seemed to speak for itself. He walked slowly forward. The girl was now in sight. Time and space seemed to pass between. The walls seemed to grow darker and farther away as he gripped her throat.

"Run!" I screamed. "Get out of there!"

The picture vanished, and a loud buzzing rang throughout my entire head. It flowed in and out of my ears, mouth and eyes.

"Shut it off, Allison!" screamed a choked-up voice.

I automatically reached over and shut off the annoying alarm. It was 6:00 a.m. Such a rude awakening this early in the morning.

Wiping the sweat from my cheeks I swung my legs over the edge of the bed. My feet felt the harsh, rough floor. Hot. I was so hot. A burning desire told me to take an ice bath.

Something turned inside my stomach. It gripped, pulled and twisted away. Running to the bathroom, I made it to the toilet just in time.

Over my moans and vulgar noises I heard my mom say, "Oh, honey, you're sick."

For the next three days I stayed home from school, sick. Sick to my stomach. Once in a while I tried to eat some of Mom's "home-made" broccoli soup, but I never seemed to be able to keep it down. I bored myself by watching exaggerated "soaps" and reading Superman comic strips. Most girls don't take Superman to be a hero, but I'm not like most girls.

Take Pia, for instance. She loves Superman more than I do. On the other hand, there's Buffy, who loves boys. Can you imagine how she got the name "Buffy"? You don't want to know.

"Feeling better, babe?" It was Mom. I think she was being sarcastic. I've never looked so bad in my entire life. Simply exhausted.

Struggling to get it out, I said, "I feel terrible. Just terrible!"

"Want to try some Jello?" She sounded concerned. "It's your favorite, lemon with kiwi."

She scooped up a spoonful of Jello and maneuvered the wiggly lemon with kiwi Jello past my wrinkled lips. Down the hatch it slid, into my turned-over stomach.

"Mom!" I shrieked. "The pan!"

I inspired her quickness by gagging. It was the most ill-flavored sensation I have ever felt. I loathed the sickening, bitter taste. Urging the rest to flow through my coated lips sapped the last of my strength. Unable to hold out any longer, I fell back onto my fuzzy pillow into a deep, profound sleep.

It had a dreary, dull grayness to the whole surrounding environment. The house looked like a neglected pile, tortured by the evil coldness. Shutters hanging at crazy angles revealed chipping paint where the discolored shutters had banged against the house, calling for help. It had a definite character to it. Pity fell upon me. Precariously, the house seemed to sway, showing all its grief and unbearable troubles. The parasitic world had cheated it in the darkness. Once flourishing in color, the victimized house was now put to shame.

There I stood in front of this house, knowing but doing nothing for the suffering girl inside. I saw her dim shadow running from window to window.

The battered stairs leading inside the house drew my attention to save her. Turning away, I ran from the house into the ever-so-bright sunset.

It's Me Again

Refreshingly awakened by the touch of a chilled, wet cloth, I felt tremendously better. Sanity told me to stay home from school one more day, but Mom thought I should give it a try.

"Give it up, Al." Tracy was so comforting. "Go to school. You can't fake much longer." She laughed and ran out the door before I threw my pillow. Kidding, of course.

I walked, dragging my behind, to the bathroom. The lights seemed to poison my eyes. Yellowness tinted my teeth, telling me it was time to brush them. Time seemed to pass by quickly as I got ready for six hours of boredom, otherwise known as school.

"Are you sure you're capable of handling school today, babe?" said Mom, practically shoving me out the doorway with a sack lunch between my teeth and books filling my arms.

"Yes, Mother," I mumbled. But the door was already closed. A sudden awareness of my being alone made me shudder. For the past three days I had been asleep or had had my comforting mother by my side. I suddenly felt trapped in a dark, black hole.

School was the same as usual, and, as usual, went by somewhat fast. Even though I banged my finger in my locker, it wasn't such a bad day.

"Ouch!" I shrieked, kicking my locker, hoping it would smash to pieces. Sticking my finger in my mouth, I turned to the drinking fountain to run cold water on it.

There he stood. Jamie. I don't know why I never mentioned him. He is really special. When I see him, my knees turn to jello and my blue eyes light up on fire. Blazing with heat, finger in mouth, all I could do was stare until I burned away to nothing but smoldering ashes. I stood wide-eyed, hoping he would walk over to me.

"Hi, Allison," said the tall, brown-eyed, gorgeous-looking figure walking swiftly toward me. "Walk you home?"

All the way home, I could not help but watch out of the corner of my eye the fantastic-looking creature who walked beside me. We didn't talk much. He was never one for conversation. I felt like expressing my deepest emotions to him, but as far as I knew, we were no more than friends. Just friends.

Depression fell upon me as my house came into view. Since today was Friday, I wouldn't see Jamie until Monday. I'd better speak up.

"How about a movie Saturday?" or "Let's do something this weekend," I thought. It all sounded so nice. What a fairytale story. I opened my mouth to speak, but the words stuck to the roof of my mouth like peanut butter. We were getting close to my house. For such a house so dear to me, I loathed the sight of it.

"Well, I guess this is it," he said. I was so spaced, gazing into his deep, brown eyes, I didn't notice that he took my hand.

Clearing my throat, I said, "Want to come in for a while?"

He followed me into the house.

"Come on in, Jamie," I said. "Sit down and make—."

I was interrupted by the ringing of the phone.

Running to the phone, I was followed by Jamie, who seemed to be curious about who was calling. I let the phone ring once more before smiling my pearls in Jamie's direction and bringing the receiver to my ear.

"Hello?"

"Hello!" said a desperate voice.

"Who's calling, please."

"It's me again."

Right away, I knew exactly who it was. I recognized her desperate call for help. For a moment, the girl was silent.

"It's me again," she said, and then pleaded, "I need your help."

I staggered. It wasn't any dream. It was real. Whimpering, the girl asked for help, again. It all came together. The girl had been beaten in the house of my nightmare, but she was just as alive and real as I. Now I knew I had to help.

Full of confidence, I answered her plea.

"I'm here. I'll help you."

There was no response but a faint dial tone. What happened? Had the enormous man gotten to her? I felt so useless. I really couldn't help. Finally realizing she would not answer, I laid down the receiver.

My Favorite Place

The next day Jamie came over to see me.

"Let's go for a walk," he said. "I want to show you my favorite place."

We walked together in silence, hand in hand. Precariously we walked on the tips of cliffs and kicked parched soil. Now, I had no qualms about our relationship. Together, we felt weightless and as one. Laughing and talking in the silence we walked to his favorite place.

"Here it is."

Instead of a small, dainty space, it ws a huge expanse of green land. It ran for miles and seemed to express loneliness. Knee-high grass came in swelling patches. It seemed to be distant and remote from the rest of the world. Jamie and I were the center, the heart. Becoming part of the beauty made my heart beat faster and faster. This, now, was my favorite place, too.

"You like it, huh?" he said. I nodded, but said nothing. Feeling invigorated, I took off and ran as fast as I could. The wind whipped my face and the grass grabbed and pulled. But nothing could stop me. Something propelled me, and Jamie behind me.

Suddenly, I saw it. The grayness took away the feeling of life and excitement. The evil grasped me. The oppressive house drew my undivided attention. The girl. She was there. I could feel her pain more than ever.

"Help me!" she called.

"Al!" called Jamie, "Wait up for me."

His words ran together. Everything was a blur, except for the house that stuck out like a sore thumb. It seemed to put me in a trance, full of restlessness. This was it. One chance.

Before I knew it I was in the house. I suddenly felt that wickedness that had gone on inside. There was a scream.

In front of me were the flimsy, mahogany stairs. I could almost see them sway, becoming more brittle by the minute.

I felt a warm, strong sensation on my shoulder. It was a hand. All over now. The unmerciful beast that had stalked these halls had killed the girl. It was my turn, now. I was the only witness. Just finishing the job. I suddenly felt defenseless and stupid. How could I have let him get me so easily? Crazy images went through my head. My mom was playing with a little girl. It was me. I'll miss you, Mom! My favorite place, I would never see it again. All because of this villain who was mentally ill. Goodbye world.

"Allison, are you OK?" It was Jamie's voice. Strength poured into me. I swung around and gave him the biggest kiss.

"I thought you were the man!" I cried.

"What man?" said Jamie, confused.

"The man that...."

Jamie's eyes turned a blood-shot red. I stared in disbelief. I had never seen him so shattered. He looked as though he was going to fall apart. My smile. The girl was hanging in his arms, battered and beaten like a paper doll

The massive beast of a man loomed over the stairs with a devilish, wicked smile. The girl was hanging in his arm, battered and beaten like a paper doll torn to pieces. How could he have done that to her!

Anger swept through me. No more was I scared or afraid, just furiously full of a need to avenge the girl. Pure hate and passion were the only things I felt for that beast.

"Jamie!" I commanded. "Get out of here and get help! NOW!"

Jamie was so shocked he followed my orders. He could feel my desire to do it on my own. Still wide-eyed, he backed out of the house alone.

"Help me," was the girl's cry before her swollen eyes collapsed.

"Yes!" screamed the madman. "Help the poor rag, but don't let me catch you."

"Come and get me, beast!" I was ready to play.

He roared, let the bruised girl fall from his muscular arms, and eagerly walked down the creaking stairs.

Blazing Smoke

What am I doing? I plead temporary insanity. The beast was at the bottom of the stairs, and he swung. Ducking, I ran into the dining room. Spider webs hung from the chandelier and the table was split in half. Where can I hide?

"Now I got ya!" The man stormed into the room. Showing his strength, he picked up half of the dusty table and threw it at me. Thank God for fast reflexes. Backing up, I backed into a cabinet filled with china. Picking up a dish and aiming, I threw it as hard as I could. The dish hit him in the arm but didn't seem to make a dent. Rage was written on his face. He picked up a chair and it immediately fell apart. The next one would be his next weapon. His eyes widened, his teeth clenched.

I turned away and covered my head with my skinny arms. Soon, the chair would smash to pieces over me and I would become his next victim.

"Hey ugly!" It was Jamie. Always-in-the-right-place-at-the-right-time Jamie.

I peeked between my arms. The beastly man had turned his back. He threw the chair at Jamie. I saw his face pound against the floor as he fell.

"No!" I screamed.

I grabbed the nearest things and chucked them, hard. A crystal dish, a candlestick, it was all the same. The seemingly undefeatable man finally fell.

Smoke, I thought I smelled smoke. The candle had started the curtains on fire. With all my strength, I pulled myself together. I helped Jamie to his feet and shoved him out the front door to the waiting ambulance and police. Running up the flimsy stairs, I helped the girl out of the burning house. I finally helped her.

Behind me, the gray, victimized house crumbled in a blazing fire. In front of me was the bright sunset.

Science Fiction

Imagine that some physical condition of life as we know it were suddenly altered—the temperature of the earth or chemistry of the brain. What would follow? Invent some such change and imagine the consequences. Think of some characters who might react to the change in interestingly different ways.

Or imagine a world that has already changed in some significant ways, that simply operates by different natural laws than ours today. Make up a story and characters that fit such a world.

Or carry farther forward into the future some current developments in technology and exploration to imagine where they might lead.

Try your story out on local science fiction fans and then try it out with some magazine or other audience.

Good Help Is Hard to Find
Peter Gast

The Benson family did not enjoy their last day of freedom for two reasons. One, they did not realize the significance it would have on their lives, and two, they were too busy waiting for their new Walter. The robot was supposed to have arrived two days earlier but had been delayed in transit.

Walter XIII arrived late Friday afternoon. He was six feet tall and dressed in the tuxedo that the Walter line always wore. He looked even more like an English butler than Walter XII. When Mrs. Benson looked closely, she could still tell it was a robot, but only when she looked closely.

She flipped open the panel on his chest, but the controls confused her. She would have to wait for Kevin to get home. He was really much better at this sort of thing. She would never get the hang of these new gadgets.

When Kevin finally returned home from school, he immediately began to program the new Walter. He had read the instruction booklet in English class instead of writing some stupid science-fiction paper. It was a matter of priorities. Kevin hurried through the task of programing Walter and finished before dinner time. Dinner that night was served by Walter.

"I entered into his data bank the weight we would like to be in eight weeks. A hundred and ten pounds for Mom, one-forty for dad, eighty-five for Brian and one-twenty for me. I know it will be hard but I think we can make it. The most important thing is that we don't cheat on this diet like we did on the last one. I told Walter not let us get away with ANY cheating."

At precisely 7:45 Walter served dinner. If you can call a plain bowl of lettuce and a small serving of cottage cheese a dinner. Even Kevin was surprised at the scarcity of the meal. No one complained but everyone left the table hungry.

The next morning Walter woke everyone at 6:45. He gave them fifteen minutes to get ready and then dragged them on a five-mile hike. When they returned home, they were treated to a breakfast of plain toast and raw eggs. The feast was followed by an hour of calisthenics.

The week went down hill from there. The meals got smaller and the exercises harder. It got to the point where they were only eating one meal and literally knocking themselves out with exhaustion. Only Mr. Benson was spared, he got to leave for work each day and sneak in a massive lunch. On Friday, the overlord noticed.

"I am afraid, sir, that you can not exercise the self-restraint necessary for a successful weight loss program. You shall require constant supervision. I have called your office and informed them that you are going on an extended leave of absence. You do not seem to realize the difficulty with this diet. It calls for you to lose over twenty pounds per week for the next eight weeks. You can not expect the diet to work if you insist on cheating."

The robot's voice went on, but Mr. Benson did not hear it. All he could hear was "Twenty pounds per week for eight weeks." The monster is trying to starve us to death. I have to get out of here, get away from it, get far away.

Mr. Benson ran frantically to the front door. It would not respond to his voice pattern. Neither would the windows. Even the phone would not activate for his use. He decided that his family must be warned. He tried to put the news to them calmly, but his heart was racing.

"I think I know what happened," Kevin told him coolly, "I must have misplaced the decimal point. It thinks I want to weigh twelve pounds instead of the one hundred twenty I really want to weigh. I think our only hope is that someone notices we're not where we're supposed to be."

"No," replied Mrs. Benson. "It has made arrangements to keep us here for weeks. It called your father's office, your school, Brian's school, anywhere we visit regularly. They all expect us to be locked up in here for eight weeks."

"Maybe we can jump it. There are four of us and only one of it," Mr. Benson suggested hopefully.

"No, it is much too fast and strong for us. It has a reaction time of microseconds and can lift a small car if it has to. We would not have a chance against it even if we had weapons, which we don't." Kevin's voice sank to a low murmur as he realized how hopeless the problem was.

"We are studying logic problems in school," Brian told them hopefully. "I know just how to blow its mind." Then he called, "Walter, come here, I need you."

"Yes, sir, how may I serve you?"

"Just answer one question. True or false. I am now lying."

"If it is true, then you are lying, which means the statement is false, meaning you are not lying, which means the statement is true, meaning...." Walter began repeating himself and stood motionless, his mind taken up completely by the paradox.

The Benson family sold Walter a week later for scrap metal. Then they sold their house and used the money to move to one of the frontier worlds where they would never see another robot again.

Reborn
Stacy Williamson

The man sat in the wheel chair, leaning slightly forward. He was only in his thirties but appeared to be much older. He sat in a well-furnished room, which was part of a nice, cheerful house. Through a nearby window, he could see the birds chirping in the summer sun and kids playing on the green lawns. The man coughed slightly, then leaned back in his wheel chair. He saw a white van pull up outside the house and two men get out.

"Martha!" he feebly shouted. "They have come!"

His wife Martha walked to the front door. She opened it and greeted the two men who approached.

"Hello," she said stepping aside. "He's in there."

She pointed to an open doorway that led into her husband's room. One of the men walked into the room and came back out pushing her husband. Her husband held onto the wheel chair's handles tightly and coughed again.

"Don't worry, Martha," he said as they left the house. "I'll be back in no time."

Martha watched from the front door as the two men loaded her husband into the van. She was of medium height, with long blond hair. She was in her late twenties, but hard work showed on her lined face. A little boy, around five or six, ran up the steps and startled her.

"Hello Mommy," he said. "Where are they taking Daddy?"

The little boy followed his mother into the house. He had short brown hair, and an air of happiness and youth followed him and seemed to linger in the air around him. His mother sat down on the sofa, and he crawled up into its warmth beside her.

His mother looked down at him and smiled.

"You know that Daddy has been sick, don't you?"

He nodded.

"Well," she continued, "They came and took him to the center."

"Oh," said the little boy. "Will I see him again?"

His mother continued smiling.

"Yes," she stated. "We will see him again tomorrow. But there is only one thing," she said as her smile faded. "He will not look the same."

'What do you mean?" the little boy asked.

"Don't worry. You will understand tomorrow."

His mother got up and walked into the kitchen, leaving behind a little boy with a questioning look on his face.

The next day the doorbell rang, and the little boy got up and walked to the front door. He had been waiting for this moment. He reached up and grabbed hold of the front door. It released its hold on the surrounding walls and swung open. A man was standing at the front door holding a briefcase. He reached down and gave the briefcase to the little boy. Turning around, he walked down the steps and sidewalk, then opened the door on a white van and left.

The boy's mother had walked up behind him.

"May I have the case?" she asked.

He gave it to her with a smile. The lady turned around and walked down the hall with the little boy following. Then she turned and opened the door to a room that nobody was allowed to enter. It was the kind of room that created questions without giving any answers. The little boy stopped at the entrance and watched his mother.

The room was white and empty, except for one object. There was a square metallic box sitting on a table. The box was a perfect one-foot cube. The boy's mother set the briefcase on the table next to the box. She then opened the case and removed an object. It was a small red cylinder that glowed an evil light. The lady carefully handled the cylinder. Stepping over to the box, she slid the cylinder down a hole in the top. It was the only marking on the whole box, and when the cylinder was pushed into the hole, the marking disappeared.

The lady turned and said to the boy, "You can come in."

The boy walked across the room to stand beside his mother and the box. He was confused and did not understand what was happening.

"Go ahead and ask the box a question," she said to the little boy. "But pretend it is your daddy."

The little boy held onto his mother's hand tightly for reassurance.

"Daddy," he asked, "is that really you?"

The box pulsated forth energy and replied, "Yes son, it is me."

The boy let go of his mother's hand and smiled. Looking up at his mother's face he said, "Daddy is home."

Naaw, Make That the Universe
Michael Kim

"Ha! Got ya' there, Jeeb! Hahaha! That gives me Alpha Centauri and the neighboring star systems!! There, that gives me ummm...," the Emperor of the Crytonian Empire frowned with the greatness in the calculation put forth upon him. Emperor Hashbrown was never good at numerical mathematics; in fact, he wasn't good at much except Crytonian Chess. With the stoutness that only an emperor could possess, he raised his chin and stroked his beard with his pectoral tentacle. "Four. Four points. Yes, that's right. Zero plus four is four. Yes, that's right. Oh, I already said that. Hehe, well, I'm beating you by, let's see, ummm...."

Jeeblebot, otherwise known as Jeeb, the Jeeb, and You-Demented-Little-Chunk-of-Rubber (for a good reason; it was true), was not patient, and was not, contrary to common belief, a tamale. Having a very low level of patience and being entirely unlike a tamale, Jeeb did not like waiting—especially not for emperors of neutron star systems—so he didn't. "Uh, er, sorry, Hashbrown. Gotta leave. Have an important meeting to miss."

Hashbrown was still working on the mind-boggling problem of how much he was beating Jeeb by. "Hey, Wait! You can't leave! Not when I'm beating you by, um...."

"Four. You're beating me by four points." And with that he left.

"Hmmm, four? Hmmm, yes, that sounds correct. I think I shall think for a while," resolved Hashbrown and fell into a coma.

"Gimme the coordinates for the nearest pub." Jeeblebot was satisfied. He didn't know why, but he was. Being satisfied with that explanation on why he was satisfied, he was satisfied.

"Gotcha, boss," energetically spoke the ship computer, "Nearing the Topwuqawuqa system."

The giant erasable pen raced across the star-speckled canvas of space.

Jeeblebot saw the emptiness outside the comfort of his erasable pen and thought how it was strange that everyone thought it was empty. "You know, it's times like this that I really appreciate being an erasable pen eraser." With that, he erased something that was nothing in particular.

"Shut up, you demented little chunk of rubber."

"Brobo!" The Jeeb nearly bounced a hole in the ceiling of his beloved pen.

"Jes' shut up, you demented little chunk of rubber."

"You still owe me some cash," solemnly stated Brobo Hecklemeyer the pi-th (as in second, third, you know). "That could possibly top Boynton Kiyt as an understatement, when he said, 'Well, sure, the Universe is a BIT bigger than my thumb.'"

"Well, Boynton DID have a big thumb," came back the helpless eraser.

"Sure he had a big thumb; that is, big compared to his hand."

"Boynton didn't have...."

"Hands, yeah. Exactly."

"Okay! So I owe you the deficit of the Whee-arinnbigtrubel colony more or less."

"More."

"Yes."

There was a total absence of silence as "I Got the Lobotomy Blues" not only went through the air like a very aerodynamic brick wall, it also took the air, mangled it, distorted it, and made it otherwise angry.

"Yes," echoed the echo (the erasable pen was giant, another understatement, I stated beforehand).

"But that's not important...."

"Of course not. Money important? Naaw! There's...." gladly added Jeeblebot.

"When did I say money wasn't important? You still owe me enough to buy a couple major suns. I'm saying there's more immediate things we must tend to."

"Whatever you say! So, what's our job?"

"Save the Universe from complete annihilation."

"Hey, man. Consider it done! Anything for a frie...." He realized the actual proportion of it and could say only one thing, "Urk!"

"The Crytonians are not pleased by the fact that their emperor is in a coma...."

"Forget it! Hashbrown's not in a coma. No, he's just working out forty-two divided by twenty-one. He was never good at long division, you know."

Brobo ignored him. "... and they think it was caused by a demented little chunk of rubber that challenged him to a game of Crytonian Chess.''

"Yeah! Hey, he beat me too! By four points.''

Brobo paused for a second. Not to think about what Jeeb had said, but to work out forty-two divided by twenty-one, ''Two.''

"Huh?''

"Never mind,'' he continued. "Anyway, the Crytonians think they must cure him of this by ending his life.''

"How cruel! How could they do that! Hashbrown has a right to live! They can't just kill him without his permission! It is his life, you know. But I SUPPOSE ... oh well, if they must....''

"By annihilating the Universe.''

"Oh,well, ummm ... Urk!''

"Urk ... ugh, I had this repulsive nightmare ... urk,'' Jeeblebot awoke.

"About Hashbrown going into a coma and the Crytonians blowing up the Universe?'' hypothesized Brobo rather correctly.

"Huh? Yeah! Hey, maybe we have that multiple dream thing I read about yesterday. You know. When two people have the same dream....''

"It wasn't a dream.''

"Huh? Huh? Urk!'' and with that he slept for a while.

Being an intelligent tissue box, Brobo followed. It was going to be a long trip.

Brobo Hecklemeyer is a very irrational tissue box, yet very intelligent. He once acquired a 314.159 ... on the GOTTAKOLD (*G* et *O* utta *T* he *T* issue box *A* argh! *K* nownothing's test *O* f *L* ong *D* ivision) test. The strange thing about that was this: it was graded on a scale of zero to a hundred. Being known as strange, irrational, and not a tamale (yes, Jeeblebot is also not a tamale. The difference is that no one thinks that Brobo is a tamale, which is true), this was not *too* strange. Other characteristics (more or less unusual) of this respectable Hecklemeyer are these: 1) He is a highly intelligent tissue box. 2) Brobo is exceedingly good at long division. 3) He is pi-th in the line of Brobo Hecklemeyers. The reason was this: his father was not very good at long division but loved multiplying things by decimals. So one day he decided to name his son Brobo Hecklemeyer after himself (being the second Brobo Hecklemeyer). "Adding one to two,'' he'd think, "is too boring.'' So he multipled two by the arctangent of one and multiplied that by four (loving multiplication the way he did). Not being very good at division, he divided that number by only two (accidentally, of course) giving the would-be Hecklemeyer III the dubious title of [+/<\+ Brobo Hecklemeyer the pi-th <\+]. To make a short story long, Brobo Hecklemeyer the pi-th became an irrational kind of guy.

Brobo woke up with the greatness of his intellect, "Ugh ... massive hangover...."

Jeeblebot did likewise. "That's funny ... no hangover."

The ship computer decided to join in the action, "Hey, gang, it looks like it's gonna be a great day!"

"Turn off your annunciators, Frooter."

"Sure boss! Just want to tell you that we're nearing the Topwuqawuqa system."

"Wait, Frooter. We're going to have to change course. Give me the direct coordinates of the Crytonian empire."

"I already told you, boss. We're nearing the Crytonian empire."

"Oh. Of course! Yeah, I knew that!"

"Crytonia is in the Topwuqawuqa system."

"Exactly. Like I said, follow the previous coordinates."

"Sure thing, boss."

Brobo spoke, "We are to meet a Kweshun Marc on Crytonia. She'll tell us where to go from there."

Jeeblebot was disappointed. "Great. First female I'm going to meet in a millenium and she's a Crytonian. I bet she shaves her tentacles."

Brobo corrected him: "Kweshun is a Dithronian."

After doing a couple of flips, the Jeeb fainted with a smile the size of his debt.

The incredibly sized erasable pen landed in the docking bay of Crytonia. There awaited Kweshun.

To Brobo, Kweshun was the only hope for the salvation of the Universe; to Jeeblebot, Kewshun had the looks and body of ... something erasable pen erasers like a lot.

Brobo introduced himself and his anticipating partner. "Hello, I'm Hecklemeyer, and this is Jeeblebot."

"Pleased to meet you both," she smiled. "There's much to be accomplished and a Universe to be saved, if I'm correct."

Jeeblebot pushed aside Brobo. "Hey, babe, how 'bout crusin' 'cross the Turnian galaxy? It's just you and me. The twin arms of Nexus and Thoyr. The...."

"You must be Jeeblebot," she frowned. To be frank, she ignored him for the rest of the story.

All Jeeblebot could say later to Brobo was, "Urk."

The gigunda erasable pen raced across the black canvas.

Jeeblebot was mumbling to himself, "Oh, you must be Jeeblebot," and sulking.

In the other corner, about a mile away, Brobo and Kweshun were planning. "Okay, so first we set up a committee who will convince the Crytonians that killing an emperor is not morally right. Then we send up a committee that will convince them that blowing up the Universe is not the answer. Meanwhile we notify the Scientists of the Imperial Galaxy of the Crytonian's plan to see if they can find a solution and the Authority Police of the Imperial Galaxy (otherwise known in its anachronic form). Maybe they'll be able to help. This is so frustrating! They could have just waited for this guy to wake up, or maybe do away with him, but no-o-o-o! They weren't satisfied with just one emperor! No! They said, 'Naaw, make that the Universe!' Now they're gonna dust us all!"

"'Oh, you must be Jeeblebot,'" continued Jeeb.

"Is he always like that?" inquired Kweshun.

"Like what? Oh, that. Naaw."

"Of course."

As the ship sped across the black canvas, a couple hundred parsecs away a man was painting on a white canvas, "Thisa weel be moiy masterpace!"

The unsuspecting artist continued to draw his "masterpace" on the white canvas. To a normal, sane person, the white canvas would appear black—for a simple reason too. It was true. The white canvas (it's very important that you know it was white) was covered with a black paint. "A masterpace!" he continued.

To a normal, sane person, it would appear that the artist was in Italy. Reason's unknown, he wasn't.

As the French painter continued to blanket the white canvas with black, he visualized the final picture, "Aoui! A masterpace!"

Later, a normal, sane person saw the painting and (being puzzled) blankly said, "My, that looks like an erasable pen."

"See, while you two were babbling away to yourselves, I was THINKING! And I have an idea. Fate being the way she is, every move is planned. So somewhere in the Universe, there must be someone who can see other places without actually being there." Jeeblebot coughed a mite and continued. "Anyway, if we can get to this guy, he could save us."

"How?" chorused the duo.

"'How?' they ask! How indeed ... how indeed ... ummm.... Can't you see?"

"No." Brobo and Kweshun almost sang it out.

"Man, you two are a regular. How? This is how! We go there and he'll tell us how! Get it?"

"No," they echoed.

"Good. Frooter, did you find this magic dude? The one with the third eye?"

"Got him, boss. Coordinates: AR94 0042G. Star system of Sol; planet Earth."

"Earth? Hmmm ... what's Earth?"

"I see nowa! You are vum a faar place and weesh to zee moiy masterpace!"

"Uh, yeah. Masterpace, yeah. Well, actually, we want you to come with us."

"To ze faar place?"

"Yeah, 'ze faar place.'"

"Vere they want to zee moiy masterpace?"

"Yeah, masterpiece. Come on."

Brobo stood high and majestic. "People of Crytonia, I bring you a teller of other places!" The crowd cheered at his reverberating voice.

Brobo started again, "He will tell you of Right and the doom you place before yourselves and all people!"

Cheer, cheer, rah, cheer.

"I bring you the Teller!"

More cheer, rah, rah!!!!!

The French painter stumbled to the podium, "Uhh, er, do you wish to zee moiy masterpace?"

Cheer, cheer, rah, rah.

He cleared his throat and brought to his side a canvas covered with a red cloth, paused, and pulled at the fabric revealing the image set upon the canvas.

It was nothing.

It was a horrible nothing. Not black, not white. Just an absence of everything, put onto a canvas.

Everyone paused.

To look at it meant to shiver, to shiver with fear.

Nobody moved. They just stared at the nothing and feared.

After the hour had passed, Brobo arose. "People of Crytonia, I once more address you. Not to introduce, but to ask of you to rid yourselves of the insane plan you created. Rid."

The second emperor of the planet slowly stood, her clothes ruffling with the movement. "We ... we hereby rid the Universe of fear. Fear of annihilation."

In the back, a pair of tentacles met. Then again. Soon, the sound of a planet clapping could be heard.

Kweshun took the chair. "People of Crytonia, we once more mention the honor of your name. Not of introduction; not of request; but of congratulations. In the splendor of this moment, let us rise. People of Crytonia, you are congratulated."

Crytonia smiled.

(At this moment, I need a pause, so stare at this period →. and count to ten slowly.)

"Hey! I'm beating you by four points! Two! Hey, forty-two divided by twenty-one is two! Haha!" Hashbrown shouted and ran down the newly made aisle to the podium, but not before he slipped on a banana. Nothing slowed, he continued.

"Welcome, Emperor Hashbrown!" The nearly inaudible din caused by the simultaneous statement of the crowd shook stars parsecs away.

"Why, thanks, gang," returned the happy emperor.

"You're welcome!" the stars rumbled once more.

Crytonia smiled.

Myth

Read some myths, then invent a supernatural story that pretends to explain something true about nature or human nature. This could take place today or in a made-up time and place. Characters in myth stand for things in life, like growth or greed, and the plot connects these things in some relationship. So what the characters do with each other shows how these forces act on each other. Places and objects also may represent things in real life—a swamp or a jewel, for example. Make your own myth to state or explain something about the world.

A simple kind of myth explains how something came to be the way it is, like how fire was first made, or how the tiger got his stripes. You might start with that type. Agree with partners to show or explain something with myth, then compare your myths afterwards. You might post or print these together.

Schooleus and School
Adrian Wenner

At one time, in the far distant past, mortal men and women had to live with their son or daughter all day and all night long. The mortal grown-ups complained. Zeus knew that people that complained a lot become rowdy and rebellious. That could be grim! So, Zeus picked a new-born immortal to be the god of a new place to be called "school." The word "cool" was "in," so Zeus made the place-name sound like "cool," hoping that boy and girl mortals would go for it. And he named the new god "Schooleus." He knew that school had to take up most of the day, but not all of it, for then the mortal children would grow up unhappy with the gods. So he decided to make two days of a regular week non-school days. He remembered the fun he experienced during his childhood with the wood nymphs, so he created summer vacation. Holidays are when Zeus and Schooleus are both in good moods.

School posed a problem. It had to serve a purpose. The mortals wouldn't be able to tell their children they were sending him or her off to school to get him or her out of their way!

"Ahhh, I know!!" thought Zeus.

Mortal children were not like immortal children. They were not born with all the knowledge they needed to make it through life, so he made it a place of learning.

"This is so great," Zeus said aloud as if he were bragging to the whole world. "It will also provide jobs for some mortals. Boy, am I smart!!"

The only trouble for the kids was that while Zeus was bragging about how great he was, his favorite window was turned into scrap glass by a young mortal's baseball. So he devised a punishment for all kids after feeding the one responsible for the broken window to the Nemean Lion. This horrid punishment was called "homework."

"Yes," he stated in a pleased tone. "I should have put this in Pandora's box. It would have fit nicely."

School worked beautifully. The adults could concentrate on their work and relax, and the children learned and worked.

All was not rosy, though, for the adults, because Zeus also developed golf and bridge, which no being, mortal or immortal, could relax while playing.

But that is another myth.

Halloween Myth
Andrea Franczyk

A long time ago life was different.

When people died their body left them, and their soul stayed.

In the beginning this was fine.

Some souls didn't like it though. They said that all they could do was "be around." They couldn't eat, smell, taste, or feel.

Deadicus, the god of dead people, proceeded to speak with Zeus one day.

"I think we should make it so that everyone lives forever on Earth." Deadicus pronounced.

"But then Earth would become overcrowded," Zeus answered.

"But souls don't like it."

"That's their problem."

"Zeus, they can't do anything but hear."

"Absolutely not," thundered Zeus.

"I'll kill Epaphus, your son," said Deadicus.

"You would never."

"Oh yes I would."

"You're not that cruel."

"Look at him right now, Zeus," said Deadicus.

Zeus looked down on the Earth.

He saw Epaphus lying in a bed very sick.

"You either let man live forever or your son dies," said Deadicus.

"We'll try it for a month," proclaimed Zeus wearily.

That night Deadicus traveled to Earth and rejoined all souls with their bodies.

All on Earth were joyous. Church bells rang and people partied all night long. Everyone was happy.

All was well on Earth except that the population kept growing and growing. No one was dead for long. When someone died they were only dead for a day and then their bodies were fixed. When someone was shot or hit by a car and their body could not be fixed they were built another.

Finally after two months Zeus called Deadicus back to talk to him. "Do you realize what we've done?" asked Zeus.

"What do you mean?" asked Deadicus.

"There is no real meaning to life because everyone is immortal. We must stop this before man tries to overtake us. If we don't I'm afraid of what will happen. There is just no more room any more.

"Even though I'm the one who thought this whole idea up I must agree with you," said Deadicus.

"Tomorrow we must start changing things back to the way they were."

"There must be a way we can enable the soul to still live in some way," pronounced Deadicus.

"I've got an idea! What if we were to make a special place in the sky where the souls could live!"

"And the bodies would stay on Earth underground," said Deadicus.

"Yes, and we could call it Heaven."

"It would be a very peaceful place."

"It would be in the clouds," commented Zeus.

"We should start building it tomorrow," suggested Deadicus.

"Yes."

One week later Heaven was done.

Deadicus traveled down to Earth. He got all the souls to bring to Heaven. On his way to Heaven some souls escaped. The souls that had escaped rebelled and haunted the Earth.

Deadicus came up with a way to scare the souls away. Once a year everyone would dress up and that would scare the souls away until next year.

It was known as Halloween.

The Beginning of It All
Karen Levine

The Beginning of Earth's Creation

Once all the stars were great big suns. They grew and grew until they exploded. As the pieces of the great suns flew, they cooled off and then fit back together as a planet.

The king of the stars, Jthoro, survived the explosions and reigned over the planet. He gave warmth and life to the hot but cooling planet, and he called it Earth, and after he named it he cried since it was all that was left of his dear sons.

Soon the life he developed began to need a shape, so Jthoro (the sun) molded humans. At first human blood was hot, but as the years went by they cooled and became warm-blooded.

While Jthoro ruled, Earth was always very hot. But when, galaxies away, more stars exploded and formed the moon, a life in itself, the moon wanted to rule the earth too. So she made it cooler. This did not please Jthoro. Since they both wanted to rule Earth they decided to compromise. Jthoro and the moon (Modera) decided that they should create night and day. They would switch posts, and where the moon was it was darker and cooler, and where the sun was it was lighter and warmer.

At night, being that it was so dark and the humans had trouble seeing things, the sun gave off sparks and they created stars. The ashes that flew from the sparks as they went to their places became clouds, and the coolness of the moon mixed with them, creating snow, rain, and hail.

The War of the Humans

At first the only creature on Earth was man. Man came in four different colors—black, yellow, red, and white. Jthoro, who had many flickering hands, managed to make humans different colors, depending on which side of him it was made on. The hottest side created blacks, the coolest whites. The reds and yellows were in between.

Now at first humans were very deformed. As they reproduced they created creatures unlike themselves, which preferred to live wildly, and they were called animals. Eventually the humans had normal-looking children, and that carried on the human race. The original reproductions went to live in the forest.

All the creatures of the earth lived on land, because that's all there was. That made Modera angry. Now it seemed that the sun had more power on the earth. So to compete with the sun she created water and cold-blooded animals that could live there. Now there were reptiles and mammals.

This of course made Jthoro mad. He made his creatures like to eat the moon's creatures. The moon then made the sun's creatures also eat the sun's creatures. The sun then made the moon's creatures eat the moon's creatures. Then there was war.

When the war ended, the sun created fire; the moon created seas out of her water. They both created diseases and death and gave all of their creatures some sort of defense—claws, teeth, and something to scrape an enemy with, or something to hide in. The stars put a reproducible spark in the human's head and that was their main defense. They had a brain. Thus they did not have to depend on the sun and the moon as much.

The Underworld

Although at first the sun and the moon were a little angry about not having as much power they did enjoy the reduced amount of work for them to do. They still were in control of the planet and knew that there was a lot more to do, but it did not deal with the life on the planet at the moment; it dealt with the death.

Modera knew that the people who now were mortal needed a place to go when they died. So she created a hell.

The sun as a sign of everlasting hatred for the moon made the underworld extremely hot. At first all the dead souls would go down there. They would get burnt up and sent to the sun in the form of ashes. There the bad souls would be picked out, put back into their soul's shape, and sent down to hell for everlasting agony. The good would go directly to the sun, and all their ashes would become a new life on earth through the sun's ray.

The leader of the underworld was Hela, a monstrous creature created by Modera. You see, at first the moon tried to create a race equal to humans in order to compete with the sun. She did not succeed, and so, being very impatient, she just gave up. So she made her creature leader of the under-world. Hela was so cold-hearted that the fierce fires of hell could not harm her, and thus she was perfect for the job.

The Earth's Seasons

Now Hela wanted to feel important. All she did was lead people to the underworld. Recently lots of people had been dying, and she was getting absolutely no breaks. Then she figured it out and told the moon and the sun that the humans were not adapting very well to the sudden changes of temperature, from night to day, so she begged them, "Go very slowly around the earth." This made summer and winter. The summer was hot and the winter was cold. The in-between times were fall and spring.

Now that Hela felt that she was important she went back to her job. However, after about a year Jthoro and Modera got angry and were exhausted. They complained to Hela, who was having a great time not working as hard. When they told her how exhausting it was for them to go so slow, she immediately thought of a solution. She took the soul of the evilest and the strongest man on earth, Axio, and made him hold it up, and spin it around, very slowly, while the sun and moon did not have to move at all.

Heaven

Now let's go up a bit to Heaven. Heavana, the sun Jthoro's beautiful daughter, also a first version of humans, was placed in heaven when after the sun created her he decided she was too beautiful to be mortal. However, unlike Hela, she was more like humans. Her job was to bring the ashes to her father, so they could be made into a new life. Before she could do that, however, she had to sort out the ashes and pick out the bad ones.

Hela of course was jealous of Heavana and always tried to cause trouble. For instance, after a person's soul was burnt, instead of sending up the ashes she would crumble them up, and thus they would not all go up successfully to heaven. Now the poor dead souls could not get into another peaceful life. These people's souls would wander around aimlessly and become what we call ghosts. The only way to help them was to burn their actual bodies and send them up to heaven by placing them on the grave.

Ghosts can take the shape of anything. Although they scare people they are just trying to tell people to help them. They figure that going to the place of their death will give them contact with people they know so that they will burn their body and give them peace. One of the many shapes that ghosts take is the wind; they blow howling in their agony, trying to tell the humans that they are not at peace. Tornados developed when miniature ashes tried to get together and get to Heaven. If they did not succeed they would all weep and howl in their agony, causing a hurricane.

When Heavana realized what was going on, she told all people on earth to hate Hela for what she had done and no longer treat her as they would a goddess but rather as a demon. That is what makes us humans hate anything to do with hell and always feel safer around something to do with the sky.

Royal Race

When the sun and the moon finally became friends and married, they had a son and a daughter, whom they placed on earth to rule the humans, who at this point were nothing but savages, and it was about time that they used their brains and started a civilization.

Now the son and daughter married each other and had many children, who grew up and ruled over more land. These children married one another also. Now, for a while this was okay. But soon the royal race began to die out, because they were only reproducing retards who did not live very long. So eventually they all died, and all that was left were the few humans who had been born a combination of humans and royalty. The humans made them their rulers, and those are the people from whom our present day kings and queens are descended.

Rocks

Once Jthoro and Modera had had their children, they took their present posts in the sky. The sun got to his place very easily, but the moon was quite fat from having the children and thus had a lot of trouble going from one place to another. So she had to lose weight before she could get to her post. She gave the evil Axio a rest while she ran around the earth 1000 times. She lost weight very quickly, and from her great body came rocks which landed on the earth. Now since her body was that of a goddess, a good many of the rocks that fell to the earth became the precious metals that we have today. Now new rocks are formed out of the dust that the moon got off her body as she ran; we call that dust dirt.

Emotions

Once Heavana had told the humans to hate Hela she realized that that was the only emotion that the humans had. Their brain only helped them to decide. People did not marry because of love, they married because they knew they had to have children so that the human race could live on. Heavana thought that she should change all of that. So she created many different emotions. She made a special rain fall, which she told all the humans to go out into, and when it soaked through their skin it caused feelings. That is what we have today. People who are seemingly evil are just descendants of the few humans who refused to go under the rain.

Done

Well, now that the earth was fully created, all the gods and goddesses made themselves unable to be seen by humans, which is why there is some doubt about there being an actual underworld. Now the people of the Earth began to live on their own and create their own inventions for their survival. However, the sun and the moon are still a main source of life. What I mean by that is that humans cannot live without the sun's warmth but need the moon's coolness to make the earth not so hot. However, every time the sun and the moon get mad at the humans they have thunder and lightning come with the rain. If a rainbow appears afterwards it means that all of the problems that were bothering them were solved. If you have ever noticed, a rainbow is an upside-down smile.

Parable

Read some parables and invent a short story that makes a general point about people but does not state the point. Draw material from either our current world or remote or imaginary times. Entertain while instructing. The point may be moral or psychological and is embodied in the story. Try your parable on others to see if your point was clear. You might read it to a group and discuss it afterwards—an especially good idea if the members of the group are taking turns reading and writing parables. Collect parables from both books and one another's writing.

The Bum
Jeannie Kim

One sluggish morning, a bum was walking, looking for at least a crumb to eat, but he couldn't find anything.

He was getting desperate, and having no other choice, he stole an apple from a small fruit stand. The owner, spotting the bum, ran after him and got hold of him. "What do you think you're doing?" the owner was yelling.

"Oh mister, I'm sorry. Please don't turn me over to the police," the bum pleaded.

"Only if you will be my slave," the owner said, taking advantage of the situation.

"I'll do anything, as long as you don't turn me in." For weeks the bum swept and mopped the floor of the fruit stand. Almost every day, the bum would steal at least four apples. This kept him full for the whole day during these weeks.

The bum was happy that he was a slave of the fruit stand owner, because he was benefitting more than the owner.

While Ahead
(Told by My Grandmother)
Michael Oretsky

When my grandmother was a young girl she was still the oldest among her brother and four sisters. It was a custom that when someone was invited to a wedding or a special occasion, the oldest child would attend. So my grandmother was able to go.

At the party she was having such a good time that when it was time to go, she insisted on staying to the end.

Soon people began to leave and the tables became empty. My grandmother cried and cried. Her parents said, "You see, now that you waited to the end, you don't go home with the memory of all the people and food, but with the memory of the empty rooms and tables."

Death No Joke
Leon Avelino

My family, all of it besides my mother, are Filipino. It seems to me that Filipinos are very fond of ghost stories and stories of the supernatural. Among several other stories that I have heard one stands out for me more than any other. The story is like a parable because the Filipinos are very strict about saying things about death, which they are terribly afraid of.

The story as far as I know was first told by my great-grandmother to teach the children not to say things about death, although I believe that it has been in my family for many years before that.

The story is about two friends who were very close. They were talking about death because they were wondering what would happen if one dies before the other, and they decided, "If I will die, then I shall return for you."

In a few years one of the friends died, and the other was alone. At the funeral they buried him in a white gown.

In exactly forty days (why forty I don't know but that's the way the story goes) the friend came back in a white gown through the village to his friend to embrace his friend, and when he had disappeared his friend died.

So every time someone made a joke about the dead my great-grandmother would silence them with this story.

Worn
Alexi Steinfink

Once there were two students. One was rich and very much into material possessions, and the other was not poor, but he wasn't rich either.

One day their English teacher assigned a major term paper which would account for a lot of the semester's grade. It was to read THE MYTH OF SISYPHUS and find the theme.

The rich one went to the campus library and found a beat-up, smelly old copy and decided to send away to a book club for a copy. The poorer one went to the library and found the very same copy and said, "Oh, what a worn-in book, this must have been used by many students. I really like 'em like this. I guess they're more human or something," and took out the book and started reading.

In the meantime, the rich one still hadn't received the book after three weeks. There were two weeks to go. The poor boy, since he had it from the beginning, started gathering together the notes he had taken.

Four days before the paper was due the poor boy was done, but the rich boy had just gotten it and was going crazy trying to finish it. Then the poor boy said, "If you hadn't judged the book by its cover, you wouldn't be in this jam."

"Yes, I realize now," the rich boy said.

He finally handed in his paper one day late and got a C+ because of the rushed job he did. The poor boy received an A for his superb job.

Fable

Read some fables, then try your hand at some. A fable is a brief story that illustrates some general truth or advice. This "moral" is stated in a separate sentence at the end. The characters don't have to be animals (although traditionally they are), and fables can be modern.

There are several ways to go about making fables. You can take some familiar saying and write a story to illustrate it. Or make a fable out of a true incident you've heard or read about that you think is a good example of something general. Or make up a moral, then invent a tale to illustrate it.

Fables are especially good to post on a bulletin board or make into a booklet. If several of you write fables to illustrate the same moral, cluster these around a little sign with the moral printed on it, or collect them in a booklet with the moral as title.

The Proof
Philip Valek

A fish swam slowly across the swamp. He just had a large meal of water plants. He was a small fish, one of the only fish that could fit in an underwater cave that had a lot of food in it. A skinny snake could also fit in the cave. The snake was a wise snake and wanted all the food to himself.

One day the snake said to the fish, "I don't think you're brave!"

"I am too!" angrily answered the fish.

"Then prove it. Go swim by the old alligator, slap him with your tail, and then swim back."

"No way," quietly answered the fish.

"You're a coward. The whole swamp is going to know you're a coward," said the snake.

"Okay," said the fish. "I'll do it."

Now the snake has the whole cave to himself.

Moral: Don't confuse bravery with stupidity.

The Gossip Columnist
Leonor Camche

Once upon a time there was a gossip columnist. Her name was Loquacious Ginger. She talked an awful lot, and everything she said wasn't true. Her main gossiping was about movie stars.

One day her boss came to her and said, "You're the best gossiper we have. Now, you have to go out there and get some good stories."

So Loquacious Ginger started to write about politicians. And write and write and write. When L. Ginger's articles came out in magazines, she was a smash to all people who liked to read good gossip. The politicians started to write to her telling her to stop. But that didn't bother her, she kept writing and writing. Soon all the other gossip magazines were offering money for her and she became famous, very wealthy, and very, very happy.

Moral: Don't get it right, get it written.

The Ostrich and the Inchworm
David Zoll

An ostrich jeered at an inchworm for the slowness of his pace. But the inchworm laughed and said he would race against her and beat her any day. "Come on," said the ostrich, "you will soon see what my feet are made of." So it was agreed that they would start at once. The inchworm went at his usual steady pace, but the ostrich was so sure of herself she got distracted easily and accidentally kicked the inchworm one inch from the finish line. The inchworm won the race by a worm's length.

Moral: Slow and steady may win the race, but getting kicked can sure help.

The Beaver and the Frog
Paul Satti

There once was a frog who was invited to a birthday party for his friend Beaver. When the frog arrived at the party, he rang the bell. "Ring."

Beaver answered the door. Frog said, "Hi, Beav" and extended his hand to shake. When Beaver shook Frog's hand, he received a shock from a buzzer.

Well, Beaver got angry and told his dad. When Mr. Beaver found out, he took Frog home.

When they came to the door, Mr. Beaver rang the bell, Mr. Frog answered the door. "Hi, Mr. Frog. Your son scared my son at the party, so I'm bringing him home," said Mr. Beaver.

Mr. Frog said to his son, "Shame on you, son. Thank you, Mr. Beaver, for bringing him home." He extended his hand to shake. But when Mr. Beaver shook Mr. Frog's hand he was shocked by the same buzzing jolt.

Moral: Like father, like son.

The Making of a Proverb
Jamar Brown

Times were hard, and Ez had discovered that working for a wage provided just a little less money than he needed to get by. Although his needs were simple, Ez yearned for a business of his own and earnings enough for him to consider a wife and family. A stroke of bad luck for a seldom-seen uncle— dying—became a bit of good fortune for Ez. The uncle's will left Ez a small house on several acres in the country and a few hundred dollars. Although raised in town, Ez saw his future on the farm.

Ez bought two hundred fowl, an incubator and a lot of chicken feed. Ez converted a shed to a chicken coop and settled in his chickens. He had obtained the incubator so that the chickens wouldn't waste time brooding their own eggs. "No sense having them sit around on the job for a few weeks when they could be laying more eggs," Ez explained. Ez could see a future farm with thousands, tens of thousands of chickens.

The chickens started producing eggs right away and Ez rushed them to the incubator. Deprived of their eggs, the chickens obligingly produced more. Pretty soon the incubator was almost filled. After three weeks Ez was piling eggs one on top of another. Still nothing had hatched. In a month many of the eggs began to spoil, and the smell of rotten eggs filled the air.

Alarmed, Ez called in the veterinarian. Since none of the eggs had hatched, the source of the problem seemed obvious to the vet. "Let me take a look at your rooster," he said. "It may be sick or too old, or—."

"Rooster," Ez interrupted. "What rooster?"

Moral: Don't count your chickens before they are hatched.

Plays

Duolog

Make up a conversation between two people that runs for several minutes if actually spoken aloud. Write the name of the speaker in the left margin, put a colon after it, then write down what he or she says. Do the same each time one of them speaks. Give the duolog a title that catches the main action or relationship. If the place and physical action can't be made clear in the speech itself without awkwardness, state these briefly in parentheses at appropriate points. (Looking at a play script will show you a standard form.)

Direct two people in a rehearsal of your script so that they can do a good reading of it for the class or another group. Make changes if rehearsals show a need for improvement. Include it in a collection of plays that others can read or perform.

Top That
Randall Peterson

A: Hi ... I'm John.

B: I'm Frank. Glad to meet you.

A: Man, I hate these flights!

B: Headed for Phoenix?

A: Yep. Going to visit an old army buddy.

B: Really? I was in the army once ... worst experience of my life. I don't know where they got those cooks, but was that food ever bad. I was always going hungry. I remember this time when a guy put a plastic vomit on his tray at the cafeteria. They charged him a quarter for it, too!

A: That sounds pretty bad. Our food was really quite good. You could have as much as ya wanted. Did they ever know how to whip up a feast!

B: Boy, did I ever get stuck at the wrong base. It was a desert down there. One day it was well over a hundred and they made us go on a hike with full gear. We had guys dropping like flies. But I suppose you had it lucky.

A: I sure did. It was practically tropical compared to my farm. The winters were so mild that we would sneak out at night and go swimming in the creek. You could get a great tan in the summer, too. The hikes *we* went on were only about as far as to my mailbox and back at home.

B: Our barracks were terrible. I was less cramped in my bathroom at home. We had eight guys in one room once. What a pain! There were smelly socks and T-shirts strewn everywhere. It sure makes work in the stock market seem easy.

A: My base was great. Our commanders were a riot. One day we were camping way up in the hills. In the middle of the night our commanders woke all of us up except one guy. We packed everything up and left him there. He could have died when he woke up. We had a great time with those commanders.

B: My commander was terrible. You couldn't get away with anything. He made us do calisthenics until we dropped. My base had no recreation at all. My college fraternity had parties all the time. When I got into the army, I couldn't believe it. There was nothing to do.

A: One thing I can say for my base is that they sure know how to entertain ya. They had a pool, bowling, movies every Friday, and a dance once a month. Yep ... times in Yuma were really great.

B: Yuma?!? You're kidding.... That's where I was.

The Smuggler
Katie Baldwin

(Two characters—a young man and an old man. The old man is sitting in a small room looking out over a bay. The young man knocks at the door and enters.

YM: Greetings, Uncle, I am most happy that you agreed to let me come to you for a little chat before I leave for my studies in North America.

OM: Sit down, young one, sit down and be peaceful in the company of an old man.

YM: Uncle, to me you will always be wise but never old. I wish I could have been an eighth as smart as you and have as much success in my life as you've had in yours.

OM: I've made mistakes in my time, don't you think I haven't.

YM: *(Interrupting.)* Oh, but it seems as if everything you have touched has always turned into gold. You went to New York to study when you were very young. That is what started you off to what you have become in your life.

OM: *(Shaking his head, to himself.)* All fools are young men. *(To YM.)* That first trip started me off all right but not the way you think.

YM: Oh, please tell me—I need your approval. I mean I have a real chance to make some money. *(He hesitates.)* You know Henry? He has a scheme—.

OM: *(Shouting, interrupts.)* No! Stay away from Henry!

YM: But Uncle, it's so easy.

(Old man gets to his feet and stomps his cane on the ground.)

OM: Now, I'm going to tell you how I was young as you are and how only by the grace of God I escaped my own stupidity. I too was poor and wanted to have a lot of money in my pocket so that when I was not studying I would have enough money to have a good time in the big city.

YM: Tell me. Tell me.

OM: We had nothing. My family was very poor. My father worked in the field, and my mother scrubbed floors to help give food to us children. I was the really bright one of the family, so when a representative from the government came to give a high school scholarship I was chosen. I did well, and then I was asked if I would like to go to college in New York. They would provide all the necessities—a place to stay, books. They would even give me winter clothing for the cold harsh winters in the city.

YM: You were so lucky like I have been myself, but I don't have all the patience that you had studying and working and saving for all those years. . . . I want—.

OM: That wasn't really my choice. I also wanted big cars, and I didn't want to wait for them.

YM: That's what I wanted to talk to you about—Henry knows a way.

OM: Listen to me first if you respect me.

YM: Yes, I will.

OM: I once had a friend just like your Henry. He told me that I could take diamonds into America. Buy them cheap here from someone he knew and then take them into America without saying anything and then sell them for a lot of money.

YM: Oh my God!

OM: I was foolish enough to take his advice. I took all the clothes the Americans had sent me and all the money I had saved up over the years. Anyway, I took it all to the diamond merchant and took off with my treasure sewn into the lining of my jacket.

YM: You were wonderful! Oh how smart you were—it's just like—.

OM: Listen, you idiot! I got to the customs line and I was very nervous, to say the least. I saw that every tenth person was being called aside and taken into a small room . . . and sure enough, they called me in.

YM: My God! My God!

OM: They took off my jacket and trousers and left me sitting there for a time which seemed like forever. I was scared to think about getting caught and having to spend my life in jail. All my hopes of having big fancy cars and living in luxury went down the drain. Just as I was about to jump out the window and put an end to it all, the customs officer came in and told me that I could go. I couldn't believe it! How come they hadn't found the diamonds! Just as I was about to leave, the customs officer looked up from his desk and asked me why I had pieces of glass sewn into the lining of my jacket.

YM: And was it glass, Uncle?

OM: Yes, I'd been robbed and saved at the same time. If my friend hadn't cheated me—.

YM: You'd have been in prison!

OM: Yes, and if I hadn't been so greedy I would have had a warm coat that first winter in New York where I almost died of cold and loneliness.

YM: But you survived.

OM: And I never again tried to be smart like that again, if you can call that smart. And nephew, what scheme was that you wanted me to approve?

YM: It was nothing, Uncle, nothing. You have answered my questions. Thank you—for all your help.

A Word with Freddy
Erik Levy

NARRATOR: One night, I was sleeping. It was a night before I had a test. Suddenly I heard a voice.

FREDDY: Erik ... Psst ... Psst. Wake up!

ERIK: Who is it?

FREDDY: It's me, Freddy, your hamster.

ERIK: Stop playing around, Serge. (*Who is my brother.*)

FREDDY: It's really me.

ERIK: I'll turn on the light and see. (*Getting out of bed.*)

FREDDY: All right, you'll see.

ERIK: Oh, my God, it really is you. How ... how are you talking? (*I was shivering because it was cold.*)

FREDDY: My fairy godmother came and gave me three wishes. And I said, "I wish I could talk, I wish I was stronger than my owner, and I wish that it would snow."

ERIK: I still don't believe it.

FREDDY: Believe it or not, I really am talking.

ERIK: Why did you want to talk to me?

FREDDY: Okay, I'll tell you. I want you to treat me better, or I'll beat you up.

ERIK: Ha, Ha, Ha. (*I started cracking up.*)

FREDDY: Don't forget that I am stronger than you.

ERIK: What kind of treatment do you want?

FREDDY: I want you to clean my cage twice a week, change my water twice a day, and get me a mate. I saw this hot hamster the other day at the pet store.

ERIK: How did you get to the pet store?

FREDDY: My fairy godmother took me there.

ERIK: I'll do my best.

FREDDY: You'd better.

ERIK: Now since you can talk, let me ask you some questions. How do you feel being a hamster? I mean, would you like to be a human or a hamster?

FREDDY: I really don't know, since I've been a hamster all my life, even though talking is coming pretty close to being a human.

ERIK: Does being in a cage bother you? Do you feel that you are confined in your cage?

FREDDY: You must remember that I am about a hundred times smaller than you. That means that your room should be about seventy-five times bigger than my cage.

ERIK: That is a very good answer. You would probably do well in my class.

FREDDY: Surely better than you.

ERIK: Shut up, or I will never clean your cage, Freddy.

FREDDY: Remember those four wishes. You know I love you a lot. I don't mean to be mean to you, Erik.

ERIK: I understand.

FREDDY: Were there any hamsters before me?

ERIK: Yes, there were. I tell you there were two before you. I'll tell you about them. The first was Frederick the First. I loved him. He lived for about three and a half years. You would have liked him. He was brown and had a little white ring around his neck. Frederick the Second was a disaster. She was frantic. She escaped.

FREDDY: Do you know which way she went? I'd like to meet her.

ERIK: I don't think it would be a good idea. I think you might find her in an unpleasant condition. She might be dead.

Let me tell you a few things about New York. The subways are very dirty. There are bums all around the place. The subways are unsafe and filthy. I try to ride them as little as I can. I have never taken you on one.

FREDDY: That is very interesting. I hope I never get to go on one.

ERIK: Let me tell you about the World Trade Centers. The World Trade Centers are these twin beautiful tall buildings. I do not know whether you would like it up there, because it is very scary when you look down.

ERIK: Okay, let's talk about the past and about all the good times and the bad times we have had together. Do you remember the time when I took you down to the pet store because you had a bad cut on your leg? The lady at the pet store told me to try to cut off your scab, but you wouldn't let me. So my mother had to take you to a vet. He gave you some medicine and you got better in about two weeks. Now there is no mark of it.

FREDDY: Yes, I do remember that. I hope I will never cut my leg again.

ERIK: I am sorry about what I did to you the other night. If you do not remember, I made a sound right above your cage and you jumped up and fell off your wheel.

FREDDY: Yes, I do remember that. I felt like biting you. You rat!

ERIK: I am sorry, Freddy, but you are the rat, I mean, the rodent.

FREDDY: Okay, okay, you win.

ERIK: Hey, you know, Fred, I have a test tomorrow and I want to get some sleep. You know, I have been up about forty-five minutes.

FREDDY: Don't worry. I have everything taken care of. Look outside. It's snowing.

ERIK: (*Now I walk over to the window.*) I don't believe it. There must be about a foot of snow out there. That means I don't have to go to school tomorrow, and that means no test. Now I see why you wished for snow. The only thing we have not gotten to talk about is the girl hamster. I will try to go tomorrow to bring her back from the pet store even though it is snowing hard.

ERIK: School or no school tomorrow, I think I should go to bed. See you in the morning.

Dialog for Three or More

Set down in script form what three or more characters say to each other during one continuous scene running for 6 to 20 minutes that develops to some sort of climax. It is better to try this after doing Duolog at least once. If your script is for film, look at a film script for terms and directions indicating camera angles and actions. If for radio or audiotape, where visuals are missing, you might use "stage directions" to indicate how lines should be read. But rely for this mainly on the way lines are written and punctuated.

If possible, have this script performed, filmed, or taped. A Readers' Theater presentation is often a simple and appropriate way to perform a script essentially depending on voice, since it requires no memorization, costumes, or staging.

Pleasing Susan
Tracy Cooper

SAM: Peter, we are friends, right?

PETER: Sure, Sam, why?

SAM: You know I like Susan, right?

PETER: Yeah sure, will you just get on with it!

SAM: Okay, well I like Susan, but Susan doesn't like me. What should I do?

PETER: Well, are you polite?

SAM: Yeah! Sure!

PETER: Can I ask you a question, Sam?

SAM: Sure, what?

PETER: I don't want to sound offensive, but why do you like Susan? I mean she is really *obnoxious.*

SAM: No, she is not. She is so pretty, here eyes are like clear pools!

PETER: If you don't mind me saying so, her eyes are more like swamps!

SAM: Swamps! How can you say something like that. I thought we were friends!

PETER: All right, it's your taste, anyway. Let's get on with it. I'm sorry.

SAM: That's better! Now what should I do?

PETER: Let me think now! *(Long pause.)* I got it! I can go up to her, insult her and you'll defend her. That always works. Come on.

SAM: Okay.

PETER: Hey, Susan, your eyes are so ugly that they turn people to stone!!!

SAM: You shut up, Peter, look at who's talking.

SUSAN: No, *you* shut up, Sam. I can fight my own battles, and besides I like men with power. *(Susan exits.)*

SAM: This will never work! *(Puts hand over eyes.)*

PETER: If she likes men with power, we'll switch it around.

SAM: What do you mean?

PETER: What I mean is that we will go up to her and you insult and I defend her.

SAM: Oh, that won't work. My life is over. *(Shakes head.)*

PETER: You're only *14.* Besides we have no other choice.

SAM: Oh all right.

PETER: Come on, before homeroom starts. *(Susan enters.)*

SAM: Hey Susan!

SUSAN: What?

SAM: You're so, *so, so, so, so* beautiful. *(Peter grabs him and pulls him over to the side.)*

PETER: What in the world are you doing?

SAM: Peter, I can't insult her, I like her too much!

PETER: Will ya' just fake it. Say, well, I got it: think like you're talking to Mary. You hate her.

SAM: All right.

PETER: Okay, let's try this again. *(They go up to Susan.)*

SAM: Susan, your hair always looks like a mop, like you *never ever* wash it!!!

PETER: Well, Sam, yours isn't so great either.

SUSAN: Yeah, Sam. Thanks for defending me, Peter. Bye.

(She starts to walk away when Sam jumps in front of her and yells.)

SAM: Listen, Susan, I've been trying to get you to like me for a long time now, and I'm sick of you being obnoxious to me. It seems you don't even care about me. Well, fine, I don't care any more. Come on, Peter, let's go. *(Starts to walk away.)*

SUSAN: Sam, I never knew you had so much guts, you made me realize how
　　　much I ignore you. I'm really sorry. How would you like to do something
　　　after school?

SAM: *(In shock.)* Sure, why not. Meet ya outside.

SUSAN: Okay. Bye. *(Susan exits.)*

PETER: That's great, Sam! She likes you, and I can't believe she has even
　　　changed a little bit.

SAM: Thank you, Peter, I couldn't have done it without you.

Exterior Monolog

*Make up a character whose way of speaking you feel confident
you can imitate. Imagine him or her telling something to
another person in a certain place. Write down only what the
character says and nothing more except brief stage directions
to indicate setting and action. To be performed in a playing
time of 2 to 5 minutes. Such a monolog calls for a situation in
which one person is speaking while another or others merely
listen and react without words. What you want to accomplish
depends on how you see such a situation being used. Consider
different media too.*

　　*For a more challenging version of this task, write your script
for pure voice—no visuals, no sound effects.*

Terri's Predicament
Jennifer Stuart

　　Beth, I'm so excited that Bret asked me to the spring prom, I can hardly
believe it. It's incredible. What a life dream! An "A" student, captain of the
football team, and every girl's heart-throb! Gosh, Beth, what will I wear?
Maybe my baby blue dress?? Noooo. That's not right for a prom. Have to get a
new dress, I guess. I'll *have* to have my seamstress fit a gown to my size. I
think I'll get a new hairstyle, change my makeup and, oh dear, Beth! Maybe I
won't change my makeup or hairstyle because what if he asked me *because* he
liked my hair and makeup? What will Candy say? She'll hate me for life! She
was sure Bret Oscar was going to ask *her* to the spring prom. Well, I'll show
her that he likes me best! Boy, will this be a shock for the school. Terri
Johnson is going to the prom with Bret Oscar. Don't those names go well
together?

　　Well at least *I* think so! I feel as light as a cloud, like I'm floating in the air. I feel so dreamy and delightful. I can't wait 'til the prom. We'll look so elegant together! I think it will be awesome. Where will we eat? Maybe the Stockyard? Or the August Lion? Who knows? We'll look so fine getting out of his white Mercedes, me in my gown and Bret in a tuxedo. Well, gotta go, Beth. Time to brush my hair 100 times! Bye!

A.A. Speaker for Today
Marisa Raphael

My family always drank a lot, especially my father. We had our own vineyard so there was never a shortage of wine in the house. My father, he would come home from a hard day at work and he would go straight for a drink. Almost always he would over-drink, and when he did he lost all control. He would throw things, scream and yell and once he . . . oh God . . . he beat up my brother. I'll never forget that night. My father came home later than usual and had an especially large amount of wine and got completely drunk. He started to yell at Mama really loudly, and me and my brothers and sisters couldn't fall asleep. I remember hiding under my bed because I was so scared. After my oldest brother, Renzo, saw us so frightened and hearing Papa yell at Mama for no reason he just had it. He went crazy. He ran downstairs and started yelling at Papa and said how he didn't care about us and that he was a stupid drunk. Papa became so mad he stood up and hit Renzo so hard he fell to the floor. Renzo started yelling with pain, but Papa ignored him and let him just lie there. Mama began to cry, but Papa just told her to shut up. I cried that night, I cried so hard I thought I'd never stop. After that night I never went near Papa. Now that my father is dead I regret making him feel like I hated him. Poor Papa . . . if only he knew how much I loved him. But he's dead; stone dead.

Then one day my two best friends came over. My family was out—some kind of outing to the city—and we were feeling adventurous. We were looking to try something new we'd never tried. We decided on Papa's wine. I was a little reluctant seeing what it did to Papa, but I didn't want to be a party pooper. I poured us a whole glass each. It was hard at first to drink, but when we got used to it it became fun. It became a regular activity, and it was sort of like a club. It started to affect my grades, and I would get constant cravings for wine even when my family was home.

We had to move to America, the land of the free, because Papa got a better job there that paid more. I had to readjust and make new friends, which I succeeded to do. My new friends also drank and I continued drinking . . . actually even a little heavier than I did in Italy. My parents started to notice something different about me. Then one day when I was 15 their suspicions were confirmed. I came home from a party and I was totally drunk. Mama and Papa were furious and mainly confused. I felt so guilty, and I lied and said that it was my first time and my last. Although they had minor doubts they believed me, which is probably the worst punishment I could get. Maybe if they had opened their eyes a little more I wouldn't be still drinking today. But they kept them closed because they didn't want to face facts . . . and you can see the results.

I've had several boyfriends and friends who have tried to get me to stop, but I just can't.

One night I came home and I said to myself this is ridiculous, I'm ruining my life, and I vowed to myself never to drink another drop of alcohol again. That night was one of the longest nights of my life. I tried, I never tried so hard, but I just couldn't stand it any more and ended up drinking a whole bottle. That's why I'm here right now. To put my life back together and never to take a drink again.

The Old, the Lonely, the Only
Kiebpoli Calnek

Today is pretty chilly, huh? Colder than yesterday. Don't let it ruffle your feathers, though, I don't mind and you're losing your body heat.

I was thinking about Langston Hughes this morning. No, he's not my husband, God rest his soul, but the poet Langston Hughes. I remember a poem that I used to love. A poem that I thought was fun to read, fun to memorize, fun to act out, but *not* fun to live. You want to know what it was called? Yeah? Well, it was called "Vagabonds." Vagabonds. I still remember it. "We are the desperate who do not care, the hungry who have nowhere to eat, no place to sleep, the tearless who cannot weep." He was my favorite poet for the one reason that whatever he wrote was *true!* and really happened to people. People were evil, people shouted, prayed, hoped and . . . and were vagabonds. I hear that poem and look at myself. Am I vagabond? A vagabond? Vagabond? A vag-a-bond? How can that be? Vagabond? Vagabonds are people who are dirty and slobber all over themselves. I have nowhere to eat and sleep, but how can I be called a vagabond?

What happened? What happened to me? Where did my life escape to? Actually where, no, *when* did it slip away from me? Right under my feet also (humph). After the movie "Bye, Bye, Baby" my life, my marriage, and my career went kaput. I mean I was a very good wife and actress, but where did I go wrong?

My husband should be here. He should be here to help me get through this time in my life. Oh, Shug, I wish you were here. I wish you were here! To share my pain and misery. You left me. You *left* me! You left me. I am alone and cannot weep. I admit defeat! *(Sarcastic.)* Aha! but I do not. I am alive and have my life ahead of me. I am at my prime of my life. I am semi-healthy and have a warm coat on my back. Come on, Mamie, come on, Mamie. Who am I kidding. There is no one here to help me or to save me. Help me? Save me? From what, that is the question. Pigeons, who is saving you? I know, humans. They feed you bread crumbs. I am definitely *not* going to pick food off of the ground. No offense to you of course. Where are *my* humane humans? Who is to care for me? I can act, dammit! I do a good job. Then why am I on the streets of New York with no one to come home to or a home to go to? I have no place to sleep. No place to eat. Pigeons, where do you sleep?

Isn't this the year 2000, or at least close? This is the hi-tech age. You know, with all them computers and robots taking over the world. Where's my robot? My robot to take care of me? Someone or something to sooth me and to make my world a better place to live in. No one, I have no one! No one! Not even a damn robot. Not even a robot to take care of me. What happened? I'm at my prime and I have no one. No one to love and no one to love me back. I am one of the fearless, the homeless, the careless, and the tearless who cannot sleep nor weep. I can't even weep.

Interior Monolog

Make up a character whose way of thinking and speaking you feel confident of imitating. Imagine him or her in some specific setting doing something in particular. Write down what the person is thinking and feeling in the exact words the person would use. Employ interior monolog for what you think it can best do. To be performed in a playing time of 3 to 5 minutes. What media would be best for your script? Write directions accordingly. Or write the script without any directions at all.

Paying Attention
Vanessa Moore

Here I am in my classroom, sitting in a chair full of splinters that are prickling my *!##. Now I'm getting hot. I think I better take off my jacket. Naw, I don't feel like walking over to the closet. Damn, now my stomach is starting to growl. I knew I should have eaten a piece of toast this morning like my father told me to, but I didn't have the time. I hope I can make it through to lunch—oh that's right, I have a Butterfinger in my bag. Naw, I better not touch it, because I know at least half of my classmates are going to ask for a piece. They should know it's only one candy bar!

Damn, this chair is still prickling my #*!#! If I try to take the splinters out, people might think I'm scratching, so I'll just suffer until the period is over.

I thought really the shade of this room should be blue, so it can represent Harbor, but what can you expect when you are in the basement?

This fingernail polish is no good; it chips right off, but what can you argue about for a 49¢ jar?

Now Loretta could have done something better with her hair than to throw a raggedy old scarf on her head. I realize she just came back from camp, but she could have fixed it up. And Jackie—she could have done something better with hers too than putting country plaits in it. She looks foolish. One day I'm going to put a hurting on her hair.

Is anybody ever going to fix that light? It really distracts me. When I look at the board, there's a dink, dink, dink of the light. One day I'm going to fix that light, right after I finish with Jackie's hair.

Rehearsing the Big One
Greg Fox

"Listen, Mom, take it easy." No, that's too forceful. "Mom, please, I don't want you to feel bad—" Yeah, this is better. "Just because I want to go away to boarding school doesn't mean I don't love you and Dad. I just feel that it's time for a change."

And then she'll probably say, "A change for what?" and I'll answer, "A change for the better, a chance to be independent, a chance to go live in a different environment, a chance to get in with the better crowd."

And she'll say, "What do you mean? We're not good enough for you? The kids that you've been hanging around with for the last five years like Walker, Jason, Ben, and all the rest—you're too good for them now?"

And I'll say, "Mom, please understand. It's not that I feel that I'm better than them or anything, it's just that I feel that making new friends can't hurt. OK, so maybe they're rich, that can't hurt."

And then my mom'll say to me, "Oh yeah, what about John? You remember John, don't you?" And I'll say, "Yes, I remember John went to boarding school and came back four years later talking like the rest of those rich so-and-so's and looking down at everybody, but, Mom, I promise I won't become like that, and the school isn't only full of rich snobs."

And she'll say, "Yeah, sure you won't come back like them. That's what John said, and look what happened to him."

And I'll say, "Look, I promise to write every day and come home every other weekend when I get a chance," and she'll start to cry and Dad'll shake my hand and say that I've really grown up and start talking to my mom and telling her it's not so bad, and my mom'll start saying, "Why, why is my baby leaving home?"

Uh-oh, here come my mom and dad. I hope this speech is as good as I think it is and works.

A Few Minutes with a Lonely Housewife
Liz Stember

Oh how lonely I am! Well, let's see what's on television today. (*Click.*) Oh, great—*Dream House!* Wow, it's already 11:30. Okay, now what's the question? Hmmmm. No, you jerk, the answer's fake! Told ya so! Oh, well (*Click.*) forget it. I'm not doomed to a day of soaps! I'm going to do something with my life! I won't stand to be categorized as a stupid suburban housewife!

But what's exciting to do here in New Rochelle? It's too early for the movies, Erma's in Palm Springs this week, and Harry's at work! I'm not used to this; when my daughter was home I was never bored like this! Only now she's away at college. Jill! That's it! I'll clean out Jill's room for her next visit home in four months. Oh, well, it's better than a day of seeing if Marcie goes for Jack or his illegitimate son! Well, it'll be fun. I'll bring back all those golden moments of yesteryear! Oh, God, I'm beginning to sound like a suburban mother now!

Huf-huf-huf. I wonder how Jill could climb all these stairs to her attic room every day? EEEK! A spider. I keep forgetting she's been away so long. Well, where should I start? How about her toy chest? That should be a real tear-jerker. Hmmmm! I wonder who that poster is of. There's three guys, one with tiny round glasses on. He's Sting? Why would a mother name her baby "Sting"? Yup, and the name of them is "The Police." And how about that poster with the five snappily dressed men on it—and the one in the middle with the big nose with lipstick prints on his face? Oh God, Jill—what have you done?

And oh no, who's that trampy woman in that rag dress? Pat Benetar— "Love Is A Battle Field"? That's right! I found that out at my senior prom. My school girl crush—Mark Bellinger. And you know what he did to me? He made a dumb crack about my date (who incidentally *was* a dip). But I still thought he was super.... Anyway, onward march to the Battle of the Childhood memories. (Oh, brother, I'm in a sappy mood today!) Well, let's see what we have here in this trunk of junk. Oh, what's this? What in the world *are* these silly little things? Well let's try and remember....

Oh, yes, it was I believe in the third grade—Jill and her so-called friend, Dinah. (*Angrily.*) They were playing one day in her yard with these Polish balls and Dinah ... Dinah ... hit Jill in the eye and she needed three stitches! I never much liked that Dinah anyway. *OOOOOH!* I was sooo mad! But let's see, how did they do these things? (*Tock-tock-tock-tock.*) Hey, I've got it! Oh no, not the china base lamp! (*Crash.*) Ah-hah, these are called Kerbangers. Now I know why! Ohhhhh-he! Now, this is great fun. I had one of these when I was a teenager too! THE SACRED HULA HOOP! Oh, God, is this embarrassing or what? All right, here we go, now, first around the waist! Ha! I can still do it! What else did Betsey Radman and I used to show off to Sam and Jason? Oh, of course—jumprope/hoop—neck, arms switching, legs, and feet. Let's try the neck—this was always my worst one.... Aaaaaakk! I haven't gotten a stronger neck in all these years? That's disgraceful! Okay, well, let's try the arms—this was always my best trick ... one, two, three, and a—Hey—Hey! I can still do it! But can I still switch arms? Yes! (*Really excitedly.*) Everyone, look at me! Erma, Harry, Jill, Betsey—*everyone!* Look at me—I'm still young at heart! Whoo. I should be on *60 Minutes*. I'd be titled: ''A Few Minutes with a Suburban Housewife/Hula-Hula Champ!'' Oh, it'd be super.

Um, well, what else do we have here? Oh, some old finger paintings of Jill's when she was three—they remind me of those psychiatrists' ink blots. Hey, I remember these, she ruined my best house dress. Anyway, let's see what else she's got stashed away in here. Hmmmm. Twister. What the ... Twister? Well, let's see what to do. It says here to spin the dial and—oh, I remember! Sure, Twister! We played this dumb game for hours at Mary Lou Shackmer's second-grade slumber party! Well, I may still be the hula hoop champ, but can my stiff joints still twist enough for Twister? Let's try it out. All right, left-hand purple. PURPLE? I was sure the only colors were yellow, red, blue, and green. Could it be a new edition? No, not by the look of it.

Well, it's probably left-hand BLUE, only this game is so old it's faded to a purplish color. Geez, if this game is that old, and I bought it for Jill when she was just seven, then that means I'm—! Humph! What else is there in here for me to remember? Hey, what's that dusty old red disc over there? Oh, it's a frisbee. Well, now let's see here, I used to be a really, really terrible frisbee-er. I guess all those lessons from that awful George McKenzy never paid off. But what can you expect from a nine-year-old boy being paid in marbles and chocolate bars? Anyway, let's try it out. Aaaaaggg! Not the china glass collectables of Jill's! (*Crash.*) Oh, no, she always treasured those, especially since Johnny Firstons (that jerk) gave them to her. It was sweet of him, but.... Oh, well, I'll just break the news to Jill in a letter, but not now—I'm having too much fun looking through all her old toys.

What? An F on a Latin test? I wonder why she never told me about that? Oh, well, what's this? A skateboard, great! I always could be seen on Park Hill Avenue, cruising on down with Marie and Tammy to the 7-11. Now, if I can't do this right, I'll kill myself.

No more. I'll sentence myself to an hour of game shows to keep out of trouble. Uh, oh, why did I say that? I haven't been on one of these since I don't know when! Oh, well. Wheeeeeeeee! This is super. Aak, not the desk! (*Crash.*) Better get out of here before I kill myself. Okay, *Dream House*, here I come.

One-Act Play

Write a script for live performance or videotaping that has several characters, lasts 20-30 minutes, and takes place in no more than three or four scenes. (Each scene is a different time and perhaps different place.) Remember that the story has to come across in what the characters say and do before our eyes. There is no storyteller to inform the audience of what it cannot see and hear for itself. Stage directions can say only how to stage the play, that is, describe physical setting and action. Directions for filming indicate angles and distance of shots and other instructions for the camera.

Arrange with your teacher or other adults to perform your play live or on film. Rewrite as needed during rehearsals. A performance can be a rehearsed reading only, in the manner of Readers' Theater, which doesn't require memorization of lines and full staging.

(For fantasy, you might try a one-act radio play or a film script meant for animation.)

Pan, Lead the Way
Nava Fader

Scene One
(Jessica's bedroom.)

RACHEL: "I drink their blood, I love blood!"

JESSICA: Dracula?

RACHEL: No stupid, *Charlotte's Web.*

JESSICA: Oh right! And speaking of nourishment I was wondering if you want any munchies.

RACHEL: "Munchies?" You mean *food!* Talk about creative! But sure, bring on the "munchies."

(Jessica ducks head down under bed and produces a bag of Ruffles Sour Cream and Onion Chips.)

JESSICA: Catch.

RACHEL: *(Begins to open bag.)* There's always so much air in these, in the top I mean. It makes me mad, I feel like I'm being cheated.

JESSICA: Yes, I'm sure Mr. Ruffles says to himself, knowing of course that it tears soul from body to see this kind of packaging—"I will do this just to annoy Rachel." And then I, of course, buy them to watch you suffer —Hey!

(Jessica gets smacked in the head by a pillow thrown by Rachel. Throws it back.)

RACHEL: "Content you in my discontent."

JESSICA: Not over sour cream and onion anyway. But can it be that you are trying to beat me at my own game? You refer to *The Taming of The Shrew*, these words spoken by *(Getting an Italian accent.)* Bianca, the sweet and beautiful.

RACHEL: Very good. To quote señor, muy bien. *(Pause.)* You know, I was thinking that no one else but you would know that. And if I wasn't with you I probably wouldn't think of it either. I don't think of books so much when I'm not with you. And it's funny, not funny *Ha, Ha,* funny weird. Most people read all the same books and they don't know or remember at all what's in them. It's kind of embarrassing if when I quote or say something from a book no one knows what I'm talking about.

JESSICA: *(Nods.)* Just a couple of days ago I said to Claire (you know how obsessed she is about her face), "And Pauline's still got a pimple on her nose," and she looked at me like I was crazy

RACHEL: That's from *Ballet Shoes,* right?

JESSICA: Right. *(Pause.)*

RACHEL: Did you see that movie with umm ... what'shisname, umm ... I can't think of it.

JESSICA: I don't know either.

RACHEL: It was horrible. Not horrible bad, but horrible sad, and scary. The government was controlling everything, even what the people read. People had to memorize books because they were prohibited.

JESSICA: Yuck! If you had to, what book would you memorize?

RACHEL: I wouldn't ever want to have to make that choice.

JESSICA: But if you had to.

RACHEL: I guess a classic, *Alice in Wonderland* or *Heidi* maybe.

JESSICA: Alice says, "I give myself very good advice but I very seldom follow it." How much do you remember from *Heidi?* Then we can see how much you have to learn.

RACHEL: All I remember is, "'Tis the mountain air that succeeds when the cook fails." How about you? What would you memorize?

JESSICA: Hmmm ... *(Looks up.)* You're getting crumbs on my bed.

RACHEL: Sorry.

JESSICA: I don't know. I guess it would have to be a book that contains all sorts of different characteristics. Happy, sad, for all the different moods I get into. Maybe I could memorize a book of poetry.

RACHEL: But who would the poet be? You'd get bored with only one kind of style.

JESSICA: I'd have an anthology, a huge collection.

RACHEL: You still might get bored.

JESSICA: I don't think so. With different points of view, as you grow older the same poem takes on new significance. Because of your own experiences—.

RACHEL: Or because growing older has made you much wiser.

JESSICA: But it doesn't always happen that way.

RACHEL: No, but you always learn something from literature. Even if you don't realize it. Something registers in your mind. *(Thinking aloud.)* I guess that's why people want certain books to be banned. They're afraid we'll learn something, even if it isn't prominent, that they don't want us to know.

JESSICA: That's really scary! It seems then that someone could be brainwashing us just by putting a poster up or saying something on TV.

RACHEL: What if someone wrote something which gave forth a thought that he didn't intend to be there?

JESSICA: Then he would learn from his work as well as others who read it.

RACHEL: Have you ever written anything you've learned from?

JESSICA: Uh-huh. When I write a poem sometimes I put in a line because it sounds good or it rhymes. And then when I read it over it really makes sense. And I didn't think of it like that before.

RACHEL: Do you feel like spouting any poetry right now? Not too profound please, this topic is getting a little too heavy for me.

JESSICA: Taking the easy way out? But OK. Which would you prefer, own or otherwise?

RACHEL: Oh "own," undoubtedly "own!"

JESSICA: *(Dramatically.)* Ahem.

One day I came upon the sea and wanted to walk along the seaside.
The scent of salt filled my nose, I saw the dancing, turbulent tide.
I knew that I was just a wave to clear the path for more
And when I left it, it would be just as it was before.
The gulls flying overhead spoke to me and they said,
"See the waves slap on the shore, they smooth it down, make room for more.
Tell your tale to the ocean's roar, then continue on your way."
And so before I left, I silently smoothed down the shore
And then it was indeed, just as it was before.

(Pause. Then Rachel softly breaks the silence.)

RACHEL: That was great. You know, it sounds just like the last line of *Moby Dick.*

JESSICA: Does it? I didn't know you read *Moby Dick.*

RACHAL: I didn't. I only know the first and last lines. "Call me Ishmael," and "... and the great shroud of the sea rolled on as it rolled 5000 years ago." That says also how nothing is really altered by what man has done. We're so unimportant.

JESSICA: *(Jokingly.)* Speak for yourself! But who's getting into heavy discussion now?

RACHEL: Whoops! *(Looks at watch.)* Hey, it's late. I have to go. Bye!

JESSICA: A bit of culture m'dear, adios!

RACHEL: And for you, au revoir!

Scene Two
(Jessica's bedroom.)

RACHEL: I don't believe it!

JESSICA: You said that already.

RACHEL: I know but this is crazy! and we were talking about banned books just yesterday. But I thought that books were banned only because they present an idea like a cult, favoring one, or if a book is pornographic. What's in *The Catcher in the Rye* that makes it a candidate for being banned? And who decides if it is one?

JESSICA: Well, I read *The Catcher in the Rye* for English, and it presents some very strong opinions. But I don't see why people have the right to ban it. As for who decides what is to be banned, I hate them, whoever they are. It doesn't matter. We have to do something to stop them.

RACHEL: But maybe they know something we don't. I'm not saying they're right or excusing them, but how can we protest if we're not sure of what's going on?

JESSICA: That's not the point. As Rush Melendy of the *Four Story Mistake* says, "It's the principle of the thing." It's the idea that the government, the Board of Education, the PTA, or whatever can take a person's opinions away from society. That's unfair.

RACHEL: If they don't want an impression made that's definitely the wrong way to do it. Making it hard to get or prohibited just arouses curiosity. Maybe people will read it now who never thought of reading it before.

JESSICA: I think it will only be removed from school and public libraries, but who knows what else they'll do. Meanwhile, we have to do something.

RACHEL: *(Reluctantly.)* Yeah, I guess we have to. Posters and stuff, petitions.

JESSICA: *(Makes a face.)* I was thinking more of a demonstration at the school library. Saturday. We'd have three days to plan it out. Someone could make a speech and then very, very dramatically we could rescue all books that might be threatened by these fiends in the future. It's all very simple.

RACHEL: You're out of your mind. That's what's simple, you're crazy! What are you, delirious? We can get arrested for disturbing the peace!

JESSICA: I guess you're all talk then, huh?

RACHEL: Now wait a minute. I never said I'd do anything. It was you that was—was flapping off at the mouth. Delusions of grandeur, visions of being a stupid hero.

JESSICA: Heroine. Look, I'm sorry. But it's not only my fault. Something's wrong, Rachel, what is it?

RACHEL: You always know when something's wrong, that's why I hate you. *(Smiles.)* That's why I like you. Jess, I'm scared. Everything like this only used to happen in the newspapers. You can't see it or even know that it's really happening. Like a war going on in Turkey or some place. It's so far away. How can I feel sorry for people when I can't see them? And now everything's starting to come out of the newspapers and being pushed right on top of me with no warning. It's getting too much, the real world. I can't push aside my fairy tales that quickly.

JESSICA: You don't have to. Not all at once anyway. But you have to take this first step.

RACHEL: But I don't want to—.

JESSICA: Tough. You're always moving. If not forward, backward. It's a game of "Mother May I?" only not so easy to master. And I know that if I keep on playing long enough I can find a castle that's waiting for me. And I'll keep on trying to climb up and up and up till I'm at the top and can raise my flag of victory.

RACHEL: But my castle's so far off the ground. Wouldn't it be easier to aim on my own level than to shoot for the stars? Instead of climbing to the top, can't I use an escalator?

Scene Three
(Outside the library.)

JOSH: Where's Jessica?

RACHEL: Outside collecting signatures for the petition.

JOSH: *(Nervously.)* Well, why doesn't she hurry up?

RACHEL: I bet she asked an undercover cop to sign and he arrested her on the charge of treason. Soon there'll be squads and squads of police coming to get us. The electric chair or jail for life. *(The door opens.)* Here they come. *(Sees it is Jessica and is embarrassed.)* Oh, hi Jess.

JOSH: Maybe we should just forget about it.

JESSICA: Oh great, just great. Let's all go home because Josh is scared out of his mind.

RACHEL: "When fear seizes, change what you are doing. You are doing something wrong." That's from *Julie of the Wolves*. But I think that Jessica's right. If you're scared that much then you should go.

JOSH: What do you think I am? A wimp? I never *said* I'd leave. I was just suggesting it for all you other guys.

RACHEL: *(Sarcastically.)* Well, isn't that generous of you. But really, I'm surprised I'm not more scared.

JESSICA: Well, you *look* scared. You're green.

RACHEL: *(Dryly.)* Thanks. You're looking pretty good yourself. Now let's go before I lose my courage.

JOSH: I can't! I have to go to the bathroom!

RACHEL: It's just nerves *(Pulls arm.)*, come on!

JESSICA: Wait! *(Turns to Rachel.)* Is my war paint smudged?

RACHEL: No, is mine?

JESSICA: No, is my hair OK?

RACHEL: No, I mean yes. Is mine?

JESSICA: Yeah, it looks great. Is my sign straight?

RACHEL: Yeah, perfect. What about my feet, I can't see them.

JESSICA: Feet? What about them?

RACHEL: Are they OK?

JESSICA: Are what OK?

RACHEL: My feet!

JESSICA: Why are you asking me?

RACHEL: You should know.

JESSICA: I should know about your feet? *(Fades out.)*

Scene Four
(The school library.)

(Demonstrators march in whistling "Solidarity Forever." They hand out flyers to the kids who are there, and with apologetic smiles and strange looks the kids all gather their books, some checking them out, and leave. Jessica and Rachel then rummage in the shelves while others march around still whistling. Jessica and Rachel form a big pile of books by each of them, and the kids form two lines in front of them and stop whistling. Then, by twos, they march forward and are each presented a book. Librarian reaches for the phone and the kids freeze.)

LIBRARIAN (HARRIET): Hello Flynn, you've got to come down here right away— Oh, excuse me. Please put the principal on the phone. Tell him it's important. Flynn? No, nothing's wrong . . . exactly. But there are some kids here . . . . Of course there always are, but . . . No, no, no, nothing like that . . . . Well . . . they're . . . . they're whistling . . . . Really!! I feel perfectly fine, thank you! Listen, trust me, OK? Please, just come down . . . .All right . . . . Fine . . . . Goodbye.

(Kids resume book distributing; then principal [Flynn] arrives.)

FLYNN: All right Harriet, what seems to be the problem? I have a lot of work to do upstairs and God only knows where I'm going to find the time to do it. And with the meeting coming up—.

HARRIET: Shh! Over there, listen to what they're saying.

FLYNN: *(Reading a sign someone is wearing.)* "Rye, not whole wheat." What is this lunacy?

HARRIET: Shhh! You'll hear in a second.

FLYNN: *(Glaring.)* I hope so.

(Kids are seated in a circle, each with his book around a spokesperson, another kid.)

SPOKESPERSON: *(Gesturing with a book.)* What you hold now in your hands is a symbol. A symbol of our rights to make our own decisions. We don't need some adult to tell us, "Don't read that, you'll make your thoughts impure." We defy you adults! We don't have to listen to you. We're capable of making our own decisions. We go only by the morals you've taught us. We want to believe them, but how can we when you violate them yourself? "Truth is Beauty, Beauty is Truth." And when the truth is ugly you want to hide it from us. So we have to hide it from you. Hide the books you want to pull the curtain over. We have to salvage them to insure our future. What is there we can't know? Whatever it is, ignorance can't make it better. A pernicious disease doesn't disappear because of ignorance. Nothing does. Whether one chooses to regard something seriously or ignore it completely, it should be their decision to do so. We don't want to fight you. We just want you to be there to help us accept the truth. We can do this through reading all those books that you've classified as "just not for children" like *The Catcher in the Rye*. Thank you.

FLYNN: Damn.

HARRIET: Why did you remove *The Catcher in the Rye* before it was mandatory?

FLYNN: I didn't think it would cause so much trouble.

HARRIET: Well, what are you going to do now?

FLYNN: Leave it to me. All right everyone, the party's over. You've had your fun. It's time to go home . . . . It's time to go now . . . . Now! Look, I don't want to bring anyone else into this, but you are creating a disruption on school property, and if I have to I will call the authorities. Now will you leave, or will I be forced to take action? . . . . Well?

(Start whistling "We Shall Overcome.")

FLYNN: This is your own doing.

Scene Five
(Jessica's bedroom.)

(Rachel smiles to herself.)

JESSICA: What's so funny?

RACHEL: I was just thinking how crazy we must have looked when the police came. Grabbing a book and clutching it as if our lives depended upon it. Shouting "liberty forever."

JESSICA: I thought we were great! Everyone played his part to perfection.

RACHEL: Yeah. Especially our spokesperson. I knew he'd get angry if the only person there besides us to hear his speech was the librarian. I thought he'd die from delight when the principal walked in.

(Pause.)

JESSICA: You know, at first it was so important to stop the banning of *The Catcher in the Rye*. I mean it is, but it's almost enough to know that we tried and took a step up.

RACHEL: I don't feel like I did. My views are more clear on this specific incident of course, but I still don't know how I'll react or think in a different one. And I *still* don't know where my castle is. Will I ever find it?

JESSICA: Well, we'll die trying won't we?
RACHEL: Yeah, I guess we will.

Changes
(TV Script)
Kioka Abbott, Galaois Cohen, Kathleen Yen

Cast:
LENARD DAVIS: Average height, heavy-set, in his forties, receding hairline and a few noticeable gray hairs.
LAURA DAVIS: 13 years old. Medium height, brown eyes, long brown hair and average weight.
MRS. GALLENTE: Italian, in her 60's, tanned, long, dark brown hair worn in a bun. Short and pudgy.
BRAD: 13 years old, medium to tall in height, light brown hair and blue eyes.

Scene I

(During credits, we see a car driving down the West Side Highway on a fall day and turn off at an exit. From car's point of view, camera focuses on a lower-middle-class neighborhood, which is run-down with kids running through the streets. As credits end, car slows down and camera switches to see the car pull up to an old apartment building. Then show Lenard and Laura getting out of the car and taking suitcases out. From a view across the street, close-ups on Lenard and Laura's faces. See Laura go up steps. Then she turns around.)

LENARD: Look at this dump. It's worse than I thought it would be.
LAURA: You mean you rented this dump and you never saw it before?
LENARD: Listen, Laura, you know I just lost my job, and this is the best I could do! Now don't complain!
LAURA: *(Softly.)* Sorry.
LENARD: Ah, never mind. Just get the rest of the suitcases. We've got a lot to do.
LAURA: All right. *(Cheerfully.)* It's going to be fun. We can fix up the place any way we want.
LENARD: Well, don't go getting too excited. Remember you're not in New Jersey any more.
LAURA: Dad, it doesn't matter how much money we have, we can still fix it up.
LENARD: Laura, we'll talk about this later. Right now, go get those bags!

(Laura goes up steps and then turns around.)

LAURA: *(Grabbing bags.)* What floor? I hope there's an elevator.
LENARD: This isn't the Waldorf. Just walk up those stairs. Fifth floor. It's good exercise.

(They go into building and Laura starts upstairs. Switch to see Lenard walk down fifth flight hall. Mrs. Gallente pokes her head out of a door.)

MRS. GALLENTE: Are you just moving in?

LENARD: Yes, I am. It's a pleasure to see such a friendly face. I'm Lenard Davis.

MRS. GALLENTE: I'm Mrs. Gallente. And I'm just about the friendliest face you'll see around here! You're from out of town, aren't you?

LENARD: Yes, how did you know?

MRS. GALLENTE: Oh, you have that look.

LENARD: Nice meeting you, but I've got to unpack.

MRS. GALLENTE: Bye, Mr. Davis. We'll see each other soon, O.K.?

LENARD: *(A little irritated.)* Whatever you say.

(Follow Lenard down hall to last door and see Laura going through boxes, unpacking inside. Then a pan of apartment. Looks small, old and dusty. Suitcases and boxes scattered around.)

LAURA: *(Trying to be cheerful.)* It looks better on the inside.

LENARD: *(Yelling.)* What are you talking about? This place is a rat hole!

LAURA: *(Timidly.)* Well, you're the one who rented it. It's not my fault.

LENARD: You ungrateful child! This is the best I could do after you made me lose my job!

LAURA: It's not my fault you got laid off.

LENARD: But it is your fault! After your mother died, I had to quit night school and work at the docks to support you. And maybe if you were a little more considerate, you wouldn't have wasted your money on clothes and going out!

LAURA: You never told me we were losing money.

LENARD: I didn't tell you because I didn't want to worry you. I wanted you to have the best life I could give you! And now you're blaming me! *(He slaps her.)*

LAURA: *(Crying.)* I'm sorry! You should have told me! I would have tried to help.

LENARD: You little lying brat! You know you only thought of yourself! *(Slaps her again.)*

LAURA: Stop it, please!

(Camera changes to see Mrs. Gallente standing outside of their door listening.)

MRS. GALLENTE: *(Turning around to go back to her apartment.)* It isn't any of my business anyway.

Scene II

(Fadeout.)

(Camera goes to clock—8:32 AM, then switches to see Laura in bed. Laura gets up and walks into bathroom. She opens the door and accidentally hits Lenard with it.)

LAURA: Sorry! Honest! I didn't know you were in there. Please, don't hit me again!

(Lenard closes the door without saying a word. Laura goes into the kitchen and makes some instant coffee. She puts in too much and puts some toast in the toaster.)

LAURA: Here, Daddy.

LENARD: Thank you. *(He takes a sip.)* What the hell is this!

LAURA: I'm sorry. I must've put in too much.

LENARD: That's all right. Besides, we haven't got time right now. We gotta get you registered into a school.

LAURA: Which one?

LENARD: Junior High 199.

LAURA: A public school?

LENARD: What were you expecting? We can't afford private school.

LAURA: Fine. *(Toast starts to burn.)* Oh, my toast!

LENARD: Can't you do anything right? Never mind. Let's go.

Scene III

(School. Back view of kids screaming down hallway. Lenard finds office. Laura looks scared.)

OFFICE ASSISTANT: May I help you?

LENARD: Yes, I'd like to register her into this school.

(During conversation camera follows Laura as she takes a few steps back and hears student #1. Then focus on student #1 and student #2 talking to one another about Laura.)

OFFICE ASSISTANT: Oh, O.K. Just fill out these forms. *(She gives him the forms.)* I'll take care of this part.

LENARD: Do you have a pen?

OFFICE ASSISTANT: Sure.

(The students are still talking about Laura; then they speak to her.)

STUDENT #1: Where'd you come from?

LAURA: I just moved here.

STUDENT #2: What school d'you go to?

LAURA: St. Paul's Middle School.

STUDENT #1: Oh, a private school. This place ain't no place for a private school girl!

STUDENT #2: Yeah, did you bring your butler with you? Where's the limo?

(Focus on Lenard.)

LENARD: Laura, come here! *(She goes.)* How soon can she start?

OFFICE ASSISTANT: Right now if you like.

LENARD: That's fine. The sooner the better.

(See Brad go by door.)

OFFICE ASSISTANT: Oh, Brad! *(Brad is a nice, clean-cut boy.)* Would you please take Laura Davis to room 613?

BRAD: Sure, no problem.

LENARD: All right then. I'll be going.

LAURA: What? Already.

LENARD: I don't see a reason to stay.

LAURA: But—.

LENARD: Don't be a baby! I'll see you after school.

BRAD: Yeah, don't worry about it. The school really isn't all that bad. The kids just have to get used to you.

LAURA: *(A little relieved.)* Thanks.

LENARD: So I'll see you after school. And come straight home. This isn't the kind of place where a little girl can walk around by herself. *(Leaves.)*

(Follow Brad and Laura up the stairs.)

BRAD: Hey, ummm where do you live? Maybe we could walk home together.

LAURA: Well, I live a couple of blocks from here.

BRAD: Do you mean downtown?

LAURA: Uhhh . . . yeah.

BRAD: Well, I live uptown, so I guess we can't.

LAURA: Are you going to be in my class?

BRAD: Yeah, Mrs. Paradis is the nicest teacher! And she's good too.

LAURA: I guess I lucked out this time.

(Follow backs of Brad and Laura into class room 613. A brief close-up of Mrs. Paradis.)

PARADIS: Welcome to J.H.S. 199, Laura. We're all glad you are in our class. Brad, will you please show Laura where she can put her coat and lunch?

BRAD: Okay. *(Laura puts her things in.)*

PARADIS: You have to sit next to Brad. It's the only empty seat.

(Follow Laura, who follows Brad to seat.)

PARIDIS: Do you have a pen and paper?

LAURA: Yes, I do.

PARADIS: All right then. We were talking about the Industrial Revolution when you came in. Have you studied that yet, Laura?

LAURA: No, I haven't.

PARADIS: Okay, then this is new for everyone.

(Fadeout.)

Scene IV

(Home. Livingroom. Lenard is looking in the Help Wanted section of the newspaper when Laura comes home.)

LAURA: Hi, Daddy!

LENARD: Hi, Laura.

LAURA: Have you found any good possibilities for a job yet?
LENARD: No, I haven't.
LAURA: I'm sure you'll find something soon.
LENARD: Well, how was your day at school?
LAURA: Oh, it was fine! I've got the best teacher in school.
LENARD: That's nice.
LAURA: And you remember that nice boy who took me upstairs?
LENARD: Barney?
LAURA: No, Brad. Well, he's in my class and he's really nice.
LENARD: Oh, so you've hooked yourself with a boyfriend already, huh?
LAURA: No, he's just a friend.
LENARD: Yeah, right, whatever you say.
LAURA: Stop that. (*They laugh.*)
LENARD: What about dinner?
LAURA: Well, what about it?
LENARD: It's your turn to cook.
LAURA: Oh, what about meatloaf?
LENARD: When did you learn to make meatloaf?
LAURA: Right now.

(*Follow Laura to kitchen.*)

COMMERCIAL

Scene V

(*Dining area. Laura and Lenard looking in the Help Wanted section at the table with empty plates in front of them.*)

LENARD: That wasn't bad for the first time.
LAURA: I'm going to my room to do my homework.
LENARD: Remember the dishes? It's your turn.

(*Laura takes the dishes into the kitchen. Lenard throws the newspaper onto the table, sighs, and walks around the room looking frustrated and glum. A crash is heard.*)

LENARD: What was that?
LAURA: Nothing, . . . just . . . nothing. Don't bother to get up.
LENARD: What's going on in here? I heard some noise.

(*Follow Lenard into kitchen.*)

LENARD: (*Sees broken dish.*) LAURA!
LAURA: I'm sorry, it just slipped out of my hands!
LENARD: You should be more careful. We haven't got money to spend on stupid dishes. (*Slaps her.*)
LAURA: I said I was sorry. I didn't mean it. (*She runs toward her room but Lenard grabs her by the arm and is about to hit her, but lets her go.*)

(*Fadeout.*)

Scene VI

(School. Focus on Laura in school with bruise on her face. Then shift to Brad looking at her.)

BRAD: What happened?
LAURA: I'll tell you later.
PARADIS: Laura, Brad, are you ready?
LAURA: Yes, Mrs. Paradis.

(Cut to lunchroom.)

BRAD: So, what happened?
LAURA: I tripped on a chair.
BRAD: You mean you fell flat on your face?
LAURA: Yeah.
BRAD: *(Unbelievingly.)* Okay.

(Dissolve to new scene in lunchroom on later occasion. Laura has another bruise on her face and on her arm too. She sits down next to Brad.)

BRAD: You fell again, like you did last week? *(Focus more onto Lauras bruises.)*
LAURA: Yeah. I'm pretty clumsy.
BRAD: Well, you aren't in school.
LAURA: Brad, let's change the subject.
BRAD: It's just that I don't like to see my friends hurt.
LAURA: Well, I'm all right so don't worry about it. I'm just a little clumsy.
BRAD: No one's THAT clumsy.
LAURA: Well, I AM, so leave me alone!
BRAD: Fine, let's eat.

(Fadeout.)

Scene VII

(Office in building on Park Ave. Scene opens with focus on street sign that says Park Ave., then focus on Lenard, who is looking at street signs and looks for a building. Finds it and checks a newspaper. Sign reads "Doorman needed." He walks in.)

LENARD: Um . . . *(To doorman.)* where can I find the office?
DOORMAN: Oh, you're going for the new job huh? Well, the office is second door on the left.
LENARD: Thanks. *(Walks.)*
DOORMAN: Good luck!
LENARD: Yeah! Thanks again! *(Enters room.)*
MAN: Have a seat.

(Fade out.)

Scene VIII

(Livingroom. Lenard's voice is heard on the phone. Slowly go up to focus on Leonard.)

LENARD: Thank you! Yes ... yes ... I'll be there tomorrow at 9:00. *(Hangs up.)*

(Lenard gets off phone as Laura and Brad walk in.)

LAURA: Hi Daddy!

LENARD: Guess what, you two! Don't take your coats off yet! We're going to celebrate. *I got a job!*

LAURA: Oh, Daddy! That's terrific.

BRAD: Yeah, that's great, Mr. Davis. I'm really happy for you. Whatcha going to be doin'?

LENARD: I'm going to be a doorman on 329 Park Ave.

(Black out.)

Scene IX

(Livingroom on another day.)

LENARD: Hi Laura, how was your day?

LAURA: Nothing spectacular. How was your day?

LENARD: *(Cheery.)* Oh, it was nice. I met the Greenfields. They are very wealthy, you know, and I think they seem to like me. Isn't that wonderful? Someone finally appreciates me.

LAURA: *(Not paying any attention to him.)* Oh ... what did you say?

LENARD: Laura, you ask me how my day went and now you're not even listening to me.

LAURA: Guess what, Dad? 'Member when Brad came over last week? Well, he asked me out on a date on Saturday night.

LENARD: What do you want to see him for on Saturday night? You see him every day at school and after school. What, are you in love with him?

LAURA: *(Teasing.)* Weeeell, I don't know, all I know is that he is really nice and cute and he likes me. I like him a lot. He's so nice.

LENARD: *(Angrily.)* That's no way for a girl your age to talk, and I won't have it. *(Slaps her on mouth.)*

LAURA: *(Crying.)* Why d'you hit me? I only—.

LENARD: I said I won't have it!! *(Punch in nose.)*

(Laura is crying hard.)

COMMERCIAL

Scene X

(Interior of school. Laura is walking to school. Brad sees her and sees her nose, which is very large and swollen.)

LAURA: Hi Brad.

BRAD: Hi Laura. Oh what happened this time? Don't tell me. Let me guess. Was it . . . the chair? Or maybe it was the rollerskates again? I know, you tripped over the rug. Poor clumsy little Laura.

LAURA: *(Horrified.)* Brad!

BRAD: Well, what was it? C'mon I wanna hear this one.

LAURA: Brad, you know what happened. Why are you being so mean to me?

BRAD: I'm just tired of your makin' up excuses! I want to hear the truth now!

LAURA: *(Quietly.)* Ever since Momma died and we moved here, Daddy's changed so much. *(Recollecting.)* He used to be so nice. We'd play, talk, and laugh, and he never hit me . . . until now. *(Starts crying.)* Now, now, he gets mad at anything I do. I try so hard, but he just doesn't seem to care. But I know that he doesn't really mean it, that he still loves me.

BRAD: I know he still loves you. I know it. You just have to give him a chance. A chance to make up for it.

LAURA: But how much can I take? I've been waiting. How much longer, Brad? How much?

BRAD: You have to understand his problems. You have to understand his losses. He lost his wife, the woman he loved so much, then he lost his job. That can tear any man apart. Not to have steady money, and then no one to talk to about it?

LAURA: But what about me? I'm his daughter. He's not supposed to beat me up. He's supposed to love me. Love me not BEAT ME!! *(She drops her books and runs toward Riverside Park. Brad retrieves books then follows Laura, running to park. Then he stops and decides that she needs some time alone.)*

(Blackout.)

Scene XI

(Home 8:00 PM. Show phone ringing then Lenard walking in door. Focus on Lenard's face when he talks on the phone.)

LENARD: Hello?

BRAD: Hi, Mr. Davis, is Laura there?

LENARD: Well, isn't she with you? Doesn't she usually go over to your house on Friday?

BRAD: Yeah, but we had an argument before school and she ran away. I haven't seen her in school.

LENARD: What! Do you mean she wasn't in school? Didn't she walk with you?

BRAD: I told you we had an argument. She was upset and ran away.

LENARD: Are you sure you don't know where she is?

BRAD: Yes, I'm sure.

LENARD: Brad, what did you fight about? *(He is getting worried.)*

BRAD: That's not important. Laura is missing—that's important.

LENARD: I know, I know . . . what direction did she run?

BRAD: Well, I don't know . . . oh yeah, she ran into Riverside Park.

LENARD: Into Riverside Park? There are so many crazy people running around in there. She could be hurt. Why didn't you stop her? Damn it!

BRAD: *(Getting upset.)* I didn't think she wouldn't come back. I thought that she needed time alone.

LENARD: Brad, talking about it is not going to bring Laura back. We've got to go look for her. Why don't we meet somewhere and go out together to look?

BRAD: How about your place?

LENARD: Fine. You know where I live, right?

BRAD: Yeah, I'll be there in ten minutes.

(Fade out.)

Scene XII

(Brad and Lenard walking frantically through the park calling "Laura, Laura, where are you?" Focus on watch 8:30 to 10:30 then on rock last.)

Scene XIII

(Lenard opening door to apartment with key. He seems very frustrated, tired and worried. Laura is seen sitting on a chair with her head on her arm. Laura hears key in door.)

LAURA: Daddy? Is that you?

LENARD: *(Door opens.)* Laura! *(Hugs her.)* Are you all right? Where were you? You had me worried.

LAURA: I'm sorry. I was walking around in Central Park and Riverside Park. I needed to think. I wasn't gonna come back, but then I realized hou much I would miss you.

LENARD: Laura, I have to talk to you. *(Sits down.)* Laura, I want you to know that I'm sorry for what I did. It was wrong . . . It's just sometimes I . . . I lose control. Tomorrow, we'll go and look for some help. You're the only thing I have left in this world. You . . . you, my little Laura.

LAURA: Oh Daddy, *(They hug. They both have tears on their cheeks. Close-up on Laura then on Lenard. Pull back to show neighborhood.)*

Musical Play

Write a play for live or filmed performance in which some of the dialog is sung. Think of a kind of story that lends itself to lyrical treatment because it has moments of feeling that are good for duet, chorus, and soliloquy. You might collaborate with one or more people as writer or musician.

Arrange to produce your musical with other students interested in performing, staging, or filming.

(The example here was written, produced, publicized, and performed on four evenings in December, 1984, by eighth-graders at Manhattan East Junior High School, supported as an in-school project of the Education Department of the Metropolitan Opera in New York City. Copyright 1984 by the Metropolitan Opera Guild.

The process used to arrive at this form of Music Theater was developed by the Education Department of the Guild, which is presently teaching it to teachers and students. This form integrates music with dramatic action. In some scenes, the music is heard throughout, whereas in other sections the music is used only for very specific dramatic purposes.

According to the permission terms, not all of the music score is included here. Those seeking further information about the process should write the Metropolitan Opera Guild, 1865 Broadway, New York, NY 10023.)

Foreign Relations

Jessamyn Backe, Galaois Cohen, Esme Montgomery, Brett Ungerleider, and Pamela Woodley. Music by Timmey Eatman.

THE SCHOOLBUS SONG

Scene 1

KAREN: "A" her name is Ann.
MISSY: See her, she's the shy one,
   She's good, she's no fun.
LULU: Yeah, she's no fun.
MISSY: Guess what . . . (*She whispers to Lulu.*)
KAREN: She likes David.
MISSY: But she always hangs out with that foreign kid!
LULU: Yeah, that foreign kid!

KAREN: "B" her name is Bella.
BELLA: (*Entering, heavily accented English.*)
   Hello, Ann. Hello, you guys.
MISSY: She's such a loser . . .
KAREN: Look how hard she tries.
LULU: Yeah, she's such a loser . . .

KAREN: At least she tries.

KAREN & MISSY: She comes from Russia.

ANN: *(To Bella.)* That's very good.

MISSY: *(Imitating Bella.)* Hel-lo, you guys.

LULU: *(Mocking Ann.)* That's very good.

MISSY & LULU: *(Mocking Bella.)* That's ve-ry good.

CHORUS

> We like taking bus rides,
> We can study, we can learn,
> We can make some brand-new friends,
> We hope this bus ride never ends.

KAREN: "C" his name is Chris.

CHRIS: *(Entering.)* No applause, just throw money.

MISSY: He thinks he's so cool.

LULU: ... and he's funny.

KAREN: *(Sarcastically.)* Yeah, real funny!

CHRIS: The party can start, Chris is here.

> Hiya, Ann. *(To Bella.)* Hel-lo, my dear.

(David enters.)

MISSY: Oh my God, have you heard the latest?

KAREN: Here comes David.

MISSY & LULU: He's the greatest!

CHRIS: Yeah, he's the greatest.

> What's up, Dave?

DAVID: Hiya Chris.

> Hiya, Ann.

CHRIS: *(About Ann.)* She's such a pris!

MISSY & LULU: She's such a pris!

CHORUS 2

> We like taking bus rides,
> We can eat, we can joke,
> We can shout and act real cool,
> We hope this bus never gets to school.

(Elaine and Fran enter.)

ELAINE: Come on, Fran. Aw don't be shy.

FRAN: But, Elaine, I'm nervous.

ELAINE: He's just a guy!

ANN & MISSY & LULU: Just a guy?

FRAN: He's just the most popular guy in school.

ELAINE: And if you guys date we'll both be cool.

MISSY & LULU: You guys cool?

BRIDGE (Gina enters.)

ANN: Is that Gina?

BELLA: Why's she here?
  She should be with her friends,
  Drinking beer.

GINA: Nothing's changed, you're still all kids.
  Here's your lunch.

MISSY: Whose?

GINA: David's.

(Huey and Irene breakdance in front of and then onto the bus.)

HUEY: My name is Huey.
  My limbs are gooey.

IRENE: He's a clean machine.

HUEY: I'm the green machine
  And I lean real mean.

IRENE: And drinks Ovaltine.

HUEY: Her name's Irene,
  And she likes to flip.

IRENE: Don't give me no lip,
  I like to flip.

HUEY & IRENE: We're the twins,
  We're next-of-kins,
  We're what's in,
  So watch us spin.

(They break.)

CHORUS 3

  We like taking bus rides,
  We can flirt and we can dance,
  We can talk and we can chat,
  We hope the schoolbus gets a flat.

KAREN: "J" her name is Jen.

(Jen enters.)

MISSY: Look, there's Jen, she acts like a bully,
  Her family's weird, I mean really!

MISSY & LULU: I mean really!

MISSY: To her *mean* is in.
  To her *niceness* is a sin.

LULU: Yeah, a sin.

CHORUS 4

> We like taking bus rides,
> We can talk . . .

MISSY & LULU: We can spy.

ALL: We can learn the latest news.

JEN: *(To Bella.)* And you can learn your two plus two's!

(All exit singing.)

> We like taking bus rides,
> We can flirt and we can dance,
> We can talk and we can chat,
> We hope the schoolbus gets a flat.

> We like taking bus rides,
> We can study, we can learn,
> We can make some brand-new friends,
> We hope this bus ride never ends.

(Seen behind the scrim, the group stands in line to pick up hot lunch.)

(They Sing:)

> Hey, isn't lunchtime boring?
> We never have any fun.
> Eating this food makes it twice as bad,
> And you don't feel so good when it's done.

> Hey, isn't lunchtime boring?
> We never have any fun,
> But look over there at Missy.
> The gossip's just begun.

Scene 2

(Cafeteria. The curtain opens and we see the hot-lunch line through the scrim at the back of the stage. Gossip and tag along enter.)

MISSY: Did you hear who got suspended?

LULU: Ah . . . no.

MISSY: You kidding? Wake up! You gotta know what's going on. Everyone knows that. Even Bella.

LULU: Even her? Well, who was it?

MISSY: Who was what?

LULU: Who got suspended?

MISSY: Lulu . . . that's old gossip. Okay, okay, it was Alfred. They found him in the Audio Visual room showing porno videos to the 7th graders. *(Reaction.) And* he was charging admission!

(They both laugh.)

(Huey and Irene enter and hear tail end of porno story.)

MISSY: Did you guys hear about Chris?

OTHERS: Huh? What? *(Etc.)*

MISSY: He got busted!

OTHERS: Really, wow, what for? *(Karen enters during this time.)*

MISSY: He dared Jen to make fun of Irene's hair-do.

LULU: What did she say, what did Jen say?

HUEY: Brillohead. If she weren't a girl I'd a' punched her out.

CHRIS: You mean you would a' bit off her kneecaps.

IRENE: You're always causing trouble. Someday you're gonna cause a real problem. *(Chris starts to say something.)* Just shut up!

MISSY: You'll never guess what I've got. Look at this. *(Reaction.)*

MISSY: It's a love note. *(Reaction.)*

LULU: Who is it for?

MISSY: Just listen! It's for DAVID! *(Reaction.)*

"Dear David: You know who I am, but you don't think of me the way I think of you. You are the coolest boy in school. Even though all the girls are hanging on you I still think you're really cool."

(At this point Fran and Elaine enter.)

Maybe we could get together some time. I think it would really be neat. Maybe a movie or something, and after that maybe we could . . . ."

ELAINE: How did you get that? *(To Fran.)* Did YOU leave that in the desk? *(To Missy.)* Don't you DARE tell David about this.

MISSY: I wouldn't tell a soul.

LULU: But Missy, you know you always—. *(Missy shuts up Lulu.)*

FRAN: David's coming. Oh, it's David.

MISSY: We were just talking about you. David, who's your favorite girl?

DAVID: *(Indicates Gina.)* You're looking at her.

LULU: Huh? But she's your sister.

GINA: Quit it, David. You guys act like a bunch of little kids.

CHRIS: Who's *your* boyfriend, Gina? *(Puts arm around her.)* I'm available.

GINA: Why do you guys think that someone always has to have a boyfriend?

(Huey and Chris share a reaction.)

IRENE: Rejection.

ELAINE: Gina! Come here, Gina. We have to talk to you for a minute.

(Elaine, Fran and Gina gather together.)

ELAINE: Do you know if David likes anyone? Who does he talk about at home. Is there anyone he talks about a lot?

FRAN: Elaine, come on, let's go.

ELAINE: Fran? Don't you want to find out?

FRAN: Not particularly, come on, let's GO . . .

ELAINE: Fran, we are so unpopular. Everyone thinks we're just drips. If you and David go out then we'll be POPULAR! Don't you want to be popular.

FRAN: Well, yeah, but couldn't we just wear popular clothes?

ELAINE: I've been unpopular for so long, I'm desperate. If you went out with David, then I'd be cool because I'm your best friend.

FRAN: Why don't YOU go out with him?

ELAINE: Well, he's not my type.

GINA: Jeez. *(Walks away.)*

ELAINE: She's not much help. Who would know?

ELAINE/FRAN: MISSY!

HUEY: I heard she almost threw Al down the stairs.

DAVID: She sure has changed. What's up with her, anyway?

HUEY: I don't know, but she better not call Irene brillohead again.

IRENE: Quiet, here she comes.

(Jen enters.)

DAVID: Is there anything wrong, Jen?

JEN: Is there something wrong with you? How would you like it if someone always asked you what was wrong when you walked into a room?

DAVID: You don't have to get all defensive. I was only asking.

JEN: You wouldn't understand anyway.

GINA: Mr. Crenshaw told me to give this to you. *(Hands her a note.)*

JEN: What is it?

GINA: It's a note you have to take home to your parents to get signed.

(Jen rips it up.)

GINA: Jen, what are you doing? They'll just send another one in the mail.

JEN: I'll rip that one up too.

GINA: Jen, you better start coming to classes.

JEN: Don't worry about me.

GINA: If you skip any more, they'll call your Mom.

JEN: Don't worry, I'll be there!

(Jen looks around. Silence from the group.)

We Dare You

ALL: Hey, isn't lunch time boring?
Let's have a little fun.
Let's find someone we can dare.
David—he's the one.

David, we dare you to stand on the table,
we dare you to lick the floor.

David, we dare you to kiss the next girl
who comes walking through that door.

DAVID: No way, you guys, that's really mean.
I don't kiss to be cruel.
Just because you take a dare
it doesn't mean that you're cool.

ALL: Of course David is so cool.
His feet are cold as ice.
He thinks making other people
happy isn't nice.
We dare ya, David.

(Chorus repeat.)

DAVID: Fine, I'll do your stupid dare.
     All right, you guys.

ALL: All right!
    Stand right here and pucker up.
    We'll get outta sight.

(Chorus to conclusion.)

(David kisses Ann.)

DAVID: I'm, sorry, I had to.
ANN: You kissed me.
CHRIS: No kidding!
MISSY: Yeah, David.
HUEY: Gettin' the rap!

DAVID: It was just a dare, okay? How was I supposed to know she would be the one to come through the door. It was just a joke!

(Ann runs out the door.)

BELLA: You . . . BAD!

JEN: Me bad? You Jane. He Tarzan. *(Group laughs.)*

BELLA: *(In Russian.)* Why did you do . . . . Why you do this? *(To David.)* Why you do this?

MISSY: Ann should be happy, Bella. After all, I heard what she told you yesterday.

BELLA: *(In Russian.)* No! Don't say!

JEN: *(Mocks the words that Bella says.)*

BELLA: Leave alone! *(To Missy.)* You stop. *(In Russian.)* Stop!

MISSY: I was in the bathroom when Bella and Ann walked in. I didn't want them to see me, so I stood up on the bowl and crouched down so I could put my ear on the door. And you know what they were talking about?

(Reaction from group.)

MISSY: And then I heard—.

BELLA: No!

MISSY: Ann telling Bella how much she loved David!

BELLA: That's secret! Not nice.

JEN: Why don't you go back to where you came from?

(Bella slaps Jen.) (Pause.)

CHRIS: I dare you to do something back, Jen. I dare you. I dare you, Jen. Go on.

(Jen crosses to the table where Bella was sitting and takes the tape recorder.)

BELLA: Not yours.

DAVID: Come on, Jen, give it back—you don't need that tape recorder.

JEN: How do you know what I need? *(She exits.)*

IRENE: What *is* eating her?

HUEY: She's changed for sure.

GINA: She's just having a bad day, all right? Give her a break.

LULU: Or maybe it's because she fell down the stairs.

MISSY: WHAT?!

LULU: Oh, I guess I forgot to tell you, it's not important.

MISSY: What? Someone fell down the stairs and you don't think it's important? Tell me! Tell me!

LULU: Well, remember the other day when I went to the nurse's office?

MISSY: Yeah? Yeah?

LULU: Well, Jen was in there. Ms. Spitzer sent her down because she wouldn't change for gym.

MISSY: She went to the nurse because she wouldn't change for gym?

CHRIS: That's what Gina does.

GINA: How do you know that I don't change my clothes for gym, Chris? *(Chris indicates Missy.)*

MISSY: Lulu, why did she go to the nurse's office—just because she wouldn't change for gym?

LULU: No-o-o-o! Because when Ms. Spitzer forced her to change she found bruises all over her body.

MISSY: And ... ?

LULU: And she told the nurse she fell down the stairs.

MISSY: And? That's all?

LULU: Yeah. I told you it wasn't very important...

MISSY: Yeah, that's not very important ...

(Whistle is blown.)

HUEY: Time to go, the whistle has been blowed. Gotta get this show out on the road.

ELAINE: *(Pushing Fran towards David.)* Go on Fran, go on.

FRAN: David ... uh, David?

DAVID: What?

FRAN: What's the math homework?

DAVID: Give it up. *(Exits.)*

ELAINE: Okay, that means plan two! We'll use your idea.

(Others leave. We see Karen and Bella alone.)

KAREN: ... your sweater. Don't feel so bad. Missy always does that. She has a need to know everything and perform it. No matter how intimate or how private. That's Missy. *(No reaction from Bella.)* Don't be mad at David. He didn't mean to hurt Ann. *(Still no reaction.)* It's Jen isn't it? *(Reaction.)* Jen needs to realize that she needs help. She's not a bad person, she just needs help.

BELLA: No ... mean. I need tape recorder.

KAREN: She'll bring it back tomorrow. You can get it then.

BELLA: But, I need tonight.

KAREN: Why?

BELLA: Need to be American. Have to talk English. I don't want them to make fun any more. Have quiz tomorrow. Need to use.

KAREN: You don't need to be embarrassed that you can't speak English all that well. *(Pauses.)* Here, you can give this to her. It's her homework pad ... in room 310 ... she'll be there tonight.

BELLA: Why?

KAREN: She doesn't want...to go home. Ask her when you see her.

Scene 3

(We see Jen making her tape. Bella enters.)

BELLA: Gimme tape.

JEN: What are you doing here? Oh, you mean this? Your English language tape. (*Rips it out.*)

BELLA: (*In Russian.*) Why?

JEN: Stick to English, or go back to where you came from.

BELLA: Why do you hate me?

JEN: Why not?

BELLA: That's no reason. Why you here?

JEN: That is none of your business.

BELLA: The tape recorder is—give it back. Not mine.

JEN: Oh yeah? Whose is it?

BELLA: Ann's.

JEN: I don't know what she sees in you anyway. You're just a stupid tourist. Go back where you came from! No one wants you here. You and that goody-goody friend of yours. What do you do for fun anyway—homework?

BELLA: I'm not failing—like you are.

JEN: How did you get in here?

BELLA: Broke window.

JEN: You broke a window? Oh no, they'll find us. Why did you come here?

BELLA: WHY YOU COME?! You don't go home—why?!

JEN: (*Grabs tape.*) Drop dead!

Trio

BELLA: Hi Ann, need . . . little . . . help.

ANN: Sure, just tell me what you need.

BELLA: Listen, help understand.

ANN: Listen to what, what do you mean?

(*Bella turns on the tape recorder. Jen sings the message from the A/V Room.*)

JEN: (*Sarcastically.*).
Dearest mom, *au revoir*,
I have gone, gone for good.
If you dropped dead, I wouldn't care,
I wish you would.

Up till now, you have treated,
You have treated me like dirt,
I don't care that you beat me,
It didn't hurt.

BELLA: (*To Ann.*) What she talking. Treat like dirt?

ANN: Her mother treats her badly,
She hits instead of talking.
She's mean—.

BELLA: Don't understand.
    She talking to her mom, that right?
    Mom treat her like dirt?
    But mom supposed to love her kid,
    And never s'posed to hurt.

JEN: I didn't mean to make Dad leave,
    I thought he loved me too.
    Because he never hit me,
    Like you do.

    I don't know why you hate me,
    You didn't hate me last year.
    And I know you never hit me,
    When Dad was here.

    Huddled deep in the dark,
    I curled up in my bed,
    And I cried.
    It hurt when you hit me,
    It hurt deep inside.
    Still I never let you see me
    When I cried.

    I don't know whay you hate me,
    You didn't hate me last year.
    And I know you never hit me
    When Dad was here.

BELLA: I don't know.
    You help, please.
    And we help Jen,
    Who needs us.

ANN: I don't know what to do with my own life,
    You don't know how hard it can be.
    And now here's a girl who needs our help.
    What can we do, you and me?

(The lights fade out.)

BELLA: I feel sorry for her,
    She has a hard life,
    But how can we make it better?
    And what will she do
    When she finds out
    That we have this letter?

ANN: I don't know right now,
    I have to think.

We'll talk some more tomorrow.
But don't let her problems
Get you down,
Or fill your dreams with sorrow.

Scene 4

(Cafeteria. Curtain opens to reveal kids seated at their lunch tables. (Huey and Irene enter laughing.)

MISSY: What are you guys laughing at?

(Huey and Irene try to answer, but can only point.)

OTHERS: What is it? *(Ad lib, etc.)*

(In walk Elaine and Fran, dressed "popular.")

ELAINE: Like hi! Like, how is everything going? I like think all of you are so tubular. You, like like our clothes. I mean aren't they awesome? . . . Oh my God! *(She looks over to Fran.)*

FRAN: Like . . . hi.

ELAINE: You can't say it like that if you want to be popular. I mean we have to be "in." You say it like this: Like, hi! Things are just so bitchin'. *(Nudges Fran.)*

FRAN: Like . . . hi! *(To Elaine.)* Is that like, better?

HUEY: Elaine, she's not with it. You can't talk like that any more. You gotta talk like this.

(Huey then quotes any rap verses. Big reaction from the group to Huey's routine.)

ELAINE: Great. *(To Fran.)* Now, we'll be popular. He's our ticket. *(To Huey.)* Teach us to rap!

(Huey, Fran, and Elaine go to a table to sit down. Karen enters with Irene.)

IRENE: I wish our parents could appreciate what we like to do—of course it's not classical ballet. Tracy does that.

KAREN: Who's Tracy?

IRENE: Our fantastic, brilliant, exceptionally talented older sister! That's what Tracy is.

HUEY: Talking about the favored one?

KAREN: Why do you say that?

HUEY: Because our parents want us to be like Tracy. They want a xerox copy family. Dad's in black and white, Mom's in black and white, so is Tracy.

IRENE: But we're colorful, and color don't come out on no xerox machines!

HUEY: This is what she says, "Children, you dress in those outrageous clothes. Why must you wear those jeans?" Or, "Irene, why not wear a dress and brush your hair?"

IRENE: I want to have my hair my way. I want to be appreciated for me.

KAREN: So why do you hide behind rapping and showing off?

(Pause.)

HUEY I try so hard to be like her. But I don't have her talent.
KAREN: But there are other talents. You have your own.
HUEY: Yeah? Like what?
KAREN: You have personality, character . . . in general, a nice person.

(Jen enters.)

DAVID: Hi, Jen.

(No reply.)

CHRIS: Don't bother!
IRENE: Feel a sudden chill in here?
HUEY: Yeah, it seems to come from that general direction.
GINA: Knock it off! Can't you see she's upset?
BELLA: *(Sings.)* What do I do?
ANN: Just go up and . . . .
BELLA: That's easy for you to say.
ANN: No really, it's simple.
BELLA: But she's so mean.
ANN: I understand.
     Sometimes her teasing gets out of hand,
     but helping is a good deed.
BELLA: How can I help her, what can I say?
ANN: A simple phrase is all you need.
     Tell everything as a simple phrase.
     Simple is the rule to follow.
     Say it with a simple phrase.
     A simple phrase is all you need
     to let them know the way you feel,
     and if you say it from your heart
     then they will know your feeling's real.
BELLA: Simple phrases aren't all bad,
     especially when they're all you have.

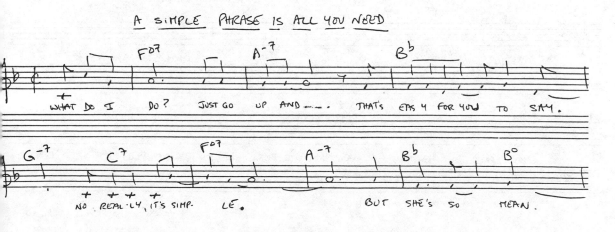

KNOW YOUR FEEL-ING'S REAL. SIM-PLE PHRA-SES ARE-N'T ALL BAD, ES-PEC-IALLY WHENS THEY'R

ALL YOU HAVE.

GINA: Bella, do you have a tape that belongs to Jen?
BELLA: Home, it's at home.
BELLA: What simple phrase?
ANN: "I understand."
BELLA: "I understand" is all I say?
ANN: Try, go ahead.
BELLA: I guess I will.
    I understand.
ANN: Go up to her and take her hand,
    and her feelings will be freed.
    Just tell her that you understand.
BELLA: A simple phrase is all that you need.
    Tell her everything as a simple phrase.
    Simple is the rule to follow.
    Say it as a simple phrase.
ANN: A simple phrase is all you need
    to let them know the way you feel
    and if you say it from your heart,
    then they will know your feeling's real.
ANN & BELLA: Simple phrases aren't all bad,
    especially when they're all you have.

    (Bella goes over to Jen.)

BELLA: I understand.
JEN: Get away from from me.
BELLA: I understand.
JEN: Now I have to go back home, and you know what my mother—.
BELLA: I understand. (Gives her the tapes.) I lied.
    All you have to do
    is tell your mom what's true.
    Don't run away from your troubles,
    a simple phrase will do.

JEN: What if I try but I can't explain why?
BELLA: Be calm, try to talk with your mom.
JEN: I need help,
  someone to tell me what to do . . . Can you?
BELLA: "I need help."
  That simple phrase will do.

(All three sing chorus. Jen and Bella walk towards phone.)

JEN: *(Looks for coin, Bella gives her one.)* What's your word for "friend"?
BELLA: Drooga.
JEN: "Drooga?" Let's stick to English, okay? . . . Friend.
BELLA: Wait.

(Pulls tape from Jen's cassette. Jen dials her mother's phone number.)

JEN: Hello? Mom? I love you. *(To Bella.)* She said it too. *(Bella and Jen exit.)*
KAREN: *(To Ann.)* A simple is phrase is all *you* need.

Scene 5

(Bus. Gina and David enter. Ann and Karen have already moved down onto apron and are in position.)

GINA: David, that was a terrible thing to do. You didn't mean that kiss.
DAVID: I know, I know.
GINA: How would you like it if someone played around with your feelings? That's not like you. It happened to me. You know it happened to me. Remember? He didn't mean it either.
DAVID: Jeff? You never got over that, did you?
GINA: No. He made me feel awful. I know how Ann feels.
DAVID: I'm going to apologize.

(Other kids get on bus, blocking David's way to Ann. Elaine gets on and does a rap for everyone—it works.)

MISSY: *(To Huey and Irene.)* How come you guys aren't dancing?
IRENE: Don't have to!

(David finally reaches Ann.)

DAVID: Sorry. I don't know what came over me. It was really . . . obnoxious.
ANN: Yeah, kinda. But don't worry about it.
ANN: A simple phrase is all we need.
  Tell everything with a simple phrase.
  Simple is the rule to follow.
  Tell it with a simple phrase.

(All others join in for repeat of chorus.)

ANN: I like you.

(David kisses Ann. Blackout.)

Poems

Sensory Poem

Take notes at some locale of your choice, as you did for
Writing Up Sensory Notes, *and look for a moment or theme*
in your observations and reactions that might make a good
poem. You might build up a mood, or a set of images, or a
story, or a reflection. These can benefit from richer language
or less common phrasing or more compact expression than one
usually expects in prose. Also, what things not at all present in
the scene you observed does your imagination connect to what
you did observe?

   Post or print up and hand out. Or collect your sensory
poems into a booklet.

Observations: 6:00 P.M.
Susannah Kaplan

As the clock strikes six a cool breeze
new to that hot day
springs up to warn everyone that
evening is here.

The sun hastens its long journey
to the west and quickly melts onto
the New Jersey skyline.

Children playing on the sidewalk
scatter one by one
to go in for supper
and long, tired afternoon shadows take their
place on the pavement.

The sky darkens
and windows and streets are illuminated
in sequence.

Fragrant smells of cooking fill the air
and many an angry stomach growls.

Rush hour is at its height as men and
women hungry for their dinners
ascend the subway stairs.

Harlem
Felicia Washington

Soul food everywhere.
Man's body.
Fish in the water,
People on the town.
Books flying all over,
City's bazaar awakening.
Bums and bag ladies lying around,
Along the edge.
Stores open and they close,
Curbs dirty with last night's beer bottles.
Streets are all getting mended
Form the tires burning holes in them overnight.
Kids eating lollipops,
And boys popping everyone by the rear end.
Boy, is this some time,
Time on a HARLEM STREET.

The Breakwater Rocks
Robert Taynton

They're slimy with the wretched smell of dead
fish. They have a disgusting feeling with moss
and barnacles clinging on them with all their energy.

They're shapeless pieces of mass with no real beauty
but in an abstract sense they're very beautiful.
It's an endless serpent with the smell of death.

People fish off of them, adding to the wretched
smell. Yet these representations of death contain
life—birds, barnacles—but in the end die and

add to that smell an eternal smell that
lasts for the rest of your life.

Women of the Sand
Lee Rosenberg

Tan women on the tan sand,
with their burnt orange skin and
light brown hair blowing in the polluted air.

A shallow smile reflecting in the sunset
as beach people walk by.

Rusty leaves fall from teak trees
onto the yellow brick road,
pleasing the beautiful models who pass by—
On their way to the rusty rocks
under the clear waters of Australia.

I become tired and fall deeply
between the bronzed legs of Paulina Porizkova.
I sigh contently and find myself in a swirl
of yellow and brown....

Now I wake up and pull the tan bedspread
up to my white neck.
I smell the good smell of toast.
The scent leaves a tan trail
through the wood house.

My brown eyes look at the walls of my room.
I see the magazine cutouts of tan women,
of tan sand with their burnt orange skin and
light brown hair blowing....

Picture Poem

Focus on some image that sticks with you and begs to be put into words. It may be something rare you glimpsed once or something you see every day, an action or object or scene or view of some person. Get across to others this image that gets to you. A comparison may help. (What is the thing like?) Make use of the resources of poetry—its unusual ways of wording things, the sounds and rhythms of language, the breaks of line endings, stanza divisions, perhaps rhyme, and so on.

Try your poem out until you are satisfied that people see the image the way you want and feel what you are trying to arouse in them. Then read it aloud, print it up and hand it out, include it in a collection, or send it to a publication.

The Ghetto
Crystal Mayers

Between the two alleys
Deep in the night
Where garbage lies everywhere
Alone one little piece of glass
Lies glittering in the moonlight.

Teddy
Deidre Garcia

His left ear is gone
'cause he got in a fight;
Max, my new puppy
chewed it off in one bite.

His nose is all flat
and so is his face
'cause Big Tommy Tucker
used my bear as first base.

His fur is all rough
and he's losing his stuffing;
the dishwasher got him—
Mom's huffin' and puffin'.

He's been spilled on and tattered,
stepped on and squeezed,
he's been laughed at and hurt,
he's always been teased.

He's filthy dirty
after all he's been through;
still he sits on the bed
a-smiling at you.

Flight
Mark Hoekstra

The Hummingbird

He darts around at the speed of light,
Maneuvering in perfect flight.
He pierces the flower with his straw-like bill.
He beats his wings and drinks his fill.

The Take-off of a Mallard Duck

His feet paddle faster and faster, and soon
He is a blur of green and orange skimming the water,
And he launches himself into the air.

The Landing of a Mallard Duck

His wings are spread like a parachute
to slow him down as he puts his jet-ski feet down,
And he slides to a halting stop.

Memory Poem

Take some memory that came up when you were writing notes for Memories and write it as a poem. Change or add facts freely to develop some feeling or story or imagery. Or transform into a poem something you wrote for your autobiography or memoirs. Or take a fresh run through your memories, letting them reel until something likely comes by. Your memory poem might feature an incident, a scene, a mood at some place, a person, a relationship, or some object. How do you feel about it? What does it mean to you? Why does it come back to you?

Let someone (or more than one) hear or read it, and ask your audience to describe to you what came across and how the poem made them feel. Improve it if you can.

Rehearse and read aloud to others, post it up, or include it in a collection of other memories or of other poems.

"Cha"
Rebecca Levi

I went to Grandma's house today.
Oh, not Grandma: Charlotte.
Only once I greeted her
with a loud "Grandma!" and
outstretched arms.
She didn't recognize this name,
didn't reply to it.

Frequent are our "discussions"
Weighing the importance
of dating Jewish boys.
"Because dating leads to marriage."
God forbid I'd be looking for a husband.
Silently I listen
While she reminisces about the dead.

But not today.
Charlotte is dating and dumping.
She dresses smartly in black,
Her favorite color.
Her hair growing out
of the blond dye.
It is now free to be grey,
a beautiful color.
Unafraid.

I left Cha's house
very content.
I feel good
like when I eat only enough
to fill my stomach.

Mirror
Rebecca Levi

I alway tried
always wanted
to see all
through my mirror.

I would stretch
my neck
as far
as it would go,

Searching for
the back hall
looking for
a missing detail.

I wanted to be
like Alice
wanted to go through.

But when I
opened the door
and ran in

the only new world
Was one of mothballs
and broken hangers.

The Sun
Alison Tucker

The world is smooth
as I skate along the edge.
"Just one more jump before I leave."
The ice swirls by my feet.
I see the sky—
        the ground—
        the sky—
blackness
staring faces.
And as I turn my head
toward the east, I
see the sun
        setting.

Garlands for the Feast
Rachel Egen

Up in the small attic
with Sara Crewe and Ermengarde.
The basket is on the thin bed.
Sara's green eyes are shining.
"These are the plates," she said.
"They are golden plates.
These are the richly embroidered napkins.
Nuns worked them in convents in Spain."
"And we can use the shawl as a tablecloth,"
        I said.

The doorbell rings.
I jump and go to let my mother in,
then return to the attic,
but I can't find it.
I was just there. I was surrounded
by those walls.
Where is it?
Then I find it, open the door,
cross the threshhold
just in time to hear Sara say,
"And those are garlands for the feast."

The Departure ... Divorce
Christina Johnson

Sitting in the living room, love all around,
With music and singing all about,
Playing, reading, and sitting on the ground—
Who knew that hate and no love was there?

Days go by but without insight.
Who knew this was going to happen?
Sleeping peaceful in the dead of night,
Who knew that hate and no love was there?

You hear them fight with each other, but it makes
     no sense at all.
You wonder to yourself, "What's going on?"
Suddenly you hear a scary scream down the hall.
Who knew that hate and no love was there!

Hearing a door slam and a terrible cry.
Next thing you know no singing and music above.
No more mummy and daddy both in the house.
Who knew that hate and no love was there?

You say to your mummy, "Why did it happen?"
Mummy doesn't know what to say except
a kiss and a hug, while the tears roll down my face.
Who knew that hate and no love was here?

No Longer Friends
Becky Lisa Bornstein

Today we had
our last fight.
You made me mad,
I knew I was right.
You got upset,
started to yell,
told me to
drop dead and
go to hell.
I said screw you
and that was the end.
I hung up, and now
we're no longer friends.

My Previous Room
Daisy Wright

I can't remember much of my
previous room,
Just that it was dark with
shadows, and full of gloom.
The walls were blue, the window
had lace,
And the trees outside made a
horrible face.
I'd let out a scream, and scream
for days,
then wake up from a dream,
and find it all okay.
I'd sit in the dark, feeling not
alone,
And think of the monsters that
would eat me to the bone.
Bodies in the closet, witches by
the moon,
Zombies in the basement, death
will come soon.

The Pasture
Anne Barthel

In the early morning haze
The air was thick with dew.
The barn so clearly visible
By the full light of noon
Was a nebulous shape in the
Far corner of the green yard.
I set my feet towards the gate
And followed the feel of the ground.
Beneath them, I could not
See five feet in front of me.
Reaching for the gate, I felt for
The rusty old latch and when
My fumbling fingers found it,
I opened the creaky gate. I
Passed through from the home yard
To the unknown world of mist

Beyond the big oak out there,
Where we would venture once
In a while to show our little-
Boy manhood, our cradle courage.
I stepped into the oak's pro-
tective shade, which I felt
Rather than saw, of course,
For the sun was on holiday (or
So the nursemaids said when we
Asked them, with childish pet-
ulance, why it wasn't sunny
Every day).
Now I was passing the old oak's
Shelter with hesitant steps,
Like a baby toddling forth for
The first time from his mother's
Arms. With the first steps I
Put everything I knew behind me
And walked alone in the pasture.
The heavy silence oppressed me,
And I longed for the boisterous
Facade of my comrades, but at
The same time I knew that I was past the
Comrades I had known, and past
All the comfort of my sweet child-
hood. Out in the pasture was nothing
But grass, weeds, rocks, a small
Stream. By the time I reached an
Outcropping of rock I felt
alone, not only now, out here in the
Pasture, but anywhere I could go,
At any time in the future, in any
Place on the vast globe; no matter
How many loyal friends surrounded
me, I would be alone.
Then I heard a voice wafting
to me on the breeze, carried from
The safety of the barnyard across
The stretch of open land to my
Ears, and it said.
"Where are you?
Answer me!"
And I tore back through the pasture,
Past the sentry oak,

To the warm kitchen,
To my mother's arms,
To my childhood.

Story Poem

Tell a story as a poem so that you can take advantage of the greater resources of poetry—richer word choice, comparisons, rhythms, sounds, rhyme, meter, and the breaking of the lines. You might read some ballads and tell your story as they do, through a series of stanzas repeating a refrain (which sometimes shifts). Your material can be realistic or fantastic.

Read aloud or record with classmates taking parts. Include in poem collections or mixed story collections.

The Dove
Jennifer Rosen

The dove sat on a willow branch,
Singing its sweet song.
When all of a sudden the man from the ranch
shot at it with his shotgun.

The poor dove, how she tried and tried
as the bullets pinged and ponged
to fly away and save her hide,
And he shot at it with his shotgun.

"Please let me go and fly away!"
The dove cried, "You've got me wrong!"
"It's rent you'll pay, if you want to stay!"
And he shot at it with his shotgun.

"O.K. I'll pay. Now will you please stop,
I can't keep this up for very long!"
The rancher laughed and jumped and hopped
And he shot at it with his shotgun.

"You'll stay but you'll stay as supper!"
The supper bell banged and bonged.
The dove breathed her last so as not to suffer,
And he shot it with his shotgun.

The Church
Shannon Mulholland

The crackling snow, half ice, half frost,
Sounded in the still cold night
As I stepped upon the tracks,
Left by the day's moving vehicles.
The church was there, half white, half blue,
As the snow covered the ground and made the tiny sanctuary of Friar Charles
Look like a steepled ghost.
The two eyes upon the door, half big, half round,
That I had seen since childhood,
That had scared me even in light of day,
Were disappearing in the dark of night
And making feet go faster in the snow.
Soon I was going, half running, half trotting,
But the distance was never ending
As a bell kept ringing,
Keeping perfect time with the zipper
Flapping on my jacket.
Two shadows appeared, half black, half grey.
I could see that one was mine,
But the twosome came following after me.
I ran faster, faster, and faster,
Into a big hallway, empty, like a box with nothing in it.
The walls came closer, half alive, half dead,
Closer, closer, they came,
Until the shadow appeared at the door
Of the empty box
As I squeezed my face
Until it was blue.

Getting Even
Jennifer Spector

It happened many years ago,
    when I was very young.
My father often would get drunk,
    and threaten me with his gun.

He kept it in a small wood box,
    underneath his big ol' bed,
and went to fetch it every time
    the booze raced to his head.

I would hear him coming down the hall;
  I'd run into my room,
away from my mean old pop,
  whose life was filled with gloom.

Once he held the big brown belt,
  I'd seen on many a night.
It slashed upon my tender skin,
  with fast and furious might.

For many years he carried on;
  Oh! I hated my father so,
I had to get *him* back for once,
  before I let him go.

I crept upon him one dark night;
  this time I used his gun.
I shot him in the head three times
  and ended all his fun.

The judge he never blamed me,
  'cause folks knew pop was cruel.
The years we'd spent together
  were one unending duel.

After Breakfast:
A Poetic Conception of the Civil War
Elisa Barston and Jodi Kanter

The Civil War,
It came and stayed,
Not just a breakfast spell,
As they thought.
And so many younguns
Were sent away
To Kill, scarcely knowing
Why they fought

The Fort that the Confederates Bombarded

In April of '61,
The Confederates bombarded
Fort Sumter
In South Carolina.
Men of the Union

Survived
For thirty hours
Without food,
Surrounded by flames.
No one was killed
Though the spirit
Of the Union
Was charred
And battered
By that last night.
Their shoulders
Slumped heavily
Against the remains
Of the fort
That the Confederates
Bombarded.

Matt

Before the war,
Matt was strong and healthy.
He gave much love
To his happy family.
He worked hard
And for long hours
Until that day
The headlines devoured
His happiness, hopes, and dreams.
The war weakened him
And changed his life.
The war punctured him
Like the stab
Of a knife.

Ellen

War has taken
Her loved ones away.
They are gone
And she is left
To pray
That someday
They will return

To soothe
The stabbing pain
Of her broken heart.
Bandages of dreams
And ointments
Made of hope
Are all she has
To mend it.

Bill Creighton—Insecure

WHY DID I LEAVE?

Now,
Sulking
In sweet mystery
Silhouetted identity,
Here
I can see that blood,
No longer isolate
In head
Or hand
Or heart
Can dissolve the sugar,
The sweetness
In the cowardice of
A homesick soldier.

Tom and Eb

War had tempted
These two young boys
Who seemed like brothers.
They couldn't wait
To get out there
And fight
And win shiny medals
And come home as heroes....
For that was what
War was like
In dreams.
But dreams
Didn't always
Come true.

Shadrach Yale (a letter never sent)

Dear Jenny,
      Each day
      Brings a new pile
      Of blood-crusted bodies
      Lying in fleshy masses
      Behind us.

      We just *leave* them, Jenny,
      Soldiers with
      Tear-glazed eyeballs
      Stark in confusion
      Stacked by their bones.

      There are arms
      That look like my arm
            in those piles,
      And I get scared.
      Today there was an eye
            like yours
      Translucent from dust
      And gunpowder
      Yet still visible,
      Sitting with the rest of the stack,
      And I realized,
      We're all in this war now.
      But until I find
      The mate to that
      Horrible, naked eye,
      Until my own bones
      Crack
      Over that ugly pile
      Left behind
      I shall dream of
      When I am sure that the eye
            is yours,
      For it rests on me.

            Yours,
            Shad

Jenny Creighton—Loving Is a Soliloquy

I wanted to be
Your lighthouse
Guiding you across
Shadow-deepened wetness
Past the deceiving horizon.

Two hopes
Hugging in
Brilliance of light
As we met at shore

Now only a landmark
Dimly lit
Beckoning soothingly
From a distance
        too far,
I can only beg
Forgiveness
Of my hidden
Other love
And pray
That I may soon come into sight
And guide you home again.

Jethro Creighton

War excited him
Before it began
When his family
Was close at hand.
He was young
And carefree
And he thought,
"It won't be—
My brothers
Will return
Unscratched."

Jethro's Imprisonment

War girdled
My freedom.
Former ambitions
Now lie trapped
In an unyielding figure
Of constant poise.

A proud soldier,
Like my brothers.
At last, MY chance to fight!
Knowledge,
Responsibility and
Youth
March free,
Until war
Capturing them all
Defeating openness
Slims me,
To half my
                    former self.

The Surrender at Appomattox—1865

A MEETING IN HEAVEN

Remember the Civil War, Sir Lee,
Remember the Civil War?
We wanted, so much
For all men to be free,
A world of race equality.
You sought land and trade goods greedily.
Remember the Civil War.

I remember the Civil War, Sir Grant
And '65, the Appomattox surrender.
I called a meeting, then another
When your ugly, heartless smother
Had gone too far. You're quite the other
Side of reason, indeed you are.
Oh yes, *I* remember the Civil War.

Remember the Civil War, dear reader,
Remember the blood and tears
Which went towards Union victory
After those five horrid years.
Remember, recount for over 600,000
Who, before getting home did fall.
And grieve for their families—
They who remember
The Civil War best of all.

Song

Write new words to a familiar tune. Just try out different words until some begin to fit that make some kind of sense or nonsense. Then follow out whatever that idea is until you have a new set of words. If you agree on a tune with partners, you can each write your own words and compare later and make a booklet giving the tune. Teach your song to a small group and sing it for others.

The next step is to make up both the words and the tune, starting with either. If you have in mind first a nice line or phrase of words, you can try to vocalize it until a melody begins to come also. Use each to draw out the other until you have a whole song.

Math Block
Jodi Kanter

Sung to the Tune of
"Over the Rainbow"

Somewhere, over the slope
Way up high
There's a sweet little axis
Floatin' horizont'ly by

Somewhere over that axis
Skies are blue,
And the dreams that your answer's right
Really do come true.

Someday I'll turn the page and look
And find the answer in the book
Will match what I got,
Where trig is known as secondhand
And no one frets o'er radicands.
That spot is my spot!

Somewhere, over the slope
Great minds fly.
Minds fly over the slope
Why then, the function, can't I?

A Drinking Song
Chris Bowdy

Come lassies and lads
O'er the field and green

An' take your lovers a' with ya!
Tomorrow you'll be smackin' the

Ale so clean, for
Pentecost's coming around ye!

"The tinker—he's shining his boots
With his spit."
"The jester he's shining his bells
With his wit."
"The swineherd he's shining his
Staff with a hint...."

"Of Pentecost's cheer around ya!"

Come lassies and lads
O'er the field and green

An' take your lovers a' with ya!
Tomorrow you'll be smackin' the
Ale so clean, for
Pentecost's coming around ye!

Poem of Feeling and Reflection

Write a poem around a certain feeling, idea, mood, or point of view. You might take off from something that came to mind when you were doing Stream of Consciousness or that you noted down in your journal, or that spun off from some other piece of writing like Personal Essay. Good poems often start with a reaction to something that happened to you recently or that you witnessed or read. Have you made some new connection in how you see things or feel about things?

Spring on a trial audience, then revise and post up, pass around, or include in a fitting book.

Visiting Grandparents
Maia Marko

Grandma says eat all you want.
Grandpa says don't eat too much.

Grandma says I can stay as
long as I want.
Grandpa says better go now
(When I don't have to go until one).

Grandma says watch TV
and have some cake.
Grandpa says read a book
and improve your mind.

I say, Grandma, you're great,
Grandpa, you're a pest,
And then I run.

Being Sick
Giovanna Hughes

Being sick is the pits
You can't go outside
Or even see your close friends
Just put it like this
She got you this time

Your mother is always pouring liquids
        into your body
Plus forcing you to take nasty
        medicine
Insisting that you stay in bed
There's nothing you can do but
        use the potty
'Cause she's got you this time,

You watch Bugs Bunny in the morning
Then soaps all day long
In the evening it's Barney Miller
There's nothing you can do
Because she's got you this time

Me

Sheshonya Rivero

color me black
with a dark ebony crayon.
color all my black inherited features
with pride and dignity
for I behold no shame.

City

David Abel

City:
bared against
the stormy sky
of things to come.

Complications

Ramon Ortiz

We wish to be in
each other's arms
and yet we stay away.
We want to share all
our love, but we can't,

not today.
We want to share our
secret with our family
and closest friends
but we are scared that
they will turn on us
and we might see the
end.
These are complications of
our love that I never knew
existed. Just too many
complications to keep our
love in existence.

Dark—Quiet—Still
Eva Braiman

The night wraps around my bed
The bird brings dark on her wings
I sit up
Afraid to lie back down
The bird isn't afraid
She lives the dark
She breathes the dark
She is the dark

Graig Nettles
Daniel Oppenheim

He plays up at Yankee stadium
And captains the team, wearing pinstripes.
This master of late inning rallies
Can get you those much needed tallies,
But it's not for his bat that he's known;
Around his glove his legend has grown.
Down the line a hit deep in the hole—
He dives and the ball's under control.
A hero of mine, old number nine.

Her Fury
Theresa Fagin

She slithers
        shiny black
iron clenched nerves
        she is furious.

Nine ten
        no help
she lashes out
        spitting words of fury

at her ache.
        Her anger is
incredible
        beyond belief

beyond reason.

It knows no
        means
she cannot control
        her flying words.

Then all of a sudden
        she collapses
a mountain of confusion
        she hangs her head.

The End
Theresa Fagin

The end of time,
of life, is drawing near.
I know it—you know it
though we refuse to
believe it.

But I know it is so—
because I have seen the end.
It is not as imagined,
war and dead bodies,
it is much different.

It is green meadows, with
the sun

shining bright
and it is a clear pool, with
fish and flamingos

and it is a river
with every imaginable
animal, whether it
has died or not.
Everyone will witness the end.

You will witness the end.

For the Simple Answer
Claudia Lewis

For the simple answer
Do not judge me,
For as paper I do yellow,
As a book I do fade,
As time I do age,
As a spirit I do flee.
Judge me as I judge you.

The Night
Alison Tucker

I am mystic about stuffed animals,
for when you go to sleep,
they rise out of the darkness,
make your head swirl.
blue fades into black and
black into white—
swirls of color
in a nightmare.
Then when you awake
   they just fall into the
glassy eyed position
   they were in before.

Black Child
Stephanie Green

Black child
Sitting on a stoop
Hangin' around till his mama comes home
from the supermarket.
Black child
Nothin' to do
Nothin' that's worth doin'
Except for lyin' and stealin'—
That's your idea of fun.
Because there's nobody to encourage your dream.
Nobody to say you're gonna make it in this world,
Not one living soul.
Except your mama.
I heard her the other day sayin':
"Black child,
That's how it is!
You can try your best,
but it'll be so damn hard.
But you'll make it.
I can see it in your eyes.
You will do the best
you could possibly ever do.
I know it."
Mama's home....

Black Child
Chandra Taylor

Black child, American, poor black child of the city.
Living in Harlem, surviving on her own,
Having fun by the fire hydrant, stepping on the tail of a kitty.
Running barefoot, with pants and shirts unsewn.

Black child, American, well-to-do black child of the city.
Living in high-rises, Manhattan, parents with money,
Having fun watching people sing, cuddling the angora kitten.
In the cupboard there's always coffee, tea, or honey.

Black child, Jamaican or Caribbean, magical black child.
Surrounded by sun, sea, and sandy white beaches,
Seeing palm trees in the wind sway untamed, wild.
Always eating: sugar cane, oranges, cherries, and peaches.

Black child, African, beautiful black child.
Surrounded by jungle, animals, and music,
Always having an open field in which to run wild.
Child of the mother of children; she is her music.

    Black child, part of all four. I come from everywhere.
    My Harlem survival, well-to-do family mind.
    Magical Jamaican ways and dark African hair.
    We are only entities embodied—I *am* the wind.

To a Poet
Chris Bowdy

To a poet (whose poems
Seem locked from a reader).
What is more difficult
Than shaping ideas and
Struggling a floating question
Like the upward staircase
That ends up in the cellar?

Should he (shying away
From humor) take the rea-
der's arm and lead him
Into his mind, or explain,
By seemingly lifting out
A textbook and explaining
The meaning of life?

Should he take the question
Of death and shove it
Back into a cemetery,
Coming back the next
Day to find the solution?
Simply to know what one is!
Now there is the burden!

Haiku
Inginio Valentin

The pale-face lady
Like a candle in the night
A glow around her

Imagination
Corin See

Images float
in the fields of our minds
        not the pink elephants
in uncorked liquor bottles
    but real images
that we never tell
floating
    at odd momemts
while we do something
else
    yellow darts fly
in delta formations towards
        a knight
    in purple armor
    and white lions
    enjoy a pawful of honey
    and churches with humming
    plums in three-piece suits
    sink into a chocolate ocean
        words screaming
"vote for Nixon" are shot by
10 bullfrogs in hunting pink
    a giant blunderbuss
fires eggs at the moon
and wolves howl for a glass
of baby liver juice
        I look at my pen,
amazed at what I just wrote.

Thinking Over

(Reflection)

Dialog of Ideas

A good way to get out a lot of your ideas on a subject or issue that interests you is to imagine a dialog about it between two or three people involved in discussing it. You can name the speakers just A, B, and C, or you can characterize them a bit by their names and their styles of speech. Use the dialog as a way to express all the points of view you can muster about the subject without having to take sides, arrive at a conclusion, or worry about contradicting yourself. Just make it up for about a half hour or so straight off, letting what one says prompt what another comes up with by way of reply. Write the dialog down in actual script form, with speakers' names in the left margin followed by a colon and using parentheses to indicate action or setting, if any.

Get a partner or two and read it aloud. Revise: cut and add ideas and rephrase for accuracy or flavor. Then let others act out your script. Or print it up or post. You might also use your dialog as the basis for another piece of writing such as an editorial, column, or other kind of essay.

Animal Rights
Bianca Santomasso

A: I strongly take the stand that animals deserve the same rights granted to humans. They have the right to live without unnecessary persecution and

279

overwhelming cruelty to their minds or their bodies. Animals have a right to live as close to their natural environment as possible without restraint or physical distress. They therefore should be respected and not taken advantage of just because their minds are not as developed as ours are or because most are incapable of communicating ideas to us directly.

In our minds animals seem to have just been put on the earth for our own personal disposal. We don't seem to care how they might be feeling, what great pain they might be experiencing when we perform brutal experiments on them or kill them for food or superfluous items such as furs and hides.

N: I don't agree with your idea that animals are our equals and that they deserve rights. With their incapability to communicate complex ideas as we do, animals are certainly not in any way equivalent to us. Dolphins and monkeys may seem quite smart and be able to pass all sorts of simple skill tests, but they still can't understand complex ideas as we can. These ideas include those behind the computer, the programs, the microchip, the building of skyscrapers and cities, the process behind elections, our government, and our space program. They can't comprehend any of these ideas and therefore shouldn't be considered on our level. It just seems natural that animals be used to promote the survival of our own species. They have a great purpose as research materials for experiments in many different fields.

A: In response to your statement that since animals can't comprehend complex ideas and therefore are our inferiors, I must say that I think you are wrong. If a creature is denied the right to life and peace just because it is not a perfect human, or not quite as intelligent as the average human, then what about our own species? In other words, if animals are denied rights for this reason, then shouldn't young children, retarded humans, and the dumb also be denied them? Well, they aren't and therefore neither should animals. Just because animals are unable to defend themselves with the use of verbal or written language doesn't mean that they should be allowed to be treated the way they are.

The theory of evolution created by Darwin states that there are no higher or lower species. If this is so then why do we continue to destroy tens of millions of conscious animals each year by starvation, heat, cold, chemical and thermal burns, trauma, surgical mutilation, poisoning, electric shock, implantation of tumors and infections, deliberate induction of neuroses, and other methods too terrible for most people to conceive? We wouldn't dream of treating a human this way. Why then do we do it to another innocent species? The experiments are not for the benefit of the animals; why then should they have to pay?

N: We perform these experiments on animals because it is a necessity. Without animal experimentation many of the major breakthroughs in medicine and science would have never been possible, and in the future our goals would remain unreached if animal experimentation were to cease. You must realize that by performing experiments on animals we are saving thousands of human lives. Without them, there would be no way of curing many diseases. Medical science could neither flourish nor advance without experimentation. The list goes on and on and on of the wonders that animal experimentation has achieved and the wonders that can possibly be achieved in the future by animal experimentation. The polio vaccine and a cure for cancer are two major diseases which are on the top of the list. Animal testing is necessary for developing new medications, and surgeons also have to practice on animals. Animals are important research tools, and it is vital they they continue to be used for our own welfare.

A: You are wrong in saying that experiments using animals are a necessity for the welfare of the human race. Much of the so-called research is not experimentation at all, and it is not only inhumane but most of it is also endlessly duplicated demonstrations; some procedures are repeated hundreds or even thousands of times! Sixty to one hundred million animals, including rats, guinea pigs, dogs, cats, monkeys, and assorted other species are used for experimental purposes in the U.S. each year. A large percentage of these are injured or killed brutally for the testing of chemicals and commercial products which are of absolutely no real importance to human survival. Lipstick seems to take priority over the life of an innocent mouse or rabbit. Then another large percentage of animal experimentation is done for the most trivial of reasons. For example a newborn monkey's eyelids are sewn together and then its whole head is bandaged in an experiment just to see what effect sight deprivation and isolation would cause. This particular experiment was totally frivolous and stupid since a detailed interview with any blind person would have sufficed, instead of permanently damaging a monkey's eyes. There are many experiments like this in which it isn't *necessary* to use animals, yet scientists don't even bother to look for alternatives simply because they don't care enough about the animals they are using. The fact above also applies to supposed successful research—in other words, using animals for medical purposes. Many of these types of experiments, surprisingly enough, are not necessary either. It isn't true that by experimenting on animals, major breakthroughs are made very often. It also isn't true that if research is stopped that we aren't going to make any progress. Nature and evolution have so far done their job. And even though there are a few exceptions to diseases cured on their own or without animal experimentation, they too could have been avoided. For example, you mentioned that we wouldn't have the polio vaccine without animal research, and this is true, but it is still false to think that the vaccine wiped out polio. Data* shows that the disease was already on a

*Acquired from the pamphlet *"The Argument for Abolition,"* published by International Society for Animal Rights.

sharp decline in the years immediately before the vaccine was introduced. The disease was actually beginning to wipe itself out on its own. In response to your statement about possibly finding a cure for cancer making animal experimentation worthwhile, this is true, yet it has been found that at least three-quarters of all human cancers are completely avoidable and that most cases are caused by smoking, heavy drinking, a meat-based diet, overexposure to the sun, and environmental pollution. Since we already know how to deal with cancer, instead of funding more research, we should devote our resources to eliminating the known causes of the disease. As for the use of animal experimentation to develop new medications, we don't need any new drugs. We are already drowning in drugs in this country, and new "wonder drugs" add nothing but enormous expenses. Finally, for surgeons to practice their techniques on animals is really not a necessity since it teaches nothing but the anatomy, which can easily be learned from a book. Also the anatomy of animals and that of humans are so different in size and configuration that there really isn't any point in doing it.

Stream of Consciousness

For about 15 minutes write down pell-mell everything that comes into your head, noting thoughts down in a telegraphic style for yourself only. Don't worry about correctness. Choose a quiet time and place that will least draw your attention to the outside world. Find out what's on your mind or under it once you suspend activity and sensations for a while. You may not be able to record all thoughts or do justice to each, but you can sample at least by just letting your mind go and witnessing it on paper. You might do this on several occasions to be sure of getting out a lot of material.

Now look over your notes and try to find a thought or image that you might want to develop, one that may be connected to further thoughts that hadn't emerged before. Or see if you can spot recurring themes or connections among thoughts that you at first regarded as discontinuous and jumbled. Make some more notes to expand or extend or link up ideas. Then shape these into some sort of essay that will allow an audience you have in mind to understand and enjoy your thought train.

(The following samples illustrate notes alone, then notes plus essay, then finally essay alone.)

Notes Only
Daniel Cuff

On the boat dock where you fish I wonder if the gas keeps the fish away or maybe you need nightcrawlers because the weekend that we went there was not one fish that showed. Oh, I think I saw one but I think I was seeing things this spring coming up or this Autumn, next time I go. I want to get to Mick's real early so we can get some worms then take our own rowboat out wet the line and see if I catch anything. I'm sure fishing can be fun if you get yourself together pretty good.

I wonder if you can go sailing in autumn I know it's cold but imagine the wind you could feel like crazy but if tip boy that would be it you'd probably freeze to death and sink to the bottom. But I'm sure I could control the boat I must admit to myself I am a great sailor I like to go out alone the then no one's screaming, "don't tip, don't tip" why would you not want to tip I can't understand this it is so much fun. You go real fast get at an angle so you're parallel to the water hold that for a few seconds and "splash!" you're in the water and pull the boat back up and go.

Notes Only
Roxanne Glass

My need is a friend. I need a friend to be able to understand me to know what I'm talking about, and to help me with my worries and confusions! I can't keep them in any longer, they're too bunched up inside. I can not tell my parents or talk to them because they would get mad at me or not understand! My sister well, she'd just go off and tell my parents or use what I'm telling her or would tell her as a way to get back at me or get me in trouble! I have one fabulous person I could talk to, David Bowen, but he's or he is 25 and maybe wouldn't understand, but then again maybe he would! But I think I'm too embarrassed or too shy and he probably wouldn't care or he is toooo busy! I just don't know what to do, but it's helping to write what I need inside. Sometimes I just want to kill myself or just disappear! Then my worries and problems would not even exist.

Notes
Nava Fader

Tall, tall bookshelf. Crammed with books of every size, shape, and color. I think of how many times I've read them. I feel sure they must know me by heart as I do them. Each full of a little magic. I think that one day the magic of each will gather together. So instead of a book with characters alive only by the words they wear I'll see them come alive and they'll take me to visit all their friends between the porous pages of a well-worn cover.

Colored paper birds, blue and red, pink and green, combinations done in bad taste. They stare at me with blank paper eyes that would never see no matter what magic filled my nest.

And my bed. The mattress always falling off, me always pushing it back on. I smell the sweetness of my younger sister lingering on the blanket with little ladybugs. There's something I always miss when she sleeps on the top bunk and I sleep on the bottom.

The light hanging overhead by my desk gives off too bright a shine. I always put too strong a bulb in it. It seems like you could walk on the path of light.

My sister's little red tricycle lying on one side. It seems sad. Like abandoning childhood to prove something. Knocking over something important and leaving it, wheels turning helplessly, pitifully comic.

Letters from friends strewn over the floor making a chain. Hopefully another link will be added soon. Letters, unfinished to a friend from camp, thanking a relative for a gift received months ago. Unfinished, like everything else.

In a Paper Cage
Nava Fader

[This is the essay based on the preceding notes.]

There's attic magic in my room. I don't know how it got there. Maybe it's because we live on the top floor of the building. Magic rises as does hot air, you know.

I look carefully around to make sure I'm alone before I open my sticker-garbed door. Inside everything is so quiet, maybe it won't happen today. Wait—what's that? I turn to see what I hope is something moving, something alive. A product of the magic's work. But no, it is only a mobile of colored paper birds drifting occasionally in a stray wind. I sigh and stare wistfully at the lifeless creatures who stare back with blank, unseeing eyes. And is it my longing, or has the magic decided to work at last? For the birds, so dull and stupid, so colorless and flat, have seemingly begun to be alive. They detach themselves from restraining cords that leave them to dangle from the ceiling and fly furiously around the room. And then they sing. They sing the song of one who has tasted freedom before and longs always to feast upon such delicacies but is encased in a cage. Whether it be metal, gold, or as in this case, paper it makes no difference. The restriction is felt.

And the blue of my walls becomes the blue of the sky, and the birds sail away. But I know they will return. Now I have to squint at the place where I last saw the birds, for my light has become so bright, almost like the sun. Is it the light or is it the sun? I remember what I read in *Mary Poppins*, "It is what you think it is," so I try hard to think it is the sun. I want the magic to continue. But the battle between thinking "seeing is believing" and thinking "believing is seeing," is strong. And alas, common sense gets the better of me. So today is not the day I travel to foreign lands or become part of a fairy tale. Today I will think about the birds in a paper cage. I smile sadly, full of regret, but then the attic magic and I exchange a wink; we share a secret.

Getting Old
Jennifer Rosen

[This is a rewritten version of the notes only.]

I'm terrified of getting old. I have written before of getting old while being alive, but I've never really written about what I think about getting old and dying.

I guess I'm kind of scared of the fact that I won't be here any more or that there may not be a place that I'll go after I'm dead and buried... BURIED.

That's what I'm scared of. Being buried underground. Not being able to see. My flesh slowly rotting until only my bones are left. I look at my arm and hand and think, "Hey! One day this won't be anything more than bones in a rotten casket!"

And my funeral. I remember my grandmother's funeral. Everyone was really upset listening to the rabbi talk about how great a woman and mother she was, bringing four children into the world. My grandmother's cousin was there. She couldn't believe that my grandmother was dead. So after we had all left the synagogue, she went back and opened the casket. My grandmother was there, all right.

The most upsetting part of that day was when they put the casket into the earth. As they covered it with soil, I realized I would never see my grandmother again. It was at that point that I cried, because until then it hadn't occurred to me that this occasion was very, very final.

Statement Through Story
Narrate any true happening that illustrates a general point you want to make. In other words, you are telling a story not only for its own sake but also to show something that the reader could apply to people and events he or she knows. This can be in first or third person and drawn from any source.

It could be included in a collection of other writings on the same theme or could be incorporated later into a large paper dealing more comprehensively with the point. Or post or print up.

Lessons of the Big City
David Hueston

New York City isn't getting any better, it's getting worse. More muggings and murders take place in a day than one would think. People in this society are getting so scared that in certain parts of the city if you saw a multitude of people you couldn't find one who wasn't checking to see who was behind them, and they have every right to. Most people think, "Well, it's not going to happen to me, so why should I care?" But when it does happen to them, it's too late. That's why you have to be careful out there. You never know when someone's going to pull you into a dark alley or put a cold blade into your back. An incident that happened to me really changed the way I feel about people on the street today.

It was a hot muggy 4th of July day. All the kids were outside playing with different types of fireworks. You could hear loud bangs as the fireworks went off all around the block. I was with my friends Trevor and Ray. We had just come out of my building, and my friend Trevor said that he wanted to buy some fireworks. So Ray and I followed Trevor over to a kid who was selling them. Trevor asked the kid the types of fireworks he had. The kid replied, firecrackers, bottle rockets, Jumping Jacks, and a few more which I can't remember.

Trevor, being very avid, pulled out the money that he was keeping in his pocket. It totaled 40 dollars. Quickly realizing that he had pulled too much money out he put 35 dollars back into his sock. Then having all that he needed he bought around six packs of firecrackers and six packs of Jumping Jacks.

All of us then went up into the back of my building. We stayed there for a while talking to different people. Then all of a sudden people started to warn us to get out of the back, though they would not say why. We, thinking nothing of this, ignored their warning and continued to stay in back. They kept on being very insistent and we decided we'd better leave.

So as we were about to go down the steps leading us into the front, two teenagers, both between the ages of seventeen and twenty, came up the steps just as we were about to go down. They were talking to each other in a very calm manner. We continued to walk on. Then all of a sudden one of them grabbed Trevor from the back and put his arm across his neck. Trevor began to struggle as the kid pulled on his neck tighter and tighter. At the same time the other kid lifted his pants and took the 35 dollars out of his sock. I did not know what to do. I froze in a confused state and just watched the pilferers take his money. My friend Ray was in the same state. The mugging lasted only 30 seconds, but it seemed to go on for an eternity. One of them quickly counted the money, then ran off with it. Tears came from Trevor's eyes as he screamed violently.

That was the most frightening experience I had ever had. After that incident I said to myself we were lucky in a way that he didn't pull out a knife or, even worse, a gun and get nervous and pull the trigger. Out of all this I've learned a valuable lesson.

A Learning Experience
Felicia Washington

Once I was walking on 112th Street near Amsterdam Avenue. The streets and sidewalks were very dirty because of the construction work that some men were doing in the street. Buses and cars traveled in all directions. The traffic lights didn't work, and the people were scattered all over, trying to get where they wanted to be.

I was all by myself, which is very unusual because everywhere I go my friend goes along with me. When I turned a corner: Boom! Bang! Smash! When I turned around I saw that a car had driven into a drugstore.

I wanted to be nosy, of course, so I peeked inside. All these people were cursing and arguing, and some were even panicking and very nervous. The manager came out, and you could tell he had already had a fit. His hair was messed up. His clothes were looking dingy, and he had only one shoe on. I guessed he ran out of the other one while getting away.

The man that had crashed into the store was a Puerto Rican addict who was on probation from a past criminal record of stealing pills, needles and other supplies from hospitals.

I know of all this because I was listening to everything the police said so I could go home and tell everybody what happened.

The next day the story about the crash that I had seen was in the daily newspaper. I could not believe it when I saw the heading. That was the first time I had actually seen something happen that was in the paper the very next day.

My mother read the article and started to tell me that I had the story all twisted up.

I told her that the newspaper had it twisted because I had seen it with my own two eyes and the newspaper was wrong. They twisted it up and had it all wrong.

I went in my room and I was talking to myself. I couldn't believe how they changed the incident like that; I mean it was just like telling a lie.

The time was changed to the night in a different hour; like an hour later. They said the man was black. They said he also was from another state. The newspaper did it all wrong. They changed the story completely. The way the newspaper exaggerates stories is unbelievable.

Every time the newspaper has to tell about something that happened they always put it in wrong or they mix it all up and have it backwards. When I read the newspaper I never believe it because half the time it does not make any sense at all. And anyway I don't even read the paper any more.

Newspaper Departments

Advice Letter

Get with some partners and make up a name for your column, like "Dear Abby," based on the name of an imaginary counselor. Write a letter to him or her asking for advice about a problem that is either real or sounds real. Provide enough detail and background to give the counselor plenty to go on. Put your letter in a box set aside for the advice column and take out someone else's to answer. (You don't have to use your real name.)

Run these as a column, perhaps a regular one, in a newspaper, make an advice bulletin board, or make a book of the letters. Get others involved and keep the column or board going.

Advice Column
M.E. (John Lipkin)

Dear M.E.,

I have a money problem. My friends snap on my clothes and they snap on my building all the time. What should I do?

Signed, No Cash Flow

Dear No Cash Flow,

Never be ashamed of your building or clothes. At least you have a roof over your head and clothes on your back. If you want extra money, babysit! If that doesn't work, start collecting bottles (5¢ each bottle).

Dear M.E.,

I have a friend who's nice to my mother and asks me if I can come over to his house. As soon as I step foot in the house, he takes advantage of me. He throws things at me, locks me in the bathroom, kicks me down the steps and he beats me. He thinks it's fun, but it hurts me. What should I do?

Signed, Taken Advantage Of

Dear Taken Advantage Of,

What is your problem in that case? You must like it if you keep going back. My advice is to tell him NO!—You won't GO.

Dear M.E.,

One of my good friends is having a party. Everyone is invited except me and I just can't go up to him and say where's my invitation. What should I do?

Signed, Staying Home

Dear Staying Home,

Check in your mail one more time. But if it is not in there, make your own party—invite all your friends but *don't* invite that person. You don't need two-faced friends like that.

Dear M.E.,

I had a job babysitting, making $20 a week. Boy, did I have it made! But then they got their phone bill. It cost $150 and they are thinking about firing me. I did make a lot of calls but not all of them, and it gets kind of lonely in a big house, so I call some friends.

Signed, Out of a Job

Dear Out of a Job,

Ask them if you could stay on the job until the money is paid off. It is your fault because you just can't go crazy on someone else's phone because you are lonely!

Dear M.E.,

My wallet is missing and I know who has it. But I just can't go up to him and say, "Give me my wallet," but it contains a lot of important things I need.

Signed, Out of a Wallet

Dear Out of a Wallet,

Try and find proof against him or try to get it from him. Other than that, there is nothing you could do.

Dear M.E.,

Last weekend I was accused of stealing something I didn't steal. It was my best friend's mother's chair. How could I have done it when I was home?

From,
Mr. Not Guilty

Dear Mr. Not Guilty,

Well, who was home with you? Use any other alibis that you find to protect yourself. Remember, you are not guilty until proven guilty.

Dear M.E.,

This year I started off on the wrong track. I don't do homework, I am very sloppy, I fail tests, and the counselor's on my case. And really, I don't understand most things that I am taught.

From,
Failure

Dear Failure,

You should get a tutor to help you with your work (it's better to get help at the beginning of the year) and try to get homework from a friend.

Dear M.E.,

I really like this girl but she likes my friend. What should I do?

From,
Lovesick

Dear Lovesick,

You should take her in a corner and explain to her how you feel. If it doesn't work, well, your friend is lucky.

Dear M.E.,

I don't have money to go on the Senior trip. It costs $80.00, and my mother's not going to give me the money because she doesn't agree it's right that we are going to stay two days.

From,
Not Going

Dear Not Going,

Well, try to compromise with your mother. If that doesn't work, then try and save your allowance until then.

Dear Ann and Louise
Karen Levine and Lisa Acevedo

Dear Ann and Louise,

My problem is I have a new ten-speed bike, and every time I ride it, I'm afraid of getting it stolen. So far I've only ridden out back where there are security guards. If I go anywhere I have to carry a ten-pound lock (which they say is the best). I need help.

Signed X

Dear X,

You have every right to feel this way. What you could do is have an adult or several friends go bike riding with you. If no one can, ask a policeman or a security guard if he/she can tell people to please buzz off if anyone bothers you. Many people have this fear. Another tip: learn to *defend* yourself, and stay *with* your bike in more crowded areas. Hopefully your bike will never be stolen.

Dear Ann and Louise,

I would really like to know how could I solve this problem: somebody gets on your nerves all the time, and one day that person steals one of your pens. You tell that person that you are going to fight her/him, but you know that if you fight you will get suspended. So, what could you do? If you go to the principal she tells that person not to do it again, and it's not fair for you. So please tell me, thank you.

Nyasha

Dear Nyasha,

I know exactly how you feel. I knew a person like that once. Tell her/him off, or ignore her/him. *If* this person does it *again* tell a teacher. Stealing is very wrong. Even if it is a pen. However do not *fight*. (You are just as liable to get hurt as he/she is.) Try speaking to the principal again.

Dear Ann and Louise,

My problem is my homework. Two days a week I go to Hebrew school. One day a week I go to special Hebrew lessons concerning my bar mitzvah, and every after-school I walk a dog for about 45 minutes.

My problem is that because of all these extra activities after school the time I get to spend on my homework is limited since my mom dislikes it when I stay up late. Please tell me what I can do.

Sincerely yours, Allen Cunnings

Dear Allen Cunnings,

What I would like to know is if it's necessary to walk the dog for 45 minutes. If not, that solves one problem. Tell your mom that the reason you stay up late is that you have to do a lot of other things. Maybe she will understand. If not, do what I always do. Make a schedule and stick to it!

Dear Ann and Louise,

There was this girl in my sixth grade class that I used to go out with and we were really good friends. Now she always calls me to tell me how she is really happy with this guy. It really bothers me, and she knows it! I don't know what to do.

Troubled

Dear Troubled,

For all you know this all could be lies that she is telling you. The only reason she is telling you all of this is because she is trying to make you jealous. If she knows she is making you jealous, she is going to keep on. The next time she calls you try not to let her know she is bothering you. Maybe she will stop.

This—Is Advice???
DG (Lisina Russo)

Dear Gabby,

I've got this serious problem with relationships (particularly mine). My problem is really boys. Everyone has a boyfriend, everyone has a date for the dance, everyone has a boy's ring or chain, everyone but me. I used to think it was acne, but that cleared up three months ago. I then thought it was my hair, so I got it cut. Now I wish I had kept it the same. My last hope for a date to the dance was gross, but hopeful, so I kissed a toad. All I got were warts! What's wrong with me? Is it personality, looks or what? Help!!

Signed, Totally Wartful

Dear Totally Wartful,

I honestly think it's not your looks or personality. I think it's all the changing around and cutting your hair. Kissing toads is not the answer! I really suggest you try cold cream to get rid of your warts, and then stay the same for a while. Give people a chance to like you....

Dear Gabby,

Yesterday I got a beautiful light blue sweater with little bears on it. My mother says I should only wear it on special occasions "because it cost *so* much." Well, I wore it to school and the sleeve ripped on the fence.... I know I will be killed if I tell her, and next Saturday my grandmother's coming over and she wants me to wear it....

Signed, "Ripped in Half"

Dear Half,

You should always tell the truth and never lie, especially to your parents. Lying just gets you into more trouble. You should explain to your mother how you were wrong and she was right, and that from now on you will listen to her. If she still won't forgive you tell her that you will try to make it up by doing chores—and remind her you love her.

Dear Gabby,

Everytime I eat meat or wear fur I feel like it's my fault the animal's dead. Some people say it's normal, but I feel like a sadist when I kill a roach!!!!

Signed, DEAD

Dear Dead,

Become a vegetarian!

Directions to Do or Make Something

Explain step by step how to do some activity such as operate a certain machine, care and feed certain plants or animals, or get from one place to another. Or, using the same step-by-step approach, describe how to make something—a model ship, a bookshelf, a patchwork quilt—whatever product or craft item you're knowledgable about.

Feed into the directions at useful points whatever background information may be required for understanding the directions. Let somebody try to follow these directions and tell you what difficulties they may have had. Rewrite as needed.

Make copies for interested people. Include in a how-to book.

How to Wash a Dog
Susie Butler

If you have a dirty dog covererd with mud and dirt, who has just come in from a fox hunt and the beauty parlor is closed, then you have a problem. But there's a simple solution. Give your dog a bath at home by yourself. All you need is a tub, water, towels, a scoop, dog soap, a dog biscuit, and of course, a dirty dog.

It's a good idea to wear old clothes so you don't ruin your nice clothes. In preparation for the bath you should do three things. First, lay out on the floor a layer of towels and then leave a pile of towels all near the tub. Second, fill the tub half to three-quarters full of warm water. Third, you must find your dog. Some dogs love water, but others dislike water and will resist the bath. So to get your dog into the tub you can lure him with a dog biscuit. Once you've caught your dog you should remove his collar.

The first thing you do once your dog is in the tub is to wet your dog, using the scoop. But avoid the ears and face area. Next, take your dog soap and put a ring of soap around your dog's neck. This will prevent fleas from getting into the dog's ears. Next, soap your dog's body, the back, stomach, legs, feet and the tail, again avoiding the face area. Now, take your scoop and using the water in the tub rinse off the dog. Once your dog is thoroughly rinsed drain the tub. Turn on the faucet. Using warm water and the scoop rinse off your dog, thoroughly! After the second rinsing run your fingers along your dog's back. If any soap bubbles appear then you should do another rinsing. When the dog is thoroughly rinsed remove him from the tub, placing him on the towels. Immediately, cover your dog with towels. This will prevent you from getting wet, because wet dogs have a tendency to shake. Next, rub all the excess water off, or as much as practical. Keep him inside for a few hours until he is fully dry. Always remember to reward a good dog with lots of praise and a dog biscuit!

How to Make Spaghetti Sauce
David Molot

I've eaten many different brands of spaghetti sauces from a jar, and it is difficult to compare my homemade sauce, which I feel is outstanding, with these other inferior sauces that are on the market. My sauce is so superior because it is made entirely from fresh ingredients and no preservatives. Today I will teach you how to make this wonderful homemade sauce.

First, sauté an onion in one teaspoon cooking oil. Then add half a pound chopped beef and break the beef apart with a fork. Cook until golden brown. Then add and stir in one cup peeled tomatoes, one cup tomato sauce, and half a cup of tomato paste. For seasoning, add and stir in half a teaspoon salt, half a teaspoon oregano, and a dash of pepper. Simmer until thickened. Serve on your spaghetti. Many people who have tasted my sauce say that I should bottle it and sell it, but I like to make it and eat it.

Review

After you have seen a film or TV program, read a book, eaten in a restaurant, or seen an art or science exhibit, evaluate your experience for the benefit of others. Write a review. It's a good idea to take notes on your impressions during the experience. The general point of a review is to make a recommendation to you reader. So while describing the thing, make clear what you consider its strong and weak points, and back these up with evidence.

Read some reviews to get ideas about how description and evaluation may be woven together. Often it's useful to compare the thing you are reviewing to others of its kind. Some background information too may be welcome to readers if they are not familiar with some things about your subject, such as facts about an artist's life or about different kinds of computers (for a product review).

Put your review in a newspaper or post up on a special board for reviews and book suggestions.

Broadway on Film
Greg Goldstein

Deathtrap

* * * ½

Deathtrap is a fantastic thriller that's a lot of fun. It's based on the great Broadway play by Ira Levin, written for film by Jay Presson Allen. It is a compilation of plot twists, scares, laughs, shocks, and suprises that all add up to a great movie. People who have seen the play (like me) will notice an additional twist added on to the end. It isn't the greatest, but it's good.

The film has a superb cast, including Michael Caine, who plays a mystery writer whose five recent Broadway productions have all been flops. His wife, nicely played by Dyan Cannon, gets worried when he says he'd "kill" for a good play. Then an envelope arrives at their house, enclosing a thriller written by one of his literary course students (Christopher Reeve). Caine realizes that the play sent is a sure-fire hit, and the story begins. I can't give away any more of the plot without ruining the movie for you, but I can tell you that nothing is what it seems.

Deathtrap is more fun than scary, and in this type of movie, that fits perfectly. As good as *Deathtrap* is as a movie, the play is better. That's because the story is designed for the theater. But it's still a clever and fun film. See it.

Annie

* * * ½

Only once in a while does a film come along so fantastic and big in scale that it can be called an event. *Annie* is such a film. Not since the late '40s has such a great musical been made into such a great movie. All musical numbers are staged and performed fabulously. It stars newcomer Aileen Quinn as Annie, the red-haired orphan who gets adopted by billionaire Daddy Warbucks, excellently played by Albert Finney. But the best performance by far is by Carol Burnett, who is superb as Miss Hannigan, the mean, undersexed drunk who runs the orphanage. Her hysterical performance is the highlight of the film. Ann Reinking is good as Warbuck's personal secretary. *Annie* has some fine supporting performances, too. Tim (*Rocky Horror*) Curry and Bernadette Peters do great jobs as Miss Hannigan's brother and his girlfriend; they pose as Annie's long-lost parents in order to get the reward money. The only flawed performance is Quinn's who, while a good singer and dancer, is a bit too cutesy to play even Annie.

At a cost of over $50 million to produce, it seems like the money was well spent. *Annie* is as elaborate as it is fun. One bad thing is that the song "N.Y.C." has been eliminated. In its place there is "Let's Go to the Movies," a number that brings them to Radio City Music Hall to see a premiere. It's not as good, but there are some new songs that are great. *Annie* is a great old-fashioned movie musical. A good see.

D.D.L. Food Show
Susannah Kaplan

There's a new show in town and its name is D.D.L. Food Show. It sells food, food, and nothing but. The prices are steep, but it costs nothing to just go in and look around, and that's exactly what I did.

The store is large and airy and pleasant. It is very attractive, with its palms and ferns and glass roof that looks out onto the sky. D.D.L. smells heavenly of bread, cheese, chocolate, spices, smoked meat, and many other delicious smells that will absolutely tantalize you right down to your toes.

There are people everywhere, most of them just looking and drooling, but some are buying.

The personnel are friendly, and they'll gladly answer any questions you have.

The only fly in D.D.L.'s ointment is that it is so glamorous and fancy that one wonders if they are interested in selling food or something else.

But if they can withstand the competition, they're sure to make a lot of bread, as well as sell it.

MTV
Jonathan Winslow

In the last year cable TV has produced many new programs, the most successful of these being MTV and the Movie Channel. I have been informed that some people must pay for MTV Don't!

It you like punk or new-wave then this channel is for you. But if your ears are attuned to Hard Rock then you would be wasting your money by buying this station.

MTV is terribly repetitious. If you watch for only an hour and a half you'll find the groups are being played over and over and over again, with an occasional slip-in of something that could only in the least sense of the word be called good.

If you enjoy listening to "Rock the Casba" and the "Do do da" then you'll enjoy it.

What's it all about? What happens is a group who has already done a record and is somewhat popular makes a video of either their band in concert or some sort of psychedelic, mind-boggling junk. They play three or four songs in a row, then five minutes of commericals, then three more minutes advertising none other than themselves. Once every hour they offer ten minutes of music news that should take only three.

So in conclusion I'll say that if you get a chance to see it, see it—but don't buy it.

Flight of the Boodles
David Zoll

Flight of the Boodles is a fun game for two humans created by C.C. Stoll. This game uses two types of pieces—boodles and grumjugs. Boodles are short, chubby humanoids who wear baggy pants. Grumjugs are lizard-like, and the position of their hands and feet is reversed.

One player takes the boodle forces, who are trying to cross the board, while the grumjug player tries to stop them. The players move their pieces around the board and occasionally fight each other. There are also rules for solo play of the game.

I like the game very much. It may look simple, but it has many possible strategies and outcomes.

Camilla
Amy Billone

Camilla, a novel by Madeline L'Engle, Newbery-award-winning author of *A Wrinkle in Time* and the Austin family series, is the story of a fifteen-year-old girl's discovery of her parents' vulnerability as she emerges from the safety of childhood and is confronted with the dangers of growing up.

Camilla's plot, while on the surface appearing to work fairly well, loses credibility under closer examination. The story consists mainly of morbid situations and unsolvable conflicts which, instead of being resolved at the end, are only intensified. My frustration with the plot, however, is not a direct result of the dissatisfying conclusion but rests primarily in an attitude of almost unrealistic optimism taken by the author. Madeline L'Engle attempts to reinforce the need for faith and the value of life by spouting optimism in a grim context. She accomplishes this not through the events of the story but through the characters themselves. As a result, the characters also fail to achieve credibility because they are used as vehicles rather than explored as human beings. Camilla, the protagonist and title character of the book, is used as a mouthpiece for the author's views. The theme of the story becomes so tangled up and intermingled with philosophical messages that it is impossible to distinguish between the two. Eventually the theme becomes a moral and, instead of growing naturally, is laid down upon the reader with such force that it becomes a kind of burden. Presenting the theme so heavy-handedly, without any attempt towards subtlety, deprives the reader of the right to discover it.

Despite these weaknesses, the quality of Madeline L'Engle's writing is very strong due to her fresh choice of words and overall command of the language. However, instead of increasing my appreciation for *Camilla,* L'Engle's verbal skill leaves me troubled: she has manipulated the language in order to influence the minds of her readers. After reading *Camilla,* I am left with a sense of loss—my childhood admiration for Madeline L'Engle, inspired by books such as *A Wrinkle in Time,* has been tarnished. While the book is directed towards junior high readers, this age group especially would resist its preachiness. For me, the magic of Madeline L'Engle has been reduced to propaganda.

Editorial

Editorials express opinions about matters currently being discussed in a community. The matters usually concern whether some action should be taken or whether something already going on is right, like a well-known building being torn down or a school rule being changed. Read some editorials in different newspapers and magazines. If you want to get in on some discussion in your school or community, or want to propose some changes, make a case by using all the reasons and evidence you can think of. Write these down in a way that you think will persuade your readers.

What's the best way to get your editorial to the attention of those you want to persuade?

The Hairstyle of the Ugly Age
Jillian Atkin

These days, people are wearing the strangest hairstyles. Some I can understand. Just regular short hair (shoulder length) and natural. But teenagers, not in this school, but in private schools and some public schools, are cutting their hair up to the nape of the neck and dying it whatever color stands out in a crowd (believe me, it works).

Kids will do anything to get noticed. I don't think Moms are too thrilled about it. Last year I tried to can (spray) my hair too, but, all in vain; my hair turned stiff.

I think kids should leave their hair natural and not dye it. Maybe cut it a little, but not too much. This is a strange age and a very ugly one too.

Testing, Cheating, Grading, and Learning
Nancy Mervish and Roberta Newman

How many times have you heard . . . "And tomorrow there'll be a test on everything we have learned so far"? We hear it quite a lot. Do tests really help you learn? Some teachers think it is a good idea to give tests so they are sure the students know the subject before they go on to another one.

Ms. Tashlik told us that she likes to use methods of teaching that enable students to learn; having students learn is her aim. Ms. Tashlik feels that learning is experiental and should have some enjoyment to it. But what do students feel?

Most students would say, "Whatever way I can get a good mark on my report card is the way I like it." Another attitude might be a concerned and conscientious student who likes to learn a lot and be challenged. Most students fear tests because they know what it all boils down to. It all boils down to their grades, and everyone wants a good grade to please their parents.

Is grading necessary? Some teachers like to write lengthy reports about each student, but that can be hard because with all the students in each of their classes, it gets tiring. Most students don't like their marks based on one or two tests, because they think it is unfair. They say, "What if I have an off day, or the test didn't really cover anything we learned," but that is the students' point of view.

Cheating is also an important factor in test taking. At the beginning of a test teachers tend to say if they catch anyone looking at anyone else's paper they will rip up the test and give them a zero. Kids often cheat on tests, and it's not because they are stupid or even because they didn't study. It's just because they get so nervous. They aren't sure of themselves, and they have to verify their answer. Also, if the kid next to them has a different answer, the person will not necessarily change his or hers, though some do. And, even though some kids say they never cheat, they must have at one time or another. Or they are not human!

Sex, Violence, and Profane Language on TV
Robbie Tewlow

When you watch television have you noticed any changes in the show's content? Do you see more explicit sex scenes? If you have, you are a victim of modern television watching syndrome.

More television shows are containing explicit sex, violence, and profane language, and many reactions aren't positive. Parents complain that exposing children to such material affects them emotionally. Psychologists and others have done studies that show sex, violence, and language on television have definite effects on adults, adolescents, and children.

Have you ever watched *Tom and Jerry, Road Runner,* or *Bugs Bunny?* Do you realize the violence they contain? Jerry blowing up Tom, the coyote falling off a cliff, or Bugs shooting Elmer Fudd? This violence is seen by many young children daily! It results in children acting violently or aggressively or doing the crazy stunts in cartoons, like jumping off a building and expecting not to be injured and things of that sort. People think that this rubs off on the children.

Many shows containing violent scenes are usually put on at 9:00 or ten o'clock. One of the more violent shows is *The A Team.* Many shows contain mature subject matter such as *Hill Street Blues, St. Elsewhere, Dallas,* and *Dynasty.* Besides dealing with mature subject matter they contain explicit sex scenes and strong language.

I asked some students: "How do you feel about sex, violence and language on TV? Does it affect you in any way?"

Tanya P.   Some shows go too far.

Jon W.   It affects me in no way, and groups like the moral majority are taking the whole subject too far.

Gillian   No comment. I belong to the moral majority.

Pedro S.   It's natural to me like ABC's and it has no effect on me.

What Do You Think?

Column

Read some columns in newspapers or magazines. Columnists often write about personal or general human interest subjects, while some write about specialized subjects like science, sports, politics, art, and so on. But the point of view is the columnist's own. A columnist often gets an idea by reacting to something he or she has recently observed, or to something that recently occurred in the field the column specializes in. So a column is a kind of personal essay, a chance to communicate your thoughts and feelings about something to whatever kind of audience reads the newspaper or magazine. You might try keeping your column going for a while on a regular basis.

If you don't have a newspaper or magazine to print it in, just share it with others as you might any other essay, by making copies, posting up, or including in a booklet of other writing.

Pet Pimples
Robin Rittenbrand

There is a very important part of growing up which you don't learn in school. This is how to cope with zits, or how to get rid of them. Some of us are even fortunate enough to get a lot of these pretty creatures.

First of all, the word "zit" has to be the ugliest word ever born. The less vulgar way of referring to them is by calling them "pimples." "Pimples" isn't as ugly as "zits," but I still wouldn't even name my pet gerbil "Pimples."

Even if you don't eat oils, sugars or chocolates and you keep your face clean, you may still awake to the frightening sight of a whitehead, blackhead, or just an ordinary zit. Zits can come alone, in bunches, or all at once, which is referred to as the "massive breakout." They usually come when you want to look your best, that is, if you're lucky. There are zits which come and go in one day, the huge zit which stays for a month, the little pimples which only you notice but drive you crazy, and there are zits which won't dry out, so you uncontrollably pick them. When it comes to picking them you can pick them with your nail, squeeze them, or stab them, which always turns out to be a disaster between bleeding and scarring.

How can we escape the powers of the zit? Eat a healthy diet, drink lots of water, exericse regularly, or do it the easy way and wear a mask!

The Main Event
Kamil Abdullah

Wrestling! The mecca of all sports! It's where the WWF, AWA and NWA all compete! There are championship matches, the Battle of the Belts, the Main Events, and Wrestle Mania!

There are pinholds, forearms, cobra clutch, head bunts, supple body slams, figure falls, scissorholds and sleeperholds. There are the tag team champions: WWF—Greg "The Hammer" Valentine and Brutus Beefcake. NWA—The Road Warriors: Animal and Hawk. The Champions of the World: Hulk Hogan and Rick Martell. Intercontinental Champion: Tito Santana.

Wrestling is a great sport, but some think it's fake. I, for one, don't think so! I mean some moves *might* be fake, like a head bunt or a forearm, but a pile driver or coming off the top ropes are not fake moves because they can't be stopped . . . no way, no-how, nowhere!

A couple of weeks ago, the "Main Event" took place. The "Main Event" is a wrestling show that comes on Channel 14 at 11:30 p.m. on specific Saturday nights. Now let's find out what took place.

The Junk Yard Dog took on Terry Funk! The Dog lost due to outside interference from a megaphone. Terry Funk hit the Dog with the megaphone, then pinned the Dog. He attempted to brand him, but the Dog caught the branding iron, threw Terry Funk out of the ring, grabbed Jimmy "Mouth-of-the-South" Heart, ripped his pants off and branded him.

Andre and Hulk Hogan fought Studd and Bundy. Andre and Hogan won by disqualification due to the Brain's interference.

Ricky "The Dragon" Steamboat took on Mr. Fuji, and the Dragon won by pinfall. But...Muraco blew salt in his eyes and they both ran.

The next card...Monday, November 25th, M.S.G. with an 8 p.m. starting time. Ricky "The Dragon" Steamboat will take on the Magnificent Don Muraco. Andre, H. BoJim and Capt. L. Albano will face Studd, Bundy and the Brain. Tito Santana and Pedro Morales will face Greg "The Hammer" Valentine and Burtus Beefcake.

Where There's Smoking There's Fire
Julie Lefkowitz

My most enjoyable experiences are the times when I go out to dinner or get on an airplane and the people next to me are a group of chain-smokers. Usually, chain-smokers seem to have memory problems. For instance, when a stewardess on a plane goes over to one of them while they are smoking, much to the annoyance of fifteen other people, and the stewardess asks them not to smoke, they argue with her until the cigarette is finished. Then they say they won't smoke. The minute the stewardess is gone, they forget what she said and light up again.

Or while I'm in a restaurant, they always seem to blow their smoke in my direction. I always wonder how a smoker can eat after getting that disgusting nicotine smell in their mouth—I know I can't after ten minutes of having to inhale their smoke. I've never figured out how they get so nervy as to ruin other people's dinner and ignore slight hints from me such as choking to death from the smoke, comments like, "My eyes are tearing from the cigarette smoke, I wish some people wouldn't blow smoke in other peoples' faces," and some other subtle remarks. I always figure, if they're going to be obnoxious, why shouldn't I? As the saying goes, "Fight fire with fire." But for this situation, I'd like to change it to "Fight fire with a fire extinguisher sprayed in their direction!"

Gotta Dance!
Daniel Cuff

Gotta dance! Gotta dance! Gotta! ... dance. Gene Kelly can move over the floor without touching and still tap. Tap, tap, tap, tap, tapppity tap! Donald O'Connor makes his feet dance like they had a life of their own.

Practice, practice, practice, in front of the mirror; get that arm perfect. Tappity tap, tap. Gene Kelly's voice to me sounds like gentle, elegant sandpaper.

Gene Kelly was married twice. He won an Emmy and an Oscar. He was in the Navy. He is 71 and his house burned down with his Emmy, Oscar, and dancing shoes.

Donald O'Connor can run up the wall and flip over. He's a great actor, and he's funny: Moses supposes his toes are roses, but Moses supposes erroneously . . . but Moses he knowsis his toes aren't roses, as Moses supposes his toesis to be.

Fred Astaire, I love him. He can tap so good it is not even funny. "I'm stepping out, my dear, into an atmosphere simply adorned with class. And I'll be there putting on my top hat, my white tie, brushing off my tails."

With his hair all greased up and combed way back, he has a manner of elegance which he captures in a very artistic way. I love the way he walks out on to the stage in top hat, all slanted, and this great smile on his face. He walks with this stride that really lets you know that he's the best, which he is.

The gentlemen all line up with their tap shoes thundering. But Fred handles it—his cane turns into a gun and shoots all the men down, smiling and tapping the whole time.

"I just got an invitation through the mail. A President requesting my presence in top hat, white tie, and tails," he sings with an air of suaveness and also a hint of glee. And then Fred takes a bow and tips his hat and walks off the stage.

The Mystery of Patmos
Rania Calas

There is something in the atmosphere of Patmos that changes our perception of people and things. The sky is bluer, the water in the ocean is clearer, and the rocks craggier than anywhere else. The houses are white-washed around Easter time every year; so are the churches and chapels that stand on every corner and on the hills. In the evening bells are tinkling from the monasteries and from herds of goats being driven over rocky pastures.

There is something about the sunlight on this island that penetrates things and makes their forms and colors appear more clearly and distinctly. I can see myself there more vividly than when I am in other places. The good things seem better and the bad appear worse. The same thing happens to a deep red hibiscus flower against the white wall of a house. It says, "Look at me! Look how beautiful I am! I am the only flower on this earth!"

Georgios, the retired garbage collector, sits on a rock in the shade of an eucalyptus tree. He is a big man, and much more than a garbage collector. His face is lined and leathery from the sun and wind. He has a beautiful smile. He cracks almonds on the stone, and the shells scatter about like grasshoppers. "Here! Have some almonds! Take them! Take them!" he says. Georgios is a very poor man, but he gives almonds like a rich man. His eyes sparkle in the light that shines through him. He, too, looks as if he were the only human on earth.

An ugly woman with most of her teeth missing looks like a witch in a fairy tale. Her voice is screechy, like that of the Wicked Witch of the West in the *Wizard of Oz*. In the wind her voice is carried from street to street. It can still be heard even after she is far up the village road.

Once an apostle came to Patmos. His name was John. He had a special vision of the end of the world. His disciple wrote down all the things John saw. It became the Book of Revelation in the Bible. He, too, saw things he might not have seen anywhere else but on that rocky island in the middle of the Aegean Sea.

A young boy passes by with his spindly, hungry goats. He stops for a moment. "What are you going to be when you are grown up, Janis?" I asked him. He throws his head back. "A priest," he says, "and you shall kiss the ring on my finger!"

I guess Janis will be a priest some day, because he is so sure of it. And after looking at his dirty goatherd hands, I am just as sure that I am not going to kiss the ring on his finger, even if he should become abbot of the Monastery of St. John!

In a nunnery, an old nun says her prayers at four o'clock in the afternoon. She is in the chapel. She says all the names of all the saints, and with each name she bends her thin body down to the stone floor. Her back has become bent from this exercise she has done for so many years, but when I look at her face it is not sad or unhappy. Just the contrary. It is a sweet face. Her eyes look happy. She does what she does gladly. The incense and the smell of the candles in the chapel, the nun's face and the way she bends down again and again form a memory in my mind that stays on and on forever. This, too, is special, different. It is Patmos.

At night, on top of the hill, a silence comes over the island so complete that you can hear your own heart beat in bed. That's when you notice too that your brain works better than usually. You remember sights and sounds of the day as if you were reliving the day all over again.

Some people get a little scared in Patmos, because they are not used to this kind of vivid perception, but once they are away from the island, they are sorry they left. In their memory remains a very blue sky, and the light that goes through everything. They remember the water so clear that one can see the pebbles on the ocean floor. They will never forget it, and the rest of the world will always seem worse than it was before they saw Patmos.

Essay

Topic Essay

Select a subject that really interests you and that you want to think more about. Focus it as a topic by fastening it in a word ("bridges"), a phrase ("the me nobody knows"), a statement ("Freedom's just another word for nothing left to lose."), or a question ("Should there be school prayer?"). Topics can come from anywhere—problems or issues of concern to you and others, some idea you heard or read, something someone said. It's just a subject or thought you want to delve into and express yourself about.

You and some partners might write on the same topic and post or print up your results together with the topic as the center.

(The titles of the following examples are also the topics.)

Old People
Michael Lora

Old people are the best story tellers, because they've been through a lot of years. They seem to be cranky, but it's not their fault. I think that old people have the right to be cranky because they're going through the last phase of their life.

When your grandmother tells your mother you are a pain and you eat a lot, don't let it bother you; that's just her new way of saying "I love you." They can also be the best advice givers. They know what mistakes they made when they were young, but we young people don't know the future, so they give us advice.

When I Feel Glad or Sad
Manny Munoz

I feel glad when I go writing on the walls. That is called vandalism, but it makes me feel good. I tag "KNOWN." Every time I write, I feel that I am getting more famous. People write on walls to get famous. For instance, if you ever see "Cris 217" that is probably the most famous writer around, even though he can't write graffiti good.

I'll probably stop at the age of sixteen. You would get in more trouble if you get caught. If you're under sixteen the police will scare you. Then they will let you go. All writers want to make it, but most don't.

The Me Nobody Knows
Katherine A. Gonzalez

There are sides of me that nobody knows. For instance, some people may sometimes think that I am very quiet and shy when they first meet me. What they do not know is that I can be a very loud person at times, and also very funny.

There is also a part of me that my parents do not know. That part of me comes out when my mother tells me to do a million things at one time, or when she is not home and she has left me a lot of things to do in the house. When that happens I get very angry and I start to hit my desk or the drawers. I hate it when she leaves me a lot of things to do in a short period of time. I get very upset and frustrated.

People such as my parents do not know that I can become very violent. I do not think I would ever really hurt my mother or father though.

I can be a very fun person and a very violent person. I treat people the way they treat me. If a person treats me nice, I will treat them nice in return. But if a person treats me mean, I treat them mean in return.

When I get angry I usually hit things, but only when I am alone. Those are two sides of me that some or most people do not know.

Should There Be School Prayer?
Maria Perez

Personally, I think we should never have prayer in school. I think prayer should be done in church or in the privacy of your home. I don't think it is needed in school, because you go to school to study and to be taught. I think you should pray and praise the Lord in church or at home.

If they make a rule that you must pray in school I will not do it. I pray every day before I come to school, and I think prayer is necessary, but I will not pray in school. I pray where and when I want to.

If they say that if you don't pray in school they will throw you out of school, I don't care what they do to me I will not pray in school. All I will do is just walk right back into the school the next day, but I will not pray. I don't care what President Reagan says.

Every night I go to church and I pray, but I will not pray in school. If those are my feelings I am going to follow them all the way to heaven.

Bridges
Gillian Shaw

Hiking across, sailing under, driving over—bridges are beautiful, strong and bold creatures. They stretch all across the rivers, the swift moving rivers. They let us travel and see the places that many of us could not see, unless we had a boat or a small plane. Bridges are heavy, and tall, bright and quiet. At night the George Washington Bridge lights up all of her bright colored lights on top and under, below. Bridges are beautiful. They carry my memories and my hopes, to a beautiful land across the river, very different from this world.

"Freedom's Just Another Word for Nothing Left to Lose"
Edie Rubinowitz

I am amazed by the truth which I have found in that quote. At first the quote seemed like a nonsensical accumulation of words, but suddenly it snapped into focus and became a pearl of wisdom.

When one has nothing left to lose, he or she must acknowledge the opportunity to make a "fresh new start of it." It is in that chance for a new life that one develops a sense of freedom.

If people are without financial situations that they must concern themselves with, relatives, or a place in society, they are unattached. They are true examples of free people. They have no one and nothing restricting them, except themselves.

I have never felt totally free, but I often think of what it would be like, particularly in times when I am very restricted.

My Favorite Place to Be
Vanessa Faria

My favorite place to be is very, very far away. You don't have to travel by bus, car or plane. You just have to sit and concentrate on whatever you want, wherever you are.

You don't share this place with anyone—it's only yours. It's not a place like the park or Paris or your room, but it is a place, a place in your mind.

I like it because it's really peaceful and quiet. Nobody can bother you there no matter how hard they try.

I can think what I want to think and no one can correct me. I can forget my problems when I want to or sort them out if I want to.

You can focus on one thought if you really try. Study it, observe it, understand it, and it will fascinate you for the first time. You can also think about a million things at once or let your imagination get away with the best of you. This can be confusing, however, because deep in your mind you begin to see things very clear. Seeing a million things clearer than you've ever seen them before all at the same time is frustrating!

So going deep into my mind—contemplation—is *my* favorite place to go.

Broad Personal Essay

This kind of essay is personal because you're writing from your own viewpoint and in your own style, but it is broad because you're writing about something that goes beyond yourself, that is relevant to other people, if not perhaps also true for them. You may well want to say when these thoughts started or how they have grown, like certain experiences you've had or witnessed. What have you concluded? Feel free to generalize.

In order to get your best thoughts on your subject, it's often a good idea to meditate on it a while. That is, get in a quiet place, sit still and relaxed, close your eyes, and focus on whatever image or feeling or thought best represents the subject for you. Don't strain to think; just let thoughts come to you because your mind is pointed at this one thing. Whenever seems a good time, make some notes of the thoughts that have come that you want to keep, including real or imagined examples of your ideas. Then write out more fully, get reactions, and revise. (Be prepared for this to come out possibly as a poem.) Post it up, pass it around, print it up, collect it in a booklet of essays.

I Wonder
Aisha Salaam

Sometimes I wonder, "Where am I going? Where is life leading me?" I go to church, and in Sunday school they tell me that after you die you will go to Heaven if you are good and obey the Ten Commandments, and if you're not good and don't obey the commandments you will go to hell.

I think that there is reincarnation, but I don't know for sure; in fact, no one knows for sure.

This is how I think reincarnation is conducted. I think as soon as we die, our souls or spirits forget everything that happened and then start over again. I think this because sometimes when I have dreams the dream actually happens later on. It seems as if I have looked into the future.

Funny Feelings
Jennifer Levi

Lately, walking down the street has not been the most pleasant thing for me to do. I feel very self-conscious because men are always looking and saying things to me. I don't think I do or say or wear anything to get myself noticed. I think it is disgusting that men feel that they have the right to say things to women they don't even know. I don't think they know how it makes women feel; I don't even think they care. All they care about is themselves and having their fun.

It makes me angry, but at the same time it makes me scared. It makes me angry that they make me feel like I can not walk around without being watched. It makes me scared because at any given moment they might hurt me.

I remember when I was just starting to develop and I was very embarrassed about it. There was only one other girl in my class that had started to develop too. I remember hearing some boys in my class talking about their bodies—they were *so* proud about their bodies, but I never really talked to any of my friends about it then. Now we sometimes talk about it, but not a lot. It seems like boys always talk about their bodies. Sometimes I even get embarrassed listening to them talking about their own bodies.

I felt real weird because in one way I was being told to be showy about my body from movies and TV. At the same time I was being told to be quiet about my body from my own fear of what other people would think. For a while I was very confused until I finally decided to go with my own feelings. Now I do not show it and I do not hide it. I just wear what I want and I do what I want to do. I don't let my fear or what I see interfere with what I do or wear.

I think that as you grow up you become less ashamed and more proud of your body (male or female). I know that men, well at least the men on the street, are very proud and showy of their bodies. Some women, the ones on TV and in movies, are showy, and some women just don't do anything either way, like me.

I know that I can not make the men on the street stop looking and saying weird things to me; all I *can* do is not make them or anyone else feel the way they've made me feel.

The Child
Vincent Evans

Oh the Child
Having fun
Not knowing the difference
Between the moon and the sun.

His mind is not cluttered
With what's right or wrong.
Whatever he does he thought of
on his own.
He'll draw a picture of a monster
Totally different than anyone else's.
He'll write a story
With different things—new races,
weapons, and places.
He walks upside down.
Then he is taught
That he can't walk upside down
and falls.
There are only some certain races,
weapons, or places,
Only a few types of monsters.
All is lost,
The imagination, everything.
Oh the child
Lost forever, now he is older.

Paper Is More Patient Than Man
Edie Rubinowitz

Silence is your truest virtue.
As for man, he speaks when
nothing is to be said.

Somehow through the silence comes
the strength of sympathy, not
measured by a clock.

Paper, I do commend you, for
time after time you wait for
my thoughts.

And man frowns, as paper
cannot, reminding me again
and again of your value.

Ambivalence
Daniel Cuff

Ambivalence is . . .
doing a pitcher's windup to do a pirouette.

Ambivalence is . . .
catching a football while doing a grande
jeté.

Ambivalence is . . .
thinking of the Olympics while trying to
keep my arm straight.

Ambivalence is . . .
skiing down a mountain while doing a
grand battement.

Ambivalence is . . .
serving a tennis ball while doing a
rond de jambe

Ambivalence is . . .
watching the ballet wondering if the
Red Sox won.

Anger
Caryn Young

Anger like a great Greek God,
controls your every thought.
It tears away at your self-respect,
destroys friendships that you've sought.

Yet anger like a gentle breeze,
can clear your mind of pain,
can turn your sorrow into strength,
can make things good again.

Overloading Women
Kathleen Yen

In today's world, we usually expect the modern woman to have a
successful career. Yet at the same time we also expect her to come home,
cook, clean the house and take care of the children. Although it is a little more
common these days for the husband or father of the family to participate in the
household chores, there probably are not that many who do so willingly. In my
own family, the work is somewhat evened out between my mother and father.
However, I think that the majority of the families still go to the mother when

there is a problem at home. The responsibility of solving these problems should be shared between the mother and the father. Older siblings can also help with any problems.

Even when there is a problem at school, the mother is usually the one who is confronted with it first. For example, how many times have you heard a teacher threatening a student by saying, "I'm going to send a note to your father," or, "I'm going to call your father!"? Not very often, if at all. The teachers seem to automatically think that the mother will handle the child's punishment. Or that she will accept all responsibility until she decides to share it with her husband.

My English teacher had been asked to help her daughter's school fund-raising committee. Her job consisted of calling up parents to talk to them about volunteering. However, every time a father answered the telephone, and heard why she was calling, he immediately said, "Wait a minute, I'll get my wife," or something like that. Why didn't he think that helping their child's school is something important? It's as if they assume that it is a "little job," and that their wives can handle it. Well, thay may not know that those "little jobs" can get awfully big and complicated sometimes. Or that their wives pick up so many of these problems that it becomes one big problem.

I have an idea as to why women accept all these little jobs. Last month, I read an article about the analysis of a woman's psychology and psychological reactions to certain situations. The article stated that women are at a certain disadvantage compared to men, because they have a tendency to accept additional responsibility for their husbands. They think that they *have* to be at his side whenever he needs them, and afterwards too. This is usually when the husband gives her these "little jobs" to help them out. This also includes the time when the husband complains and tells all his problems and aggravations to his wife. And then the wives react to these aggravations, usually by thinking that they have to apologize for the incidents even though they may not have had anything to do with them! It happens all the time, and a female reader might be able to identify with this feeling.

It even shows up in advertising. There is a commercial for a coffee where the mother has to remind the teen-age daughter not to be home late, find her husband's briefcase, and get breakfast and take her son to school because he missed the bus. Why couldn't the husband find his own briefcase? But there it is. The mother who does it all and doesn't mind. Perhaps the reason for this is that we don't know that we have all these problems, and we just leave them there like dirty clothes on the floor for our moms and wives to pick up. Or, the mothers and wives don't know that they are taking in these problems and reacting to them. This is not something that occurs only with older women; it is something that affects young women and girls too. I know that when something wrong happens in school, like a friend failed a test or didn't do well on a report, I feel awful although I might not have had anything to do with the incident. Sometimes a great amount of guilt overcomes me and weighs down my mind for a considerable amount of time.

There are many times when the man or men will use this sort of situation for their own good. They will sense that a woman is at a disadvantage and then they will assume control of the situation. Eventually they will only succeed in blowing up their own ego. It seems that they only do this when they know that the situation is in their favor.

So you can see that a woman has a lot to deal with. She sometimes is carrying a burden that she is not even aware of. As far as a remedy for this goes, I can only think of one, in the future, as children and husbands, as members of families we should try to burden our mothers and wives less now that we are aware of the situation.

Teenage Pregnancies
Eunice Richards

Teenage women of today have more problems than ever. One reason they have these problems is that they try to hold their boyfriends by having their baby. Teenage women feel that if they have their boyfriend's baby, the boy will stay with them forever, but it does not work like that. Teenage women must understand that the faster the woman gets preganat, the quicker the man leaves her.

The cause of these teenagers getting pregnant is that their parents do not talk to them about sexual intercourse while they are young. Teenage women get hung up in these incidents because the do not know what to look out for as they are growing up. There are teenage men of today that are outrageous. They convince a girl to have sexual intercourse with them, the girl gets pregnant, the boy wants her to get the baby and she will because she feels that if she has the baby, the boy is going to stay with her forever. Now the girl is caught in a trap; she's pregnant.

Some teenage women go looking for someone to love them because they get let down too many times. When teenage women go looking for love, they will love anyone just to get some affection. That's when the hurting part comes in. The teenage woman will most likely get her feelings hurt because she has now fallen in love with this teenage man, but he did not fall in love with her, he just wanted her for that night. Again the girl gets let down, and she still goes out and does the same thing until she really finds someone to care for her.

Some teenage women want to grow up so fast because of their environment. There are certain things that make a teenager want to be a woman, for example the record "Like a Virgin" by Madonna, "What's Love" by New Jersey Choir, and a couple of other love songs. There are also commercials, television shows and books. A commercial like Hostess Donuts, where the woman has breakfast ready for her husband and children might convince a girl, too, because she might want to have responsibilities like that woman has.

Television shows also can convince a teenage woman to have sexual intercourse too. For example on *Miami Vice* someone makes love on every episode. The young teenage woman looks at other people making love and she sees how good it looks and then she might want to try it 'cause she is going to have a good time.

These things are some of the reasons why teenage women want to grow up and get pregnant so fast.

Being Thirteen
Lorraine R. Mazelis

Being Thirteen
is not being a kid any more,
no longer able to get away with playing with dolls.

Being Thirteen
is to look at the doll that used to be your favorite
          and remembering.

Being Thirteen
is remembering,
remembering when the worst thing that happened
          to you was losing your Teddy Bear.
And laughing until the tears roll down your face,
          missing those times
      but thanking God they're over.

Being Thirteen
is discussing bra sizes,
      and finding out you're the third to the smallest
And one girl doesn't even think you need one.

Being Thirteen
is talking about maxi pads,
      "What kind do you use?"
and not being able to answer,
      to not know what to say.
And wishing,
      wishing
You'd get your period already
even though you know it will be a pain.

Being Thirteen
is being able to wear blue eyeliner
and not having to worry that someone
          might laugh at you,
      because now you're old enough.

Being Thirteen
is to worry about your hair,
　　　cutting it, dyeing it, perming it,
and then letting it grow out again.

Being Thriteen
is being jealous of the girl that's popular
　　　　and smart and pretty
　　　and has tons of boyfriends.

Being Thirteen
is being madly in love with a boy,
　　　along with 50 other girls,
　　　　he, perfect,
　　　and you're surprised he even remembers
　　　　your name,
and you know he never thinks about you.

Being Thirteen is going out with a boy because he's nice.
　　　Everyone else thinks he's a nerd,
probably because he's not *that* cute,
And finally dropping him out of embarrassment
　　　and then wishing you hadn't.

Being Thirteen
is fighting with your parents
　　　and sometimes really hating them.

Being Thirteen
is having fun with your friends
　　　and then going home to cry
because you think everyone hates you.

Being Thirteen
is having a best friend
　　who will care,
　　who will talk to you and listen
when you won't shut up.
Being Thirteen
is fighting with your friends
　　　and never hating them
　　　　like you used to.

Being Thirteen
is going crazy, jumping around, dancing,
　　　　laughing,
　　　　　crying,
　　　Having food fights.

Being Thirteen
is being in between a kid and
          a grownup
     and not belonging
     and being confused.

Being Thirteen,
is a sudden change.
     You were just a kid,
playing with dolls, carefree,
          and having fun,
and all of a sudden there's a change,
     A big change,
from being happy, and laughing all the time,
from just a boyfriend who never kissed you
     To a world where everything and everyone's
          different from before.
Everyone's experienced and tough,
          and cool.
One, two, many people doing bad things,
          being stupid,
but still a little of me left inside.
Well,
     at least there's still a chance,
          maybe.
I could try real hard,
          maybe,
Maybe, if I try,
          maybe.

Being Thirteen
     is trying,
     and finally having what you waited for,
          for so long,
     then losing it, or wanting something else.
     But you know,
          you have a good chance.

Being Thirteen
is growing up.